PRAISE FOR *THE THINKING FAN'S GUIDE TO WALT DISNEY WORLD: MAGIC KINGDOM*

I really enjoyed reading this book. It offers a different way to look at the park and its attractions, not your traditional guidebook route. I was curious going in to see what is considered a Thinking Fan's guide… and as luck would have it they think like us geeks think! … Also be sure to spend a few minutes checking out the footnotes. I found many of the observations and references there to be just as interesting as the main pieces of the book.
    Jason Dziegielewski, *DisneyGeek.com*

I have to say this might be my favorite Disney book to date! … I love Aaron Wallace's writing style. It's intelligent, with a hint of humorous mixed in for good measure.
    Heidi Strawser, *Heidi-Strawser.com*

Ever wonder why the Disney parks are so successful? A new book called *The Thinking Fan's Guide to Walt Disney World: Magic Kingdom* goes a long way toward answering that question… While you hardly need to know the history or various possible levels of meaning behind Disney's attractions to enjoy the theme park, it's fun to know that someone took a deeper look.
    Rudy Maxa, *Rudy Maxa's World*

…There was plenty of new insight to keep me turning the page. And that's the thing here, *The Thinking Fan's Guide* is insanely readable. Through personal experiences and opinions Wallace is able to keep the reader grounded in the real world, while still taking time to look back at the history of the attraction.
    Andrew Tipton, *DisneyHipsters.com*

Few could come to the same brilliant conclusions.
    Alex Reif, *LaughingPlace.com*

Personally, I have a new appreciation for several rides (Jungle Cruise, anyone?) thanks to the book.
    Anthony Markham, *WDW Happy Place.com*

I actually found the notes section the most interesting place in the book, and any readers of Wallace's book should not bypass this wonderful section. Wallace has mini biographies of influential individuals, comments on the nomenclature in the parks, and even includes the full Shakespearean verse that gave rise to the phrase 'Grim Grinning Ghosts' (wonderful!). ... [The book is] a perfect introduction to the wonderful depths of artistry that so many eyes overlook.
    David Younger, *Theme Park Theory.com*

[A] book we would highly recommend to you — all our Readers — regardless of how many times you have personally visited the parks here in Central Florida. In fact, this book will not only increase your knowledge of the rich history and all the great attractions that the Magic Kingdom offers, but will also enterain you and give you an overview of the park you love... from another fan's perspective.
    Sam Carta, *Orlando Theme Park News*

[Wallace] is able to introduce attractions in a way that doesn't make old WDW vets feel as though they are being talked down to, but also allows the uninitiated to understand what they are looking for without even having seen the actual attraction itself.
    Charlie Hensel, *NJ Biblio*

Aaron supplies fans (new and old) with a refreshing take on Magic Kingdom... he has an amicable way of making his information feel accessible and fun.
    Estelle Hallick, *This Happy Place Blog*

The Thinking Fan's Guide to Walt Disney World is like giving every Disney Guest who reads it their own Disney historian as a guide
    Natalie Reiner, *Ink and Paint Blog*

The descriptive, contemplative views of each ride are so comprehensive that *The Thinking Fan's Guide to Walt Disney World: Magic Kingdom* is recommended for erudite armchair travelers, as it is for starry-eyed tourists!
    James A. Cox, Editor-in-Chief, *Midwest Book Review*

Also by Aaron Wallace

The Thinking Fan's Guide to Walt Disney World: Epcot

One of Tomorrow Society's "Top Five Books for Epcot Fans"

Recommended by UCF's Theatre M.F.A. Themed Experience Research Guide

"It's rare to read such a fair assessment of Epcot... each chapter offers a surprisingly nuanced take on every aspect of the attraction [and] a down-to-earth style. ... There's a wealth of great material packed into these pages," — Dan Heaton, *Tomorrow Society*

"I've been visiting Epcot for years, but after devouring *The Thinking Fan's Guide to Walt Disney World: Epcot*, I felt like I was gifted a brand-new theme park to discover all over again." — Jeff DePaoli, *Dizney Coast to Coast*

"Aaron's guide to Epcot embodies the 'edutainment' ideals of the park's original mission. It will make you see Epcot for what it truly is - an immersive world of history, innovation, culture, and imagination." — Courtney Guth & Emily McDermott, *Book of the Mouse Club Podcast*

"Legitimately teared up." — *GoodReads* reader Alexandra

"Aaron Wallace does it again. He is insightful, educational, and entertaining. Cannot recommend enough." — *GoodReads* reader Emily Dean

"His arguments are always researched, thought provoking, and beautifully explained." - *GoodReads* reader Peter Wright

Hocus Pocus in Focus: The Thinking Fan's Guide to Disney's Halloween Classic

As featured in The Washington Post

One of New York Daily News' "6 Spooky New Books for Halloween"

"Love *Hocus Pocus*? Then you need this book. Terrifyingly knowledgeable... accessible and smart, packed with fascinating stories, facts, and analysis." — *Den of Geek*

"More lit than the Black Flame Candle." — *Buzzfeed*

"Honestly, my first thought was, 'Awesome! I love that movie - but is there enough material for an entire book?' As it turns out, there is." — *WickedHorror.com*

"A scholarly dive into the making and meaning of the film." — *New York Daily News*

"A treasure trove of insight... nothing short of a magical experience." — *LaughingPlace.com*

"The chapters are all cleverly titled... with his colloquial tone, fresh perspective and well thought-out ideas, Wallace makes this an interesting and easy read." — *The Movie Guys*

THE THINKING FAN'S GUIDE TO WALT DISNEY WORLD: Magic Kingdom 2020

AARON WALLACE

Copyright © 2013, 2015, 2019, 2020 by Aaron Wallace. All rights reserved.

THE THINKING FAN'S GUIDE TO
WALT DISNEY WORLD: MAGIC KINGDOM

Published by Pensive Pen Publishing, Orlando, Florida
www.pensivepenpublishing.com

All rights reserved. No part of this book may be reproduced or transmitted in any form or by any means, electronic or mechanical, including photocopying, recording, or by any information storage and retrieval system, without the express written permission of the author, except for the inclusion of brief quotations in a review.

This book makes reference to various copyrights, characters, properties, trademarks, and registered marks owned by The Walt Disney Company and Disney Enterprises, Inc. or its affiliates or subsidiaries. They are used in this book solely for editorial purposes. Neither the author nor the publisher makes any commercial claim to their use. Note: for purposes of readability, the official names of some entities, including but not limited to Disneyland® Park, Walt Disney World® Resort, Epcot®, Disney's Animal Kingdom®, and Disney California Adventure® Park, are occasionally referred to in the abbreviated or colloquial forms by which they are commonly known to the public. These marks are the sole property of the The Walt Disney Company and Disney Enterprises, Inc.

The views and opinions expressed in this book are solely those of the author. They do not necessarily reflect the views of The Walt Disney Company or any of its affiliates or subsidiaries. This book is not authorized by or affiliated with The Walt Disney Company, its affiliates, or subsidiaries. It has not been submitted for their review.

Third Edition
Printed in the United States
Cover design by Rob Yeo, www.RobYeoDesign.com
ISBN: 978-0-9980592-2-8
Library of Congress Control Number: 2019948354

About the Author

Aaron Wallace is a writer, podcaster, and attorney who studies movies, music, television, theatre, theme parks, and why we love them. He is the author of three bestselling books about Disney travel and entertainment.

Aaron first started writing about The Walt Disney Company while at The University of North Carolina at Chapel Hill, where he earned a Bachelor of Arts degree in both English and Communication Studies (with a concentration in media and film). While there, he taught a recitation course in analyzing children's literature, with an emphasis on Disney's adaptations in theme parks and movies. He later pursued an interest in law, earning a Juris Doctorate from Wake Forest University and practicing as an attorney before transitioning full-time to his career as a writer, critic, podcaster, and public speaker.

Disney fans know Aaron as the host of *On Main Street with Aaron Wallace*, the web's longest-running Disney fan podcast, recognized by Apple as a Featured Podcast and a fixture in the Travel Top 10. He also reviews live theatre and conducts celebrity interviews as a Contributing Editor at *BroadwayWorld.com*, the web's #1 source for live entertainment coverage. His more than two hundred movie, music, and television reviews have reached an audience of millions across multiple outlets, including the popular *DVDizzy.com*.

He has been featured in *The Washington Post*, the *New York Daily News*, *Buzzfeed*, *Attractions Magazine*, and *The Orlando Sentinel*, among other publications, and is a frequent guest on podcasts such as *The Mad Chatters* and *Dizney Coast to Coast*.

Today, Aaron lives in Orlando, Florida, where he visits the Walt Disney World Resort on at least a weekly basis and shares his adventures on Twitter (@aaronwallace) and Instagram (@aaronhwallace).

His website is available at www.AaronWallaceOnline.com.

Dedication

Jesus Christ, the fount of blessing.
Rodney and Karen Wallace, my parents who taught me love.
Nichole Wallace Jackson, my amazing sister and a mom
to three incredible kids.
Mike Sullivan, a dear friend gone too soon.

And to the late Charlie Ridgway, a Disney Legend in every sense of the term and a friend. Thank you for helping to make this book happen. You'll always be a part of it.

Table of Contents

Introduction	13
Chapter 1: Adventureland	21
Jungle Cruise	22
Walt Disney's Enchanted Tiki Room	27
Swiss Family Treehouse	33
The Magic Carpets of Aladdin	37
Pirates of the Caribbean	40
Chapter 2: Frontierland	47
Country Bear Jamboree	48
Big Thunder Mountain Railroad	54
Frontierland Shootin' Arcade	58
Splash Mountain	61
Tom Sawyer Island	67
Chapter 3: Liberty Square	73
Liberty Square Riverboat	75
The Muppets Present... Great Moments in American History	79
The Hall of Presidents	85
Haunted Mansion	95

Chapter 4: Fantasyland — 103

- Peter Pan's Flight — 105
- It's a Small World — 110
- Prince Charming Regal Carrousel — 114
- Mickey's PhilharMagic — 118
- Enchanted Tales with Belle — 123
- Under the Sea ~ Journey of The Little Mermaid — 127
- Seven Dwarfs Mine Train — 132
- The Many Adventures of Winnie the Pooh — 139
- Mad Tea Party — 146
- Dumbo the Flying Elephant — 149
- The Barnstormer — 154
- Cinderella Castle — 159

Chapter 5: Tomorrowland — 165

- Tomorrowland Transit Authority PeopleMover — 166
- Buzz Lightyear's Space Ranger Spin — 171
- Tomorrowland Speedway — 176
- Astro Orbiter — 179
- Monsters, Inc. Laugh Floor — 182
- Space Mountain — 185
- Walt Disney's Carousel of Progress — 190

Chapter 6: Main Street, U.S.A.	209
Main Street, U.S.A.	210
Walt Disney World Railroad	213
Sorcerers of the Magic Kingdom	216
Disney Festival of Fantasy Parade	223
Happily Ever After	227
Notes	235
Index	269
Acknowledgements	279

Introduction

If I've done my job, you'll never think about theme parks the same way again. This book is different from other travel guides you're used to, and it's designed to make your time in Walt Disney World more rewarding than it's ever been before. Too often, we get caught up in the frenzy of trip planning and then rush into the parks on a mission: ride everything as quickly as we can. There's some fun in that, but if you stop to think about Disney's rides and shows for what they are — incredibly detailed stories and experiences unfolding in a three-dimensional environment — you'll find there's so much more to enjoy than you found on first glance.

Whether you're planning your first trip to a Disney resort or your hundredth, I hope this book will introduce exciting perspectives and new ways to think about The Most Magical Place on Earth.

You probably wouldn't plan a trip to Egypt or France without reading a bit about them first. I submit that a Disney vacation should be no different. The Disney parks are the world's most visited resort destinations, and they enjoy that status for a reason. One of this guide's major goals is to understand *why* we love these attractions and keep coming back to them in the millions, year after year.

This book, the first in a series about Disney theme parks and entertainment, focuses entirely on Magic Kingdom. Of all the theme parks in the world, Magic Kingdom is the most visited by a comfortable margin.

Setting aside meet-and-greets and minor diversions for the time being, it is home to 39 major rides and shows. In the pages that follow, you will explore each of those in depth.

You'll learn the intriguing history behind the attractions. Together, we'll ponder their appeal. On the rare occasion when an attraction doesn't quite measure up to the high Disney standard, we'll take a playfully irreverent look at what went wrong. And we will think about "Disney magic" as something that can be both felt and understood. While we all have our favorite attractions, the aim of *The Thinking Fan's Guide* is to lend insight by creating new prompts, tools, and frameworks for thinking about Disney entertainment in a whole new way, however you might feel about a given ride or show.

There are six chapters in this book, each devoted to one of the themed "lands" in the Magic Kingdom — Adventureland; Frontierland; Liberty Square; Fantasyland; Tomorrowland; and Main Street, U.S.A. For the most part, we'll move clockwise around the park, starting in Adventureland, and ending on Main Street, where the park's wonderful nighttime festivities are staged.

As we walk through the park, I will recommend movies and television shows that complement each attraction or illuminate its major themes. You'll find these in the 'Watch This' box after each attraction. Some are Disney titles, some come from other studios, and many of them are "outside the box," relating to the park in unexpected or surprising ways. As this book goes to press, Disney is on the cusp of launching its new online streaming subscription service, Disney+. It is likely that many of the movies recommended in this book will be available to stream on that platform throughout 2020 and beyond.

Finally, while this is not a traditional "guidebook," each discussion will open with the nuts-and-bolts information you need to plan your day in Magic Kingdom.

Endnotes

Beyond citations, the endnotes in this book include additional commentary on Magic Kingdom and the Walt Disney Company. Many of these notes are extensive and simply too long for the bottom of each page. Accordingly, you'll find all the notes together in one section at the back of the book.

Many readers prefer to wait and read the endnotes after each chapter, but the right approach is the one that works best for you. That's all you need to know about the book's layout, but a small dose of "Disney 101" might be helpful too.

The Disney Story in Four Paragraphs

Walter Elias Disney was born in Chicago on December 5, 1901 and moved to the small town of Marceline, Missouri with his family when he was four. The Disneys faced financial struggles throughout Walt's childhood, moving around the country in search of work. By the time he was 18, Walt was an amateur cartoonist, occasionally finding small successes. In 1928, his life changed forever with *Steamboat Willie*, which introduced the world to Mickey Mouse. Mickey was a smash success and paved the way for the first-ever animated feature film, *Snow White and the Seven Dwarfs*. Widely expected to be a dismal failure, *Snow White* surprised everyone in 1937 by becoming one of the biggest box office achievements of all time, a distinction it retains to this day.

Walt made many more movies after *Snow White*, but his studio faltered throughout World War II. Then came the 1950s, when audiences suddenly clamored for anything and everything Disney. Walt also hit it big on television, a market most film producers still didn't want to touch. "The Mickey Mouse Club" and serials like "Davy Crockett" took the country by storm. It was also during the 1950s that Walt opened Disneyland.

There are two Disney resorts in the United States. The first began as a single park, Disneyland in Anaheim, California. Americans were no strangers to carnivals, but Disneyland was the world's first true theme park. It opened on July 17, 1955. Nearly a half-century later, in 2001, Disneyland would expand with a second park, Disney California Adventure, along with a new luxury hotel and the Downtown Disney complex, transforming Disneyland into the Disneyland Resort.

Disney's other U.S. resort, of course, is Walt Disney World, located just outside Orlando, Florida. It opened on October 1, 1971 with only one park, Magic Kingdom, essentially Disneyland replicated on a larger scale. The resort has added three more theme parks since then: Epcot, Disney's Hollywood Studios (formerly the Disney-MGM Studios), and Disney's Animal Kingdom. There are also two water parks, a massive outdoor retail district called Disney Springs, a variety of recreational facilities, and more than 20 resort hotels. Today, the company is the biggest entertainment corporation in the world, with additional theme parks in Tokyo, Paris, Hong Kong, and Shanghai.

Throughout the book, I use several terms of art that apply to theme parks in general and Disney parks in particular. They will be familiar to Disney fans and many others, but for the benefit of those who may be new to theme park culture, here are some brief definitions.

A Brief Glossary

Audio-Animatronics. A registered trademark of Disney Imagineering referring to the robotic technology used in Disney's rides and shows.

backstory. A literary device commonly used in books, television, film, and theme parks, backstory is a narrative or collection of facts about the history of a character, attraction, or fictional universe. A backstory may be entirely fictitious or based on historical fact. Disney's Imagineers (see below) have a reputation for creating extensive backstory for each attraction, even if the backstory is not always made readily apparent to guests.

cast member. In Disney parlance, *all* employees, and especially those working in the theme parks, are called "cast members."

dark ride. Traditionally, an attraction in which two-to-four-person vehicles move slowly along tracks through a darkened interior where black-lighted story scenes create atmosphere or construct narrative.

E-ticket. A long time ago, Disney theme park tickets were sold on a per-attraction basis, and the most desirable rides required E tickets (lesser exhibits took A, B, C, or D). Over the years, "E-ticket" has evolved into a phrase meaning "most popular" or "the best of the best."

Imagineer. An employee of Walt Disney Imagineering (WDI), the branch of The Walt Disney Company responsible for planning, designing, and constructing Disney's parks, resorts, attractions, and other such endeavors. The division was established as WED Enterprises by Walt Disney himself in 1952 (the acronym a reference to his full name, Walter Elias Disney) but later became WDI. The term is a portmanteau of the words "imagination" and "engineering."

meet-and-greet. An opportunity to interact with a costumed character from the Disney universe, usually at a pre-designated location.

narrative. Though it is a word with many important meanings, for our purposes here, "narrative" is best understood as the way in which a story is presented. Whereas "plot" refers to what happens in a story, "narrative" refers to the way in which that story is told: the sequencing of events, the use of flashback, where the story begins and ends, etc. When filmmakers or Imagineers construct a narrative, they make many decisions about how to tell their story (and just as importantly, how not to tell it).

queue. The designated space in which guests wait in line before beginning an attraction. Disney theme parks are known for building elaborately themed queues, which sometimes contribute to an attraction's backstory.

text. When we refer to a movie or attraction as a "text," the idea is that we can "read" it like we read a book. When we read books, we look "between the lines" and consider literary elements such as a foreshadowing, mood, tone, implication, etc. We also ask questions about what the text says to its audience. We can apply this same concept to theme park attractions, film, stage shows, and many other kinds of art.

weenie. A term used by Walt Disney and adopted by the Imagineers to denote massive theme park landmarks that draw visitors' attention from a distance. Cinderella Castle (*Chapter Four*) is a prime example.

Terminology and Style

This book references both attraction names and movie titles. When talking about Disney, the names frequently overlap. To avoid confusion, I will italicize movie titles (including short films). Attraction names will be capitalized without italics. Where a movie and attraction are one and the same (e.g. Mickey's PhilharMagic), it will be capitalized without italics. Song and TV show titles will appear in quotation marks. If an attraction features a show-within-a-show, the latter will appear in quotation marks (for example, "The Declaration of Independence" in The Muppets Present... Great Moments in American History). This book otherwise conforms to the publisher's house style.

As is common practice, when referring to Walt Disney the person, I will generally use "Walt." When referring to the Walt Disney Company or the executives and creatives representing the company collectively, I will generally use "Disney," except where context dictates otherwise.

A Word on Accuracy

Everything in this book is, to the best of my research and knowledge, accurate as of the time it goes to press. Disney's parks are constantly changing, however, and that's never been truer than now, with the company making new and large-scale investments at every Disney resort around the world. Should anything in this book strike your curiosity, or if you happen to find anything you believe to be in error, please contact me directly with questions or suggestions at **book@aaronwallaceonline.com**.

You can also contact me on Twitter (**@aaronwallace**) or Instagram (**@aaronhwallace**). I encourage you to visit my website, **AaronWallaceOnline.com**, and sign up for the online newsletter to receive important updates.

On MyMagic+ and FastPass+

Walt Disney World uses a complex vacation-planning system called MyMagic+, which relies on the My Disney Experience (MDX) website and smartphone app to handle everything from hotel and dining reservations to current wait times. MDX is available to all guests at no charge.

Disney's popular FASTPASS, which allowed guests to bypass the standby line in certain attractions at no additional charge, is now known as FastPass+, for which initial reservations are made online and 30 days in advance (or 60 days prior to check-in for guests of WDW resort hotels). Reservations can be modified later, even while in the park.

At Magic Kingdom, guests are allowed to make up to three initial FastPass+ reservations per calendar day. After experiencing your first three attractions using FastPass+, you can reserve a fourth FastPass+ (and then a fifth after redeeming the fourth, and so on, subject to availability).

In this book, FastPass+ attractions are assigned one of four priority rankings: top, high, medium, and low. (Note: the Mickey Mouse and Princess Fairytale Hall meet-and-greets, while not covered in depth in this book, should also be considered a top priority for those eager to greet those characters. Likewise, the meet-and-greet at Ariel's Grotto in Fantasyland is a medium to high priority, while Tinker Bell's post on Main Street ranks as a medium to low priority.) There is a lot more to know about FastPass+. For the very latest, www.easywdw.com has some of the best updates and strategies around.

Thank You

In writing and researching this book, I've fallen in love with Magic Kingdom all over again. I sincerely hope you come away from the reading experience with a newfound appreciation for what I believe is a very special place. Should you find anything new to admire about this wondrous vacation kingdom while spending time in these pages, I will take great satisfaction in my efforts here. Happy reading!

Aaron Wallace

Chapter 1

Adventureland

"Here is adventure. Here is romance. Here is mystery. Tropical rivers — silently flowing into the unknown. The unbelievable splendor of exotic flowers... the eerie sounds of the jungle... with eyes that are always watching. This is Adventureland."

Walt Disney, "Dateline: Disneyland," July 17, 1955

Walt Disney reportedly planned to install a plaque with these words at the entrance to the original Adventureland. It never happened, maybe because Adventureland speaks for itself. Still, the inscription does nicely capture the essence of the park's most exotic realm.

There are many kinds of adventure, but Adventureland concerns itself only with those that might unfold in the "other" — other eras, other languages, other cultures, other locales. A blend of Africa, Asia, Arabia, the Caribbean, and the South Pacific islands, the land is an immersion into things balmy and foreign to the American mindset. Home to ferocious beasts, bramble, and colonies in the wild, Adventureland is a jungle nook teetering on the dicey edge of civilization. That's the illusion, anyway, and it's put together by five major attractions — Jungle Cruise, Walt Disney's Enchanted Tiki Room, Swiss Family Treehouse, The Magic Carpets of Aladdin, and Pirates of the Caribbean.

In between them, the sound of steel drums and the smell of pineapple fill the air. Street vendors peddle their market goods and a camel spits at visitors as they walk past thick and flourishing foliage and a towering, thatched pagoda. Expeditions, sword fighting, and tree climbing await. The place feels like Walt once described it — "the wonderland of nature's own design."

Jungle Cruise

Type: Boat ride
Duration: 9 to 10 minutes
Height Restriction: None
Popularity/Crowds: Moderate to High
FastPass+: Yes; medium priority
Fear Factor: 1 out of 5 (gun effects; darkness at night)
Wet Factor: 0.5 out of 5 (light mist; splash of water on very rare occasions)
Preshow: None
Boarding Speed: Moderate
Best Time to Visit without FastPass+: Early morning, late evening, or during fireworks or a parade. If you find it crowded, try again later.
Special Notes: During the holidays, Jungle Cruise becomes Jingle Cruise. It's the usual experience, dressed up with yuletide humor and décor.

Every Disney ride begins with a familiar warning: "Keep your hands, arms, feet, and legs inside the vehicle at all times." While on the Jungle Cruise, you'll need to keep your tongue inside your cheek too. This outdoor adventure ride is Disney's most self-deprecating attraction, steadfastly refusing to take itself seriously. Originally conceived as a more grounded encounter with real animals from the wild, Jungle Cruise has evolved into something that revels in its artifice instead. In so doing, Disney pokes fun not only at itself but at us as well.

The Jungle Cruise is quintessential Adventureland, its *raison d'être*. While Walt Disney's career as a film producer is best remembered for animated classics and live-action musicals, his studio also took a successful stab at documentaries, most notably the *True-Life Adventures* series. Beginning in 1948 and running through 1960, Disney released 17 *True-Life* titles to theaters, where they scored with audiences and critics alike. A full half even won Oscars. The documentaries sought to make viewer-friendly narratives out of real-life nature footage, stamped with distinctly Disney music and voice-overs. They gave birth to a popular comic strip in the 1950s and, more recently, a theatrical renaissance in the "Disneynature" brand, best known for its debut film, *Earth* (2009). Its most enduring legacy, however, is as the impetus for the Jungle Cruise.

When plans for Disneyland went into motion, the first section off the main castle hub was to be called True-Life Adventureland. Its star attraction would be the Jungle Cruise, a boat tour through re-created habitats featuring many of the live animals seen in Walt's *True-Life* films, narrated by a cast member at the helm (the "skipper"). But by the time Disneyland opened in 1955, the real-life animals had been substituted with robotic replicas, and the "encounter with nature" vibe had been dialed down to an "encounter with plastic" instead. As it turns out, mixing real people with really aggressive animals isn't the most practical idea, or at least it wasn't in 1955. Decades later, Disney's Animal Kingdom park would leverage new technology and additional acreage to fully embrace Walt's original vision of bringing man into the wild. In Disneyland, though, that face-to-face wasn't to be.

Today, the ride is more Comedy Central than National Geographic. How did that change come about? Jungle Cruise always had a wry sense of humor, echoing the lighthearted levity of the documentaries themselves. The 1950s were a less sardonic time, though, and the mere spectacle of riding through a man-made jungle was enough to delight. The skippers might have intoned a sense of bemusement toward the Audio-Animatronics, but their script took the show scenes seriously enough.

Enter Marc Davis, the legendary artist whose hand had given life to Disney characters from Snow White to Tinker Bell.[1] He was shifting gears toward theme park design in the early 1960s, when Disneyland's Jungle Cruise was due for an update. His inherent cartoon wit made him a natural for sight gags, and he had plenty dreamed up and sketched out for Jungle Cruise.

Like your funniest friend who changes the energy of the room whenever he joins the party, Davis's concepts redirected the ride's tone and soon cemented it as a guest favorite.

That's probably why Magic Kingdom asked Davis to take the reins for its own version of the Jungle Cruise a few years later. *This* Jungle Cruise *screams* Marc Davis. While it borrows much of the original 1955 design, it adds scenes and characters all its own, and by "its," I mean his. Davis's vignettes are proper jokes, complete with setups and punchlines, all of it communicated visually. Verbally, though, there was still nobody telling jokes. Even in 1971, the ride's official script closely mirrored 1955's.

Then came the cast members. The boat drivers' deadpan wisecracks and one-liners slowly worked their way into the official script, which is today all but an open-mic routine. To some extent, their contributions and inflections matched the sentiments of new generations, which now had newer-model mechanical animals in their local pizza parlors. But let's not underestimate the influence Marc Davis's own personal and professional sense of humor has had on the ride and those steering it. It's hard to introduce a boatload of tourists to explorers whose backsides are a mere millimeter away from a rhino's horn and *not* crack a joke. Davis's sensibilities are prone to droll wit, and in large measure, they are Disney's sensibilities too.

There's a certain kind of humor pervasive throughout the Walt Disney World Resort. It's a dry brand of tongue-in-cheek comedy that isn't afraid to come dangerously close to the audience's threshold for corny jokes. It's wordplay; it's parody; it's pointing out the obvious as if it were breaking news. You find it on the hilariously morbid tombstones outside Haunted Mansion. You find it when Statler and Waldorf tell their audience they're bolted to their seats in Hollywood Studios' Muppet*Vision 3D (literally, they are). You find it when the pre-show in Animal Kingdom's Dinosaur ride warns you it might get "a little bumpy" as you see a family flung around and screaming for dear life. And you find it in nearly every moment aboard the Jungle Cruise. There may be no other attraction more representative of the Disney theme parks' personality.

Today, purporting that everything in the ride is real would cripple it with pretense. If clearly artificial animals are to be used alongside a live human tour guide, they must be brought front and center and celebrated for what they are — fakes. And that's the genius of Jungle Cruise. The ride is lavishly detailed and filled with visual treats, but its entire substance is a sendup of those same sights. Its punny irreverence has become the thing people love about it most.

More than any other ride at Disney, the Jungle Cruise experience hinges entirely on the cast members leading it — the skippers, your personal emcees. They dress in khaki, they steer the boat, they forget to steer the boat, and they deliver one poker-faced pun after another into a tiny radio microphone at the boat's bow. Armed with improvisational license, they mold the assigned script to match the moment and their own ingenuity. The act isn't easy to pull off, but in the hands of a capable comedian, it can make for one of the resort's most memorable experiences.

The trick for skippers is to come off as just cynical enough to sound comically jaded but still cheery enough to let on that they're actually having a good time — to add just enough of their own material to make returning guests feel they've heard something new, but not so much as to make the passengers fear they have a renegade on their hands. If the skipper errs too far to one end, they sound uncomfortably bitter; too far to the other, and the ride becomes saccharine and rather lame. I've seen it all on my many cruises through these peculiar jungles, and it's only the very best and the very worst that stay in mind. Good or bad, that variance guarantees the Jungle Cruise will be a different ride each and every time. This is no broken record. It's always a new release. Even for a once-in-a-lifetime visitor who rides the Jungle Cruise only twice during a week in Walt Disney World, that makes an important impression.

No matter whom you have as your guide, there are a few things you can almost always count on hearing. Your skipper will lament that the skull-on-a-stick remnants of a tribal gathering is "kind of a dead party." You'll learn the Nile River got its name because, as the world's longest river, it goes on "for Niles and Niles and Niles..." You'll meet a crocodile named Ginger — "she's one tough cookie, but watch out! Ginger snaps." And the skippers will be sure to tease you with a carefully timed sequence of water-squirting elephants, which always look like they're about to erupt right beside you... but only occasionally do.

The foundation for this banter is the idea that it's fun to ridicule the absurd — and let's face it, there's something about riding around in a boat on tracks and looking at fake animals that is a little bit absurd. But we aren't laughing at the plastic animals so much as we're laughing at ourselves. Or, rather, Disney is laughing at us by proxy through the skippers, and we laugh along with them.

As mentally stimulating as the Disney parks are, they're also commercial enterprises built on make-believe. To really enjoy the nirvana of dreams come true and wishes fulfilled that makes Walt Disney World so special, you've got to shed your cynicism and buy into that fantasy. You've got to check your disbelief at the door. The Jungle Cruise is that door. Geographically, the ride sets itself up to be the first that many guests will encounter. For the rest of your time in Walt Disney World, you're going to embrace all that is faux and farce-funny, but before you do, you've got to come to terms with your own "too cool for school" mentality. How better to do that than to kick things off with a hearty laugh at yourself? That's what the Jungle Cruise does. It proudly presents its just-barely-moving robotic creations and its "hardy-harhar" puns, and it boasts, "Yes, it's fake, it's a little corny, it's all a little simplistic… but you love it, don't you?" Your defenses melting away, you sheepishly grin and relent with an exuberant "Yes!"

Welcome to Walt Disney World. Please keep your cynicism, skepticism, and disbelief outside the vehicle at all times.

WATCH THIS - The African Queen (1951)

Conventional wisdom might tell you to watch *The African Lion*, a feature-length *True-Life Adventure* documentary that was especially influential in the Jungle Cruise's creation. Come July 24, 2020, you'll probably also want to watch Disney's long-promised, big-budget Hollywood adaptation of the ride (à la Johnny Depp and *Pirates of the Caribbean*) starring Dwayne "The Rock" Johnson and Emily Blunt.

But if you really want to see the spirit of the Jungle Cruise captured on film, you'll watch a movie that doesn't have anything to do with Disney. Released just four years before Disneyland opened, *The African Queen* served as something of a model for the attraction. One viewing of this classic starring Humphrey Bogart and Katherine Hepburn and you'll see why. The stars spend most of the movie in a small boat, encountering all kinds of peril as they race down a long and winding river. Sound familiar? Ride the Jungle Cruise and it will!

Here's some good news: this once-elusive classic is now readily accessible. Despite ranking high on many critics' lists of the all-time greatest movies, the unforgettable adventure film went decades without a home video release in the United States. Then in 2010, Paramount opened up its vault and brought *The African Queen* to both DVD and Blu-ray at long last. An HD digital release followed. Now it's easier than ever to experience a little bit of Jungle Cruise at home.

Walt Disney's Enchanted Tiki Room

Type: Theater show

Duration: 12 minutes

Height Restriction: None

Popularity/Crowds: Low to Moderate

FastPass+: No

Fear Factor: 2 out of 5 (darkness; storm effects)

Wet Factor: None

Preshow: Outdoor, standing-room-only dialogue between two Animatronic birds

Best Time to Visit: Anytime

For more than a decade, guests avoided Adventureland's only theater performance like the plague — or, to use a more appropriate metaphorical epidemic, the avian flu. That's because corporate meddling had turned the park's once-beloved bird show into a caustic schlockfest. As luck would have it, the unpopular edition ultimately went down in flames — literally — prompting cheers from parkgoers as Disney deigned to return the show to its original glory. Phoenix-like, a whole new bird arose from the ashes of disaster. This is the story of the Enchanted Tiki Room.

When it opened in Disneyland in 1963, the Enchanted Tiki Room marked Disney's first use of Audio-Animatronics, the robotic creatures that populate many of its attractions today. What was originally to be an interactive restaurant experience became a theatre-in-the-round instead, with a harmonious host of birds cracking wise and singing songs from the rafters above the audience. It's been substantially the same ever since in Disneyland, where it lives on as a perpetual favorite of the California park's guests.

Florida's Magic Kingdom called its version of the show Tropical Serenade, but it was essentially identical to California's original. The East Coast performances were warmly welcomed when they began in October 1971, and they ran mostly unchanged for more than a quarter century. By the mid-1990s, though, attendance at Florida's Tiki Room had slumped while California's stayed strong enough. In response to the decline, Walt Disney World closed its Tiki Room in September 1997 and reopened it seven months later with a new name and a brand-new show inside.

The Enchanted Tiki Room — Under New Management presented a "hipper," more contemporary twist on the original production, or at least that was the idea. In the new version, Iago from *Aladdin* and Zazu from *The Lion King* were the stars of the show. The brightly feathered headliners announced they'd been recruited to bring renewed life to the Tiki birds' dying act. That was Corporate Disney's way of saying, "Out with the old and in with the slightly less old."

By the time Under New Management opened in 1998, *Aladdin* and *The Lion King* had already left the New Release shelves. While both films remained unquestionably popular (and still are), the assumption that these supporting characters could alone rejuvenate interest in an attraction that had very little to do with them was far from bankable. It didn't work out.

Instead, audiences resented the changes. Loud-mouthed Iago was now interrupting the classic theme song to brashly declare that it (and, by implication, anyone who still loved it) was washed up and lame. How rude. It didn't help that the production felt instantly dated either.

The new show came across as a musical game of badminton, with birdies bouncing back and forth from classic to contemporary and frequently getting lodged in the mid-'80s in between. Its soundtrack included radio relics "Hot, Hot, Hot," "Conga," and "Get on Your Feet." Of all the songs ever made, that Disney chose three that are relegated to local car sales commercials and the back of karaoke books is indicative of the low standards for the Tiki Room reboot. With no disrespect to the Gloria Estefan songbook, one can't help but question the use of not one but two of her songs back-to-back. The latter half of the show turned into some kind of Fowls' Salute to the Miami Sound Machine, and you started to wonder if you were even in Walt Disney World anymore.

For a long time, the most exciting thing about Under New Management was the race it launched between my eyes and Walt Disney in his grave to see which could roll faster. That changed on January 12, 2011, when a small fire broke out in the attic of the Tiki Room and forced guests inside to evacuate unscathed. The doors closed, Heaven smiled, and the interrupting Iago was never to be heard from again.

Disney has been tight-lipped about the fire's cause and origin, though fans were quick to espouse theories of their own.[2] Whatever happened, the damage was severe enough to keep the Tiki Room closed for seven months, just long enough for Disney to decide the original show should return later that year. To fans, this was divine intervention. One of the park's most despised attractions had — quite randomly and without explanation — burned down, and Disney was pledging to bring back the esteemed original in its place. Even better, rumor had it the infamous Iago Animatronic was nearly completely destroyed in the fire. This must have been how Dorothy felt when the Wicked Witch went down in a puddle.

At long last, on August 15, 2011, the attraction reopened as Walt Disney's Enchanted Tiki Room. The founder's name in the title signaled a return to form. In Disneyland, it had been called Walt Disney's Enchanted Tiki Room because it was literally Walt Disney's — he owned the attraction himself, separate and apart from Walt Disney Productions.[3] Obviously, that's not the case today, but Florida's newest incarnation certainly has the tone and quality of Walt's personal touch. Save for a few unfortunate but ultimately minor abridgements, the new Magic Kingdom edition mirrors its Disneyland counterpart almost exactly. Only the outdoor preshow is significantly different.

Standing in a covered lanai while waiting for the doors to open, guests meet two toucans named Claude and Clyde. Their witty waterfall banter reveals that they and their winged friends haven't always been able to talk. They were apparently spellbound while living deep down the rivers of Adventureland (in the Jungle Cruise, perhaps?), but a gong beckoning entry into the show hall interrupts them before they can finish their story. We never get to find out exactly what led to their enchantment, only that it has something to do with the room we're about to enter, a room they call the magical Sunshine Pavilion.[4]

All we really need to know is that what we're in for is anything but a real-life bird show. These are fantastical forktails, after all, and they enjoy some sort of mysterious relationship with the easily stirred Tiki gods. Their Sunshine Pavilion is beautiful, lush, and exotic inside. The low lighting, bright colors, and instant air conditioning extend an immediate invitation to relaxation. We take our seats on backrest-equipped benches and settle in for what turns out to be a lighthearted and admittedly strange variety show.

The casual parkgoer might be surprised, upon seeing Walt Disney's Enchanted Tiki Room for the first time, that this is what all the fuss was about. There is nothing especially show stopping here. Modestly mobile birds sing a few simple songs, and then the audience goes on its merry way. The seats do not move. There are no sudden surprises and no 3-D. Not a single princess waltzes in for brand recognition. Even the jokes are pretty gentle and unlikely to prompt guffaws. So why was anyone demanding to see this thing again?

The Tiki Room's magic lies not so much in its fanfare or technological razzle-dazzle — though it did receive several upgrades and a remastered soundtrack when it reopened — but in the way it transports our subconscious to Hawaii. The show is a concert of soothing music set to seductive rhythms. The entire building is constructed to bring those sounds to life. The wood on the walls opens its eyes to become a living Tiki totem. Flower beds descend from their high-up perches to coo calming harmonies. All around us, nature sings. That's what Polynesia feels like, or at least what we fantasize it to feel like. By cueing those connections for us, and massaging our senses with breezy lullabies, the crooning cast of Tiki dwellers can coax us into a Hawaiian state of mind.

The attraction doesn't necessarily set out to simulate a tropic retreat. There's no exposition to that end in the script or its backstory, and on a surface level, the show is focused more on the novelty of singing birds than the theme of Polynesian paradise. And while the room does draw from the isles of that region — principally Hawaii, Fiji, Tonga, and the Cook Islands — the central theme song incorporates Latin American and European influences too. But as we take respite from all the walking we've done outside and enjoy the crisp air conditioning in a darkened room, letting those easy tempos and choral, floral melodies wash over us, our imaginations drift to a place of tropical pampering. The Tiki Room is a vacation from our vacation, even if for only twelve minutes at a time.

The production reminds us of a different era, largely because it is the product of one. From the subtle references to jazz singers like Louis Armstrong to its relatively primitive technology, the Tiki Room is alive with the zeitgeist of the 1960s. For the most part, the humor is universal enough and the arrangement of its score organic enough for the presentation to avoid falling over that fine line between "classic" and "dated." But with emphatic announcements for each successive act, the script almost seems to expect audiences to be more wowed by the sights and sounds than they are likely to be today — a reminder of a time when we were perhaps less insistent on major spectacle for our entertainment.

José, the lead Animatronic, begins each program by waking from an ever-shortening siesta and greeting the real-live-person cast member as "señorita," regardless of their gender.[5] The salutation is simultaneously campy in its lack of sophistication and politically incorrect in its assumption that the host is female. The same can be said for French fowl Pierre's catcall to the women in the audience during the early part of the show, a whistle he ostensibly intends for waking up his friend but winkingly directs toward the ladies. So far, those exchanges have proven harmless enough to avoid any widely registered offense or major calls for protest. A new generation might even find the nostalgia of those moments charming, or embrace José's disregard for gender as either progressive or amusing in an ironic sense. Then again, sentiment could go the other way, and revision might await us in the future, as has been the case elsewhere in Adventureland (more on that later). Ultimately, whether such banter is insensitive or not, it probably does contribute to a certain yesteryear allure. These quips would never find their way into a newly scripted production, so it's instructive and maybe even escapist to return to a time when they did. We aren't just traveling to Hawaii; we're traveling to 1960s Hawaii. It's two trips in one.

All the romance of a 1960s aloha gets shaken ever so slightly, however, when later in the show those aforementioned Tiki gods start to rouse. Chanting, wailing, and the quickening beat of drums turn the tone almost violent during the luau finale, capped off by a veritable storm inside the theater. Here, nature is singing again, but this time it's a different kind of song. Storms on the shore always have a beautiful drama about them, and this scene taps into that feeling with its memorable Tiki cloudburst. Tropical thunder is as important as seaside serenity in getting the full Polynesian experience.

You can find plenty of luaus like this throughout Hawaii, but you won't come across one done by talking, singing birds. That only happens at Disney. Now that the original show has been resurrected from its enchanted Tiki tomb, audiences can again enjoy an experience that is thoroughly unusual and yet also quintessentially Walt. That's especially true in the closing moments of the show, when the birds rush the audience out to the tune of "Heigh-Ho," the anthem from Walt Disney's very first movie and a song as timeless as the Tiki Room now feels again. It is a bit of a shame, I suppose, that things had to end this way, with the otherwise likeable Iago burned up and his audiences burned out. Perhaps the Imagineers could still find a place for him as a part of the show — locked in a cage at the exit, maybe. If nothing else, it would serve as a reminder that some things are best left unchanged.

WATCH THIS - The Even Stevens Movie (2003)

An unusual recommendation for an unusual attraction. "Even Stevens" (1999 - 2003) ran for 65 episodes on The Disney Channel before bowing out with a feature-length TV movie. The series was one of the network's best, but you needn't see a single episode to enjoy this comedy adventure, which stars Shia LaBeouf, Christy Carlson Romano, and Tim Meadows, along with a cameo appearance by "Full House" star Dave Coulier.

> The harmlessly dysfunctional Stevens family gets talked into an exotic getaway on an uncharted island, its region not quite specific — but then that's part of the mystique. Once they arrive, they find that the wildly wardrobed natives are far from friendly. Throw in the occasional Tiki god and you've got yourself a screwball escapade on the order of Walt Disney's Enchanted Tiki Room! There's even some corporate meddling to make a mess of things in the middle. It's like a page right out of Adventureland history.

Swiss Family Treehouse

Type: Walk-through environment
Duration: Usually 10 to 15 minutes, but tour at your own pace
Height Restriction: None
Popularity/Crowds: Low
FastPass+: No
Fear Factor: 1 out of 5 (heights)
Wet Factor: None
Preshow: None
Best Time to Visit: Anytime

Like any large and sprawling tree, the Swiss Family Treehouse[6] has centuries-old roots — not in soil, but in literature and pop culture. They date back to 1719, when Daniel Defoe published *Robinson Crusoe*, believed by some to be the first proper novel written in English. Nearly a hundred years later, in 1812, Johann David Wyss retold the story in his own adaptation, *The Swiss Family Robinson*. Wyss's rendition has itself been adapted dozens of times since then, never more notably than in Walt Disney's 1960 live-action classic of the same name.

Two years after its theatrical release, Walt introduced his film to Disneyland with the Swiss Family Treehouse, which Walt Disney World re-created for its opening. That makes the Magic Kingdom's Treehouse the clone of an exhibit inspired by a film version of a retelling of an original English novel (which was itself based on several pre-existing true-life accounts).[7] Phew! With that many popular iterations out there, one might assume Swiss Family Treehouse is as familiar-feeling an attraction as any in the Magic Kingdom. On the contrary, I'd wager that many guests remain oblivious to the existence of Walt's film, making the attraction unique for not only its design but also its lack of commercial appeal.

Swiss Family Treehouse doesn't fit into any of the usual theme park attraction categories. Neither ride nor show nor playground nor really even an exhibit, the walk-through tour is exactly what its name suggests: a tree house. Then again, "tree house" might imply playfulness to many, while the Swiss Family's quarters offer only a slow-moving expedition up and down a long series of stairs, with minimal interactivity along the way. Guests moving through the tree house, which consists of platforms built on several levels, will find the family's imaginatively makeshift living quarters. Bedrooms, a kitchen, china sets, musical instruments, and an elaborate pulley system for fetching water all create the appearance of home life. Small signposts along the way provide a minimalist recounting of the *Swiss Family Robinson* story.

When the Treehouse opened in 1962, *Swiss Family Robinson* was fresh off an overwhelmingly successful box office run. Walt was a master promoter, and in-park exhibits trumpeting his newest movies were hardly uncommon. *Babes in Toyland* and *20,000 Leagues Under the Sea* had each gotten their own, and even Sleeping Beauty Castle, the Disneyland icon with a diorama tour inside, was designed to promote a movie that wouldn't hit theaters for another four years. But while the *Leagues* and *Toyland* sets stuck around just long enough to create a little buzz for those movies and capitalize on their success, the Swiss Family Treehouse has stayed much, much longer. Of course, those smaller exhibits paled in comparison to the grandiosity of the Treehouse. It is so massive and impressive a structure that its removal even decades later would be an enormous and surprising undertaking.

Still, Disney makes a point of keeping its parks current, sustaining guests' interest and allowing the company to sell merchandise in a way that feels organic. Unlike *Mary Poppins* (which, incidentally, doesn't have a theme park attraction anywhere in the world), *Swiss Family Robinson* has not endured as a fan favorite and you'll be hard-pressed to find it celebrated in any but the most comprehensive Disney anthologies. There's no gift shop at the Treehouse's entrance or exit, no surprise camera inside with instant printouts sold as souvenirs, not even a small booth nearby for selling copies of the movie on DVD.

Why keep the Robinsons' residence around, then? That's a question Disney executives have asked themselves, and they've answered both ways. Disneyland closed its original Treehouse in early 1999 and reopened it four months later under a new name, Tarzan's Treehouse. Ditching the Robinsons and adopting hot-off-the-presses *Tarzan* characters as residents instead, the new attraction differed little from the original, adding only some window dressing, a stronger storybook framework, and a few additional interactive elements. When Hong Kong Disneyland opened in 2005, it opted for *Tarzan* from the get-go. But at Walt Disney World, the Robinsons still rule the roost.

Maybe the mixed reaction to Tarzan's Treehouse in Disneyland persuaded Disney executives that the change would be unwelcome. Maybe keeping the classic Treehouse was Disney World's tradeoff with Disneyland, which got to keep its original Enchanted Tiki Room show (discussed later in this chapter). Or, with three other theme parks to worry about, including the then-still-new Animal Kingdom, maybe Walt Disney World couldn't justify spending money on the overlay at the time.

Whatever the reason, the Swiss Family Robinson storyline lives on in Magic Kingdom, where guests continue to enjoy the attraction even though many probably have only distant memories of the movie at best. Familiarity with the source material really isn't always a prerequisite to fully appreciating an attraction.

The Robinsons' plight — shipwrecked and alone, forced to work with what little they had in order to survive — is made manifest in the expansive and fully functioning home they're said to have constructed out of necessity. The attraction confronts the individual guest with his or her own potential to adapt, innovate, and survive. That theme of survival was incidental in *Tarzan*. In *Swiss Family Robinson*, it's paramount. Like history's greatest castaway stories, the Treehouse encourages visitors to ponder their own capacity for inventiveness and resourcefulness, should they ever be summoned to harness it in this technological age of convenience.

Kudos to Walt Disney World for keeping a classic in place these nearly fifty years. With a remake of the 1960 movie supposedly on the way,[8] Disney just might reap the benefits of the Swiss seed it sowed and nurtured all these years, bringing newfound commercial import to an underrated Magic Kingdom classic at last.

> **WATCH THIS – "Lost" (2004)**
>
> Common sense dictates that you ought to start with *The Swiss Family Robinson*, especially now that it's available in Digital HD, on Blu-ray (from the Disney Movie Club), and on a fully loaded, low-priced "Vault Disney Collection" DVD. But you know what else makes for a nice thematic match with the Swiss Family Treehouse? "Lost." And yep, it's Disney too.
>
> In this TV drama-mystery-adventure series, produced and distributed by Disney and broadcast on Disney-owned ABC, plane passengers find themselves stranded on a mysterious island after a crash landing — the modern day equivalent of a shipwreck. Faced with their own mortality, they tap instincts they didn't realize they had, making the most of meager resources and one another to survive.

The Magic Carpets of Aladdin

Type: Aerial carousel
Duration: Under 2 minutes
Popularity/Crowds: Low to Moderate
Height Restriction: None
FastPass+: Yes; low priority
Fear Factor: 0.5 out of 5 (moderate heights)
Wet Factor: 0.5 out of 5 (spitting camel squirts the occasional guest)
Preshow: None
Boarding Speed: Slow
Best Time to Visit without FastPass+: Anytime, but come back later if you find it crowded.

The Magic Carpets of Aladdin hasn't had a warm reception among many Magic Kingdom fans. But hey, Aladdin himself didn't strike anyone as particularly worthwhile either, and he soon proved there was more to him than meets the eye. We might say the same for his Magic Carpets in Walt Disney World. Though no diamond in the rough, it does have hidden gems. You'll just have to overlook the inherent simplicity and redundancy to find them.

The Magic Carpets of Aladdin is a typical carnival-style flat ride known as an uncovered carousel or a "spinner." A lever inside each vehicle allows us to control how high or low our vehicle "flies" during its very short, very slow rotation. Fantasyland has something similar. There, we ride Dumbo. Here, we ride carpets.

For that matter, Tomorrowland has one too: Astro Orbiter. So when Magic Carpets of Aladdin opened in Magic Kingdom in 2001, it was the park's *third* spinner. That same year, Disney's Animal Kingdom opened its own version with TriceraTop Spin. For a resort that specializes in the unique and impossible, that's a whole lot of a very simple ride. Worse still, making way for Prince Ali meant leaving less room for the thousands of other guests to get through Adventureland's old bazaar. Fans were quick to decry the ride as a street rat of a copycat.

While the topic of walkway width is worthy of debate (Walt Disney World's propensity for spacious paths stands in contrast to Disneyland's intimate and clustered design), so are ride mechanics. On that score, Aladdin's flight fares better in a carousel-for-carousel comparison than its ill repute might suggest.[9]

The Magic Carpets seat four, for starters — and comfortably, I might add. Anyone who's flown on Dumbo knows that even two there is a tight squeeze. There's also the benefit of added control, since the carpets feature joysticks that not only raise and lower the vehicles but tilt them forward and backward too! It's hard to argue that older incarnations are superior when Aladdin invites whole parties to ride together and gives them more to do during their flight.

There's also more to take in. While all of these hub-and-spoke rides employ some beautiful scenery as a backdrop, The Magic Carpets of Aladdin really uses the land around it to bring its narrative to life.

The fictional city of Agrabah, filled with street vendors, crowds, and canopies, originated in 1992's *Aladdin* but took its cue in part from *One Thousand and One Nights*,[10] better known as the "Arabian Nights" tales. With the construction of The Magic Carpets came an entire "village" within Adventureland, one that houses gift shops that do a pretty decent job masquerading as the actual streets of Agrabah. The effect is that guests aren't just flying in circles around Genie's lamp to get a bird's-eye view and hear a few Alan Menken[11] tunes — they're getting the chance to fly over the same city that Aladdin and Jasmine flew over and on what appears to be the very same rug. In this way, the otherwise simple ride is effective at bringing a memorable story to life.

So while The Magic Carpets of Aladdin hardly takes us to "A Whole New World" of ride technology, its integration within a nicely detailed perimeter area makes it a more fully realized experience than other flat rides, at least. Undoubtedly, magic carpet escapism could be better achieved in a more dazzling ride — to borrow from Epcot, a "Soarin' Around Agrabah" attraction could be an E-ticket — but this centerpiece of Adventureland makes do with what it has. Given three wishes, I doubt you'd use one of them to ride this, but at least it gets you close to the lamp.

WATCH THIS – The Thief of Bagdad (1940)

One Thousand and One Nights has inspired many works, including literally every *Aladdin*, *Sinbad*, and *Ali Baba* movie ever made. Prized among them is the 1940 British fantasy, *The Thief of Bagdad* (an old-style spelling of Baghdad).

Distributed by United Artists, the film is now available in the U.S. on DVD as part of the esteemed Criterion Collection and on region-free Blu-ray through international distributors.

Disney's *Aladdin* borrows liberally from *Bagdad*. The animated hero is a composite of the 1940 film's two central protagonists: King Ahmad (John Justin), who takes care of the princess wooing, and Abu (Sabu)[12], who isn't a monkey as in Disney's version, but rather an adventurous young man in the role of Ahmad's thieving, street-rat sidekick.

Bagdad's influence is especially apparent in some of *Aladdin*'s mirror-image scenes. When the evil vizier Jaffar (Conrad Veidt)[13] attempts to convince the Sultan (Miles Malleson) to give him the Princess's (June Duprez) hand in marriage, for example, or when Abu enters a cave to steal a treasured gem, the older movie will feel familiar to younger generations better acquainted with Disney's telling.

One of the most notable differences is the role of the magic carpet, which appears much later in *Bagdad* than in *Aladdin* but assumes greater significance in the former, making this a suitable companion piece for a ride on The Magic Carpets of Aladdin.

Pirates of the Caribbean

Type: Boat ride

Duration: 8 minutes

Height Restriction: None

Popularity/Crowds: Moderate

FastPass+: Yes; medium priority

Fear Factor: 2.5 out of 5 (darkness; ghost themes; weapons effects; small drop; loud noises)

Wet Factor: 3.5 out of 5 (Recent changes to the boats increase your chance of getting wet, sometimes very wet.)

Preshow: None

Boarding Speed: Fast

Best Time to Visit without FastPass+: Mornings or evenings

What's a story before it's told? A place, maybe — the setting. The people. The conflict. The mood, the theme, the tone. That's Pirates of the Caribbean: the who, what, when, where, and why (and aye), but *not* the plot. Because dead men tell no tales. No, Pirates of the Caribbean is the rare Disney classic to eschew traditional storytelling in favor of story*feeling*. It does that by combining two narrative devices that we will consider in some detail here, especially in light of recent changes to the ride: time travel and *in medias res*.[14] To that end, we're going to take a slightly deeper dive into Pirates of the Caribbean than we have our other attractions so far.

In Magic Kingdom, our anti-story begins in Adventureland, where we step inside a Spanish fortress called Castillo del Morro[15] — our first clue that *this* version of Pirates, unlike the original in Disneyland from 1967, is not set in New Orleans — and through the barracks a pirate crew once called home. Along the way, steel bars and dark recesses obscure the sight of bony dungeon dwellers. Whether they are the remains of long-expired prisoners or living skeletons is hard to tell, but their upright posture and a grueling game of chess suggest that they're something less than dead. If ye be scared of ghosts, ye'd best turn back now.

There are docks at the rear of the fortress, where a boat will take us into the foggy darkness of endless caverns ahead. Inside, we find waterfalls, shipwrecks, and a few more sword-wielding bags'o'bones. The black tricorns atop these skeletons tell us they are pirates of the past. There's not a living soul to be seen outside our boat, and the eerie calm, punctuated by a haunting echo — "dead men tell no tales" — is positively tomblike.

But all that changes in an instant as we topple over one of those waterfalls and plunge into the epic crossfire of cannons, the environs suddenly springing to life. The very same fortress that served as our entry to port is now under siege by pirates! Hold on to your fanny packs, folks, and prepare to be plundered, because that waterfall just took us back in time.

From here on, debauchery and violence will set the scene, but none of it too graphic or visibly shocking to the conscience. Gulping down one spirit-filled jug after another, bands of buccaneers revel in their lawlessness, oblivious to the chaos surrounding them. Guns fire, men fight, and buildings go up in flames… and still, the carousal goes on.

They're always running, always chasing, always carousing. There is no beginning or end to this journey, just middle. We might think of this as a story *in medias res*, a Latin term meaning "in the middle of things," often used when a story opens in the middle of the action and then works its way backward, or else proceeds from the midpoint while using exposition to catch us up on what's already happened. There is no proceeding in Pirates, though, because our journey here is confined to a single flashback, beginning with the waterfall that took us back in time. Before there's the chance for any exposition or a plot point, we're headed up a lift hill and back into the present day at the end of the ride.

By resisting a narrative and concentrating on total immersion in its environment, Pirates of the Caribbean walks us through the existential life of a pirate. The ride's iconic theme song reflects that mission — "Yo ho, yo ho, a pirate's life for me." Need it say more? That is precisely what this attraction offers us: a pirate's life for we. The rest of the lyrics reinforce that same idea, describing with rapid fire the various hobbies of piratedom — "We pillage, we plunder, we rifle and loot… we kidnap and ravage and don't give a hoot." These aren't storytelling lines, but rather, descriptors of a more general story world.

The combination of time travel and *in medias res* is more important than it seems to be because of the moral that this attraction *must* impart if it is to be anything other than deplorable. In order to enjoy the rebel-rousing, we must *first* know that these pirates get their comeuppance in the end. They die and rot away in the fog of a forgotten cavern, alone and with no one to tell of their plight. Dead men tell no tales.

It's a subtle moral, often overlooked. This quality has led to some misunderstandings about the ride from guests and critics who've read it as an adventure quest rather than as a fable. The ride's moral message might have changed the way we understood the old scenes. For example, the one where the pirates chased women through the town (altered in the 1990s so that the women chased the men instead). Or the one where the pirates auctioned off imprisoned women as brides, shouting, "We wants the redhead!" (altered in 2017 so that the redhead is now part of a pirate crew, taking prisoners of her own and forcing them at gunpoint to trot their prized possessions out to the riverbed, where she's auctioning the items off to her rival raiders).[16] Disney didn't offer an official reason when it made those changes, but it is probably safe to assume that evolving cultural norms were at play. Maybe the ride's subtle morality play was getting lost in the fog.

Be This Arrrt, Aye?: What Kind of Art Is a Ride?

How are we to reconcile these kinds of alterations with our understanding of Pirates of the Caribbean as a classic work of art? If theme park rides are indeed works of art — and I cannot find a reasonable argument that would distinguish them from our understanding of what art is — then we are right to worry when they are reworked, revised, or removed. More worrisome still is if the changes arise out of a misguided or poorly considered interpretation of the art. Then again, if we accept that this *is* art, who's to say which reading is right?

Perhaps we can concede at least this much: a theme park ride is surely distinct from other forms of art, just as a painting is distinct from a movie, which is distinct from a song, and so on. Rides are probably more akin to live theatre than they are to motion pictures. Like theatre, a theme park ride is a new release every single day. So Pirates of the Caribbean speaks to its audience not only from 1967 or 1971 but also from 2020, and 2021 to follow, and so on. When audiences sit down to watch *The African Queen*, they know it's from 1951; when they ride the Jungle Cruise, even though the setting is in the past, the presentation is happening in the present day, no matter when it was first staged.[17]

An instructive point of comparison is Broadway's *Peter Pan* (not to be confused with the Disney film). Originally staged in 1954, it has been revived countless times and has seen changes to some of its offensive Native American stereotyping over the years. Some of those changes have been embraced as improvements on the show. The same is true for Rodgers & Hammerstein's *Cinderella* (again, not to be confused with the animated Disney film), which has been changed so many times on stage and screen through the years that it is essentially impossible to point to any one production as the definitive or "true" play.[18] All of this is accepted as a normal, healthy, and even vital part of the art form that is live theatre. Perhaps the same is true to some extent of theme park rides. Like a play, theme park rides are forever and inextricably staged in the present no matter when they were first scripted or built. Just as there's no way to go back and watch a Broadway show once its run has ended, there's no way to experience an original theme park ride once it has been altered or destroyed. YouTube videos and the hope of revival (read: rebuilding) will have to suffice.

Walt Disney chimed in on this topic once. He said:

> *"A picture is a thing that once you wrap it up and turn it over to Technicolor, you're through. Snow White is a dead issue with me. The last picture I just finished—the one I just wrapped up a few weeks ago—it's gone; I can't touch it. There's things in it I don't like? I can't do anything about it.*
>
> *"I wanted something live, something that could grow, something I could keep plussing with ideas, you see? The park is that. Not only can I add things but even the trees will keep growing; the thing will get more beautiful every year. And as I find what the public likes— and when a picture's finished and I put it out—I find out what they like, or they don't like, and I have to apply that to some other thing; I can't change that picture, so that's why I wanted that park."*[19]

Today's Walt Disney Company has probably been guilty of using this quote to justify a few too many cost-cutting or crowd-pleasing changes.

But to Walt's point, if an increasing number of people don't like what they see in an attraction, there isn't anything in our understanding of Walt's philosophy — or in our understanding of theatrical art — to prohibit a change. But one would hope that change will always be for the better, not only in terms of societal mores but also in the context of the attraction itself. Surely it is possible to avoid offense without settling for second-rate showmanship. If the women are to chase the men, the new scene must still make for an easy read that adds to guests' understanding of the world they have entered. If the redhead is to be a pirate instead of a prisoner, Imagineers must make sure the vignette never stands out as "less than" the others in the ride. If Johnny Depp is going to pop up out of a rum barrel, it had better make sense in the world around him.[20]

Change is never easy. It's only human to mourn that which is now confined to a memory. Guests disagree as to how the new scenes play. To my mind, the women chasing the men is a joke that works so well Marc Davis[21] could have conceived it himself; the redhead is more interesting as a pirate and her new scene reads as easily as the old one; and Captain Jack's commandeering of the ride works without compromising the ride's anti-story *in medias res*. His presence here merely hints at the silhouette of a story that really requires seeing the movie to follow. If anything, the alterations underscore how rich this story world was in the first place. If the ride's fictive landscape hadn't been so remarkably and authentically detailed, there could be no *Black Pearl*... or at least not one that rings so true.

Then again, the chicken jokes in the new auction scene aren't half as witty as the old ones, and it's a little bit of a bummer that we can't experience this 1960s-era attraction without a 2000s-era movie on our mind.[22] You might have your own list of things you do like about one version and don't like about another, just as we might get up in arms over whether Angela Lansbury or Bernadette Peters was Broadway's better Mama Rose. The debatability is part of what makes it art.

Finding the Hidden Treasure: Rummaging Up the Ride's Appeal

Pirates of the Caribbean was a masterpiece well before Jack Sparrow and the retooled redhead ever sailed in on the seas of change. How do we explain its fundamental appeal?

In his memoir *Life on the Mississippi*, Mark Twain wrote of his boyhood days, "Now and then we had a hope that if we lived and were good, God would permit us to be pirates." We all know what it was like to be fascinated by pirates as children, just as we all know the truth about the fascinations of youth: they are diminished but never finished.

As we grow to understand the evils of the world and what buccaneers really were, piracy loses its luster. Still, even (and especially) as adults, we must all wonder what kind of mind it takes to cast one's cares to the wind and embrace a life of lawlessness. The ride makes it comfortable for us to explore that question because we've already seen that the pirate's life ends in tragic misfortune. So on some level, Pirates of the Caribbean's appeal is not unlike that of a murder mystery or a true-crime show. Experts assign our interest in these things to instinct: catharsis, escape, self-protection, self-control, schadenfreude, the desperate need to understand that which is different, and the euphoria of adrenaline.[23] In Pirates of the Caribbean, we come face to face with violent criminals but escape unharmed.

Clamor and peril are part of the package: swashbuckling, gunfire, and flames. There are elements of horror, too: flickering lights, howling wind, human skulls, and voices without faces. It can be strangely exciting to flirt with the paranormal, and Pirates thrusts us into that courtship early on. Inasmuch as ghosts are part of pirate lore, the supernatural elements lend a literary quality to the ride. The nighttime setting, so impressively conveyed by a moonlit canvas high above us, only makes it richer. Everything seems more dangerous, more ominous, and even more romantic at night. But Pirates keeps its frights light, a careful balancing of moods. Even its theme song is a duet between an intimidating bass singer and a silly, warbling, hiccupping fool.

Theme park theorist Kira Prince writes that, while fans are quick to call Pirates immersive, it's "the *way* it immerses the rider into those environments and story" that sets it apart. "Experiential immersion," as Prince calls it, is an effect that maximizes the "kinesthetic and emotional impact" of the ride's design through pacing and induction. It's responsible for the trance-like effect that anyone who has experienced Pirates of the Caribbean has surely felt. It's the "blissful sensation of forgetting yourself" such that we "feel" a story even if we aren't told one.[24] This marriage of immersion and motion gives us a sense that we've gone through something with a beginning and end when all is said and done, even if there was only ever middle.

There's so much more to a ride like Pirates than set dressing and story. Walt and his team, led by Imagineer Marc Davis, created one of the most engrossing story worlds in all of fiction, with the bold goal of letting guests indulge in the world for what it is, leaving the tale-telling to our own imaginations. The particular stories that screenwriters Ted Elliott and Terry Rossio conjured up for the blockbusting film series are but examples of the innumerable sagas that could unfold within that universe. The writers were able to work within this fully realized environment to develop plotlines so popular that the masses demanded their addition to the ride that inspired them in the first place. That achievement is a credit to Davis's and Disney's extraordinary success in *not* telling one heck of a story.

WATCH THIS – Blackbeard's Ghost (1968)

Released to theaters less than a year after Pirates of the Caribbean opened in Disneyland, this pirate comedy begins when young Steve Walker (Dean Jones) moves to a coastal town in North Carolina, where he's been offered a position as the new high school track coach. He happens to arrive during a rally to save Blackbeard's Inn, a local hotel under threat of acquisition by a casino developer. While rummaging through some of the inn's artifacts, Steve stumbles upon an old spell book and accidentally summons the ghost of Blackbeard himself (Peter Ustinov). As luck would have it, Walker is the only one who can see or hear the famous pirate's apparition.

Like Pirates of the Caribbean, *Blackbeard's Ghost* is a hearty pirate tale tuned into the supernatural side of buccaneering. Ustinov's interpretation of Blackbeard could easily have been an inspiration for Johnny Depp's Jack Sparrow (though Depp's true muse was Rolling Stones guitarist Keith Richards). Both legendary actors lend their conniving captains a delightful blend of the silly and unsavory.

Chapter 2

Frontierland

"Frontierland: it is here that we experience the story of our country's past — the color, romance and drama of Frontier America as it developed from wilderness trails to roads, riverboats, railroads, and civilization — a tribute to the faith, courage, and ingenuity of our hearty pioneers who blazed the trails and made this progress possible."
                        Walt Disney, "Dateline: Disneyland," *July 17, 1955*

Walt and his team designed Frontierland to "give you the feeling of having lived, even for a short while, during our country's pioneer days." It's easy to think about Frontierland as a place for action, where they put the extra "wild" in the Wild, Wild West. More than that, though, it is a living period piece. In Frontierland, life moves at more of a saunter than a gallop.

Oversized porches and rope-bound logs make up the storefronts and walkways of Frontierland, where the wooden-plank sidewalks are raised off the ground to keep all that imaginary dirt off the lads' boots and the lasses' billowing dresses. The steady-flowing river and its slow-rolling watercraft set the pace for this olden town, and so does its music.

With peacefully plodding tunes like "Home on the Range," "Git Along, Little Dogies," and "Oh My Darling, Clementine," there is an attractive laziness in the climate here. At home, you could fall asleep to the background music loop, but in the park you'll be engrossed in the ambience of Frontierland and its five cardinal attractions — Country Bear Jamboree, Big Thunder Mountain Railroad, Frontierland Shootin' Arcade, Splash Mountain, and Tom Sawyer Island. It's a place for slinging guns and toppling over waterfalls, for woodland hoedowns and do-si-dos. It's a place for eating cinnamon-coated churros like there's no tomorrow. And at the end of the day, it's a place for loafing in the take-it-easy tempo of Disney's American Frontier.

Country Bear Jamboree

Type: Theater show
Duration: 11 minutes
Height Restriction: None
Popularity/Crowds: Low to Moderate
FastPass+: No
Fear Factor: None
Wet Factor: None
Preshow: None
Best Time to Visit: Anytime

If you're like me, you just don't get the Country Bear Jamboree. Or, I should say, if you're like I used to be. The attraction is a disappointment to many, a glorified Chuck E. Cheese where the pizza must be eaten before you come inside and the only arcade game in sight is a simple, not-included-in-the-price-of-admission shooting gallery that even the NRA might pass up. During my many jaunts through Frontierland, if I went inside (and usually I didn't) it was because a travel buddy of mine insisted on it or because I needed an air-conditioned nap.

In the not altogether unlikely event that you haven't taken your own journey inside the Country Bear theater, all you need to know is that the roughly 11-minute show parades a series of bears on and off a multi-platform stage as they perform one old-time ditty after another. A top hat-wearing bear named Henry serves as emcee, engaging his fellow bears in backwoods banter that is the very paradigm of campy humor.

That hillbilly tour de force never appealed to me, thus my infrequent attendance. Over the years, though, my reluctant jamborees added up, and after countless rounds of forced laughter and sarcastic applause, I one day found myself doing something I hadn't done before — I was singing along. Through no fault of my own, my subconscious had tuned in and learned every twangy word to every corny song in the show. No sooner had I found myself synchronized with the bears than another, more sickening realization dawned upon me: I wasn't just participating. I was enjoying it. *"Heaven help me,"* I thought, *"I'm a sellout."*

Years of ardent derision gave way to a healthy, albeit moderate appreciation for what is perhaps Walt Disney's World's most divisive, love-it-or-hate-it experience.[1] That appreciation isn't necessarily easy to share, particularly if your first visit to Walt Disney World came under the presidency of anyone after Jimmy Carter. If that's you, then allow me to draw from my own Country Bear journey to change the way you think about the Jamboree so that you, too, can anxiously await its next stale punch line with bated breath.

Walt Disney himself worked on the Country Bear Jamboree but died before he could see its debut as part of the Magic Kingdom's grand opening on October 1, 1971. A Frontierland original, the show enjoyed instant popularity, becoming an integral part of the new Walt Disney World experience that the media devoted so much attention to in the early '70s. That warm embrace led not only to a replica in Disneyland the next year but also an entire land in the California park dedicated to the show's stars, Bear Country.[2] Various incarnations have come and gone on both coasts over the years but while Disneyland's closed its doors for good at the dawn of the millennium, the original show still runs every day in Florida's Magic Kingdom.

The show opens with the promise that it will be a "jamboree featuring a bit of Americana, our musical heritage of the past." That places the attraction very nicely in the crook between nostalgia for our own past and reverence for historical traditions that frame the Magic Kingdom.

Musically, the show is reminiscent of the recordings of "old-timey" traditional folk music made popular in the 1930s and '40s. The Carter Family comes to mind. Of course, the Carters and their ilk were artists of a not-so-distant past for the parents and grandparents visiting Walt Disney World in 1971. For many, the show was likely a pleasant reminder of the homegrown musicianship they knew before the rock era and the vast reach of mainstream radio. Naturally, those who know traditional country music as an important part of popular culture are fewer and farther between today. The diminished relevance that the passage of time casts upon the genre showcased in the attraction might in part explain why its popularity has also faded with time.

But even to those who are hearing the plunk of a banjo for the very first time inside the Country Bear theater, the music has something important to offer. The lands of the Magic Kingdom are each designed to transport their guests to a different point in time. That goal is most effectively achieved by a drastic change in aesthetics — take one step out of Adventureland and into Frontierland and everything you see and hear is suddenly radically different. As any Disney parkgoer can tell you, music is a pivotal part of that experience. That's where the Country Bear Jamboree comes in.

"The American Frontier" probably most accurately describes the first three quarters of the nineteenth century and accordingly, Disney's Frontierland attractions set their sights primarily on the mid-1800s. The Country Bear Jamboree is therefore a kind of live soundtrack for the world you've entered. You might very well have seen this kind of show somewhere in the Midwest in 1875, so it makes sense to sit down and enjoy it while you're pretending you've gone back in time. Granted, you wouldn't have found singing bears back then, but if anthropomorphic animals breaking into song are too far out there for you, you might need to spend your vacation time somewhere else.

There's something Jim Henson-esque about these bears. Henson's Muppets are, after all, a motley crew of well-meaning creatures intent on staging a show and entertaining an audience but failing spectacularly in the attempt. The Country Bears are doing the very same; they want to stage a musical revue but keep falling short. Like the Muppets, their charm lies in their capacity for failure. That's why the absolute highlight of the show, a slurred ballad called "Blood on the Saddle" performed by the laughably oversized Big Al, scores Al-sized laughs every time.[3] Kermit and his gang fail because they're either too self-absorbed (Miss Piggy, Sam the Eagle) or too talentless (Fozzie Bear) to get the job done. Henry's bears fail because they're just a little too backwoods and a little too bottom-of-the-class to keep things together. As an audience, we know they mean well, though, so their efforts make them adorable, no matter the result.

There's also something to be said for the value of country music in the show. The country-western genre works because it speaks to the common problems of the everyman, and it does so in a simple and honest way. Twang isn't everyone's cup of tea but few will struggle to find songs in the country music repertoire to which they can easily relate. That innate appeal is central to the Jamboree, a showcase for the early country-western style. Self-deprecating lyrics like "My woman ain't purty but she don't swear none; she's kind of heavy, don't weigh a ton" and "All the guys that turn me on turn me down" are funny because they speak to anxieties that most people have connected with at one time or another.

But for all the charm I've recently found in the Country Bear Jamboree, there's no denying that the show continues to bewilder a good portion of its audience. That the attraction isn't going to be the hit sensation today that it was in 1971 is arguably inevitable, but for years, the theater was a bit of a fix-me-up. Lyrics and puns were hard to make out thanks to an audio system that couldn't compete with the factory speakers in most cars. I suspect that the lackluster technical presentation has been a significant factor in the underwhelming of many guests over the last decade or so. Of course, the pace dragged just a tad, too.

Fortunately, the attraction received a woefully overdue refurbishment in the fall of 2012, reopening on October 17th with brighter lights, more vivid colors, newly enhanced audio, and an entire cast of dazzlingly redesigned Animatronics. Bits of clever dialogue were regrettably truncated, two of the show's less memorable songs were completely excised, and several other performances were slightly abridged, but that all seems a small price to pay for a new lease on life. Change is never easy for fond-hearted fans, but at the risk of bruising nostalgic affections, I can't help but think that casual guests might actually start to care about this show again now that it feels zippy, bright, and alive. And if the public doesn't start caring, well, I shudder to think that the Bears' act might someday fold up for good.[4]

I wouldn't endorse the update if I thought it didn't retain the heart and soul of the original presentation, but in my evaluation, it does. The Bears are still showing us that even their very best is a bit of a laugh, and it's as easy as ever to fall in love with them along the way.

Of course, there's no guarantee that a shorter show and new polish will change the public's puzzlement regarding the Country Bear Jamboree. It remains something of a cultural head-scratcher for many. Maybe there's more Disney could do to prevent the show from drifting into the realm of the "A-ticket," once allocated for the park's least-in-demand items. For starters, welcoming food into the theater could breathe new life into the place. With no counterpart to Disneyland's Golden Horseshoe Saloon,[5] the Magic Kingdom is in need of a dinner theater. Why not let an old favorite fill that much-needed role? Granted, an 11-minute show doesn't allow a lot of time for Disney's many food-loving guests to stuff their faces full to satisfaction. With the Pecos Bill Tall Tale Inn and Café right next door, though, and plenty of snack carts around, inviting guests to bring their outside food indoors for an 11-minute show should make for a happier and ultimately less disappointed audience. After all, the way to a tourist's heart is through his or her stomach.

That said, a few minutes without food haven't kept millions from embracing the attraction for nearly fifty years. There's a reason the Country Bear Jamboree is one of the best-known productions in Disney Parks history, but if that reason has eluded you until now — well believe me, I can relate. The next time you're passing by the log cabin with those tired old bears inside, though, give it another try. If you're a first-timer, go in with an open mind. Pay attention to the understated throwaways, clap along when the beat feels right, and allow yourself to enjoy the sometimes silly, sometimes droll entertainment that the Animatronic performers are serving up for you. If you do all that while thinking about the show in the context of the Magic Kingdom and its presentation of the American Frontier, you just might find it more ...er... bearable than you ever have before.

WATCH THIS - Westward Ho, the Wagons! (1956)

Sure, there is a Disney movie out there called *The Country Bears*, directly inspired by the attraction... but if its measly $16.9 million domestic gross and 30% Rotten Tomatoes score[6] are any kind of a gauge, you probably won't like it (then again, I happen to enjoy the movie more than most). Instead, try this slightly more obscure Disney film — if you can find it. *Westward Ho, the Wagons!* is a grandiose Western musical made in Technicolor and Cinemascope, two beautiful filmmaking processes that were expensive and rare in 1956. Originally written for TV, Walt upgraded the movie to theaters following the enormous success of "Davy Crockett" and "The Mickey Mouse Club" (*Wagons* stars Fess Parker[7] alongside a slew of Mouseketeers).

After they left theaters, Disney movies in those days were often broadcast as an edited, two-part TV special and featured on the popular "Disneyland" anthology series. That's how *Wagons* made its TV debut in February 1961. When the movie later came to VHS in 1986 (and again in 1997), it was only in its TV form, edited for time and cropped from Cinemascope. The VHS is long out of print today and the movie has never been revisited for DVD, perhaps due to its sometimes-unflattering portrayal of Native Americans. Eager viewers are in luck, though, as this enjoyable little product of it time still turns up as an inexpensive rental through online Video on Demand services (still only as the TV edit) and might soon be available on Disney+. That's good news because *Westward Ho, the Wagons!* is a ready-made primer for the Country Bear Jamboree.

For starters, the Country Bears sing the "Davy Crockett" theme as part of their show. That song isn't a part of *Wagons,* but the man who played Davy Crockett does sing a number of tunes that fit right into the Country Bears' musical palette. Even though some of the better numbers were dropped for the TV airing, there's enough left for a meaningful sample of simple folk songs in their native Frontier setting. Besides, if you've seen the movie, Disney will reward you with a subtle nod on your way out of the door. Just across from the Country Bear exit is a food wagon with a sign that reads "Westward Ho Refreshments." Eat, sing, and be bear-y!

Big Thunder Mountain Railroad

Type: Roller coaster
Duration: 3 to 4 minutes
Height Restriction: 40 inches or taller (adult riders can switch off)
Popularity/Crowds: E-ticket
FastPass+: Yes; high priority
Fear Factor: 3 out of 5 (sharp turns and slight drops at moderately high speed; heights)
Wet Factor: 0.5 out of 5 (occasional light mist)
Preshow: None
Boarding Speed: Moderate to Fast
Best Time to Visit without FastPass+: Early morning or late night

Big Thunder Mountain Railroad might be Magic Kingdom's most conventional roller coaster experience. That's saying something, given that it zips through a towering desert landscape and beckons guests to Frontierland from the park entrance and beyond. At Walt Disney World, it seems, even convention gets spruced up with panache. The level of visual detail in Big Thunder gives the coaster an "it" factor that turns this super-sized upgrade of the standard mine train[8] ride into the "wildest ride in the wilderness."

The first Big Thunder Mountain opened at Disneyland on September 2, 1979. One year later, an even bigger one boomed at Walt Disney World. Since then, Tokyo Disneyland and Disneyland Paris have each added the attraction to their respective mountain ranges as well. But even though it officially debuted in California, the attraction actually traces back to right here in Florida.

Big Thunder is the brainchild of Tony Baxter,[9] former Imagineer and an official Disney Legend in his own time. After Pirates of the Caribbean opened in Disneyland's New Orleans Square in 1967, Disney wanted a ride-through experience of the same scale to give East Coast America a glimpse of the West in the same way that Pirates had given West Coasters a taste of the Caribbean. Plans began for a major "cowboys versus Indians" ride to serve as Walt Disney World's answer to Disneyland's Pirates hit. The new ride would be called The Western River Expedition. When heavy attendance in Florida required rapid production of crowd-swallowing attractions, though, Disney decided to scrap those plans. The Imagineers pulled out their ready-to-go Pirates blueprints instead and built an economy-sized replica as a quick means of crowd control.

Still needing an E-ticket, Disney World asked its Imagineers to fill the large plot of Frontierland with something special. Tony Baxter listened and thus Big Thunder Mountain Railroad — his first major Imagineering project — emerged from the plans for what was once to be The Western River Expedition. But because science fiction was all the rage in the 1970s, Disney's attention shifted to the Space Mountain project in Florida, putting Big Thunder on the back burner. That's how Baxter's mine train ended up in Disneyland first. The Magic Kingdom didn't wait too long, though, opening its own version in the fall of 1980.

At Disney World, the mountain is modeled after the earth-toned sandstone towers and buttes of Monument Valley in Utah. Those who have visited the Valley (or who've at least seen it in films like John Ford's classic *Stagecoach*) will note the resemblance. Big Thunder immediately impresses with its man-made majesty, the secret of which is that the roller coaster housed within the mountain is barely visible from the outside. Baxter's primary design objective was to make the rock look like it existed before the rail track was put in place, and he pulled it off with style.

Standing at the foot of the mountain, one can catch only fleeting glimpses of a reckless locomotive lurching around one of Big Thunder's many bends, creating the appearance that the train is traveling across a real rock formation. The illusion continues aboard the train itself, where there's far more rock than track to be seen. Passengers are treated to sweeping vistas of intricately striated columns as they barrel in and out of the mountain's caves. Where the track is visible, it's disguised as aged wood set atop the rocky surface.

That attention to detail jells superbly with Big Thunder's backstory. It's never made readily apparent to the railroad traveler and there are numerous differing accounts out there, each with steadfast adherents. The central gist remains the same in most, however, and it's surprisingly easy to follow, even while holding onto the safety bar for dear life. This is Disney's Gold Rush ride, an homage to an essential part of the American Frontier myth.

The ride is set in the fictional town of Tumbleweed, established as a gold mining site in the late 1800s. The settlers built a mine train and enjoyed some success, but unfortunately for them, a Native American curse on the land ensured that the good fortune was short-lived. Tumbleweed was destroyed and the miners haven't been heard from since, save for an elderly rainmaker who still hangs around. Their train track lives on, though. The Haunted Mansion isn't the only thing haunted along the Rivers of America; Big Thunder too has its fair share of spirits from regions beyond. The same Native American curse that caused the settlers' demise keeps these now-possessed trains racing around the mountain and through the ruins of Tumbleweed. Lucky you, you get to climb aboard for a wild survey of the wilderness.

Populating the landscape are props that bring this narrative to life. Abandoned buildings, old equipment, and animal bones are scattered throughout the mountain. Whether guests know the backstory before boarding the train or not, there are enough visual cues to inform them that there is a definite history to the environment they've entered. The beautiful design of the attraction and Disney's faithful adherence to a solidly developed story work together to create a very organic experience.

In the fall of 2012, Disney enhanced the ride's narrative with a post on its website, recounting the fictional tale of Barnabus T. Bullion, president of the Big Thunder Mining Company. This newest layer of the ride's mythos posits that the mines we encounter when we board the ride are part of Bullion's ongoing efforts to uncover the mountain's hidden gold, which he believes to be his family's birthright. Unfortunately, Big Thunder's curse keeps getting in his way... but that hasn't stopped him from trying. To contribute to the Bullion tale, the Imagineers created an interactive queue for the ride, which includes, among other things, a portrait of Barnabus Bullion himself. Incidentally, he looks almost exactly like Tony Baxter.

Big Thunder Mountain Railroad is a classic example of Disney magic (that is, attention to detail) at work. Plenty of amusement parks offer a mine train roller coaster, but at the Magic Kingdom, guests ride rock rather than steel — or at least, that's how the story goes. The wonderful thing about Disney's Imagineers is that they make the story so very easy to buy into.

There's also something intrinsically thrilling in the ride's evocation of lost control. Walt Disney World runs on two things: boats and trains. To enter the Magic Kingdom, you travel on either a monorail train or a ferryboat. The first attraction you pass is the Walt Disney World Railroad. From then on, you'll spend a good part of your day in the park either on water or rail (or both). Walt Disney himself had a lifelong fascination with trains, which manifests itself in the theme parks he created. His millions of guests in the years since have been able to relax and enjoy themselves while onboard his trains because they're generally smooth and easygoing. But in the back corner of the Magic Kingdom is Big Thunder Mountain Railroad, an attraction that is all about trains — and premised on the idea that they've gone completely out of control. What could be more delightfully terrifying than a challenge to the very sense of security that gets you through your time in the World?

If thrill rides were weather forecasts, Big Thunder wouldn't warrant a trip to the cellar, but the thing sure feels fast as lightning, careening out of our comfort zones at full steam ahead.

WATCH THIS - The Apple Dumpling Gang (1975)

Get a taste of the Wild West with Disney's classic live-action comedy, in which Russel Donavan (Bill Bixby) agrees to pick up a shipment for an old friend but soon regrets it when the package turns out to be a bundle of three orphans. He reluctantly agrees to care for them until his friend returns, attracting the assistance of the no-nonsense delivery lady, Magnolia (Susan Clark). For some reason, her name amuses Russel, and a strange kind of romance quickly blossoms.

Meanwhile, their town is targeted by a bumbling pair of would-be crooks, Theodore and Amos (Don Knotts and Tim Conway, respectively). The hilariously inept criminals are in search of gold and the kids take an interest in it too. Set in California during the mid-1800s, that makes this a Gold Rush story, not unlike Big Thunder Mountain Railroad, which now happens to pay homage to the Dumpling Gang in its new queue. Both the movie and the ride spend a lot of time inside structurally unsound mines, and the film's village looks a lot like Tumbleweed! The movie even includes a great runaway mine cart scene!

Frontierland Shootin' Arcade

Type: Shooting gallery
Duration: A few minutes per session (play at your own pace)
Height Restriction: None
Popularity/Crowds: Low
FastPass+: No
Fear Factor: 1 out of 5 (gun play; ghosts)
Wet Factor: None
Preshow: None
Best Time to Visit: Anytime
Special Comments: $1 per session (not included in park admission)

Walt-less Disney has always been a little gun-shy. In the last few decades, for instance, *Melody Time* came to DVD with its shootout segment missing and the Jungle Cruise has seen its skippers' fully functioning guns go away and then come back. Throughout all the trigger trepidation, one bit of gunplay has held its ground — the Frontierland Shootin' Arcade. One of the rare Disney attractions to charge a small fee on top of admission, it's left off many a vacationer's itinerary. Tucked between the Diamond Horseshoe Saloon and Country Bear Jamboree, the wooden veranda looks at first glance like a mere sideline diversion, but there's more to this graveyard arcade than you might think.

For starters, a round of target practice here connects us with a surprisingly rich tradition of interactive Disney arcades. Guests visiting Disneyland in 1955 had three arcade options (four if you count the Crystal Arcade, but that's always been just a retailer hiding behind the façade of an arcade). Let's take a quick look at those three, only the first of which was ever replicated in Florida.

That was the Main Street Penny Arcade, home to old-timey and inexpensive gaming. When Florida's Magic Kingdom opened in 1971, its Main Street also had a Penny Arcade, but that closed in the spring of 1995 to allow for a larger Emporium. California's Penny Arcade, on the other hand, stands to this day but has evolved into more of a place to shop than play.

In 1955, Disneyland added the Main Street Shooting Gallery (a small toy-gun firing range) and a Davy Crockett shooting gallery. Main Street's lasted until 1962, when it folded into the Penny Arcade. Davy Crockett's is technically still open, but only as a retailer: Davy Crockett's Pioneer

Mercantile, a name it assumed in 1987 after a two-year stint as the Davy Crockett Frontier Arcade. Neither gallery was ever replicated in Florida.

The fourth arcade at Disneyland, The Frontierland Shootin' Gallery, didn't open until 1957. It is the only gun arcade still operating in Disneyland, where it's been known as the Frontierland Shootin' Exposition since 1985. Florida's Magic Kingdom has always had something similar, but here's it been called the Frontierland Shootin' Arcade from Day One.

A myriad of others have come and gone in the parks through the years. Among them were a Country Bear joint with games custom-made for the show, a pirate-themed shooting arcade with electric guns, and the Jungle Cruise's safari-themed version of the Frontierland gallery. While there are still a few video game parlors to be found on both coasts, the Frontierland Shootin' Arcade and its California counterpart are the last remaining vestiges of what were once among Disney's more popular pastimes.

For the price of one dollar, guests today get a chance to relive a time when costumed outlaws staged gunfights atop the roofs of Frontierland and guests were so musket crazy that Disney put up nearly as many shooting galleries as food carts.

It's a time machine in more ways than one. Besides looking back into Disney history, the gallery also sets the scene for the Wild West. The firing range is set against a sprawling desert backdrop, the towering buttes in the horizon instantly reminiscent of Big Thunder Mountain. The township boasts a jailhouse, a shabby bank, a rickety hotel… oh, and don't forget the skeletons pulling themselves out of their sandy graves just past the city limits. Clearly haunted, this little boondocks foreshadows the bedeviled town of Tumbleweed, tiny but as authentically detailed as any full-scale Disney environment. It is, essentially, a microcosm of Frontierland. There's even a bit of railroad track in the diorama, and the creepy sounds bellowing over the gunfire are quite like Big Thunder's bat, coyote, and storm effects.

The Frontierland Shootin' Arcade is the perfect primer for this part of the park. (The PeopleMover plays a similar role in Tomorrowland, as we'll see in *Chapter Five*.) Guests are thrown into the middle of the action and tossed a gun for protection. They'll need it. The Frontier's a'crawlin' with bandits and spooks, and a cowboy's gotta know how to handle his pistol. Here's your training ground — a place to hone your survival skills and fully indulge yourself in the illusion of Frontierland from the get-go. Who says you can't get anything for a dollar?

WATCH THIS -
The Adventures of Bullwhip Griffin (1967)

There are probably at least one hundred live-action Disney movies that most people haven't heard of, let alone seen. Among the better ones is *The Adventures of Bullwhip Griffin*, a charming semi-Western featuring a cast of Disney regulars, including Suzanne Pleshette, Roddy McDowall (as Bullwhip), and Hermione Baddeley (*Mary Poppins'* sassy housekeeper, Ellen). Another Gold Rush comedy, this one follows an English butler (McDowall) as he mistakenly finds himself westward bound and in search of gold. He and one of the children in his care manage to get their hands on a treasure map, but when the villainous Judge Higgins (Karl Malden) swipes it, they have to modify their itinerary in order to get it back.

Bullwhip Griffin doesn't have as much gunfire in it as, say, the "Pecos Bill" portion of Disney's *Melody Time*, but it does feature some very clever dialogue, including a sharp exchange between Bullwhip and Judge Higgins on the rules of gunmanship. The movie's wonderful Western vibe is a pleasure to spend some time in. It's more a family adventure than a traditional Western film, but just as the Shootin' Arcade offers an ideal overview of Frontierland, *Bullwhip Griffin* beautifully captures the area's atmosphere.

Splash Mountain

Type: Log flume ride
Duration: 10 to 11 minutes
Height Restriction: 40 inches or taller (adult riders can switch off)
Popularity/Crowds: E-ticket
FastPass+: Yes; a top priority
Fear Factor: 4 out of 5 (steep drops; tall heights; deliberate suspense)
Wet Factor: 4 out of 5 (most riders get a little wet; some get soaked)
Preshow: None
Boarding Speed: Moderate to Fast
Best Time to Visit without FastPass+: Early morning or late night (or during midday to cool off, but expect crowds)

Splash Mountain is the world's most popular attraction based on a movie that nobody has seen. The elaborate log flume ride is faithfully inspired by *Song of the South*, Walt Disney's hit 1946 musical that, like any successful and acclaimed film, is kept under lock and key where the public can't find it. There's a politically charged taboo surrounding the movie, but that hasn't kept its thrill-ride representative from becoming one of Disney's most celebrated attractions. The paradoxical relationship Splash Mountain shares with the film it's based on is arguably the most interesting facet of the whole experience — but it's one amazing ride, too.

Following two quasi-movies that were produced with educational and promotional aims, *Song of the South* was Walt Disney's first real effort at a full-length live-action film. Released in the fall of 1946, the movie adapts the famous Uncle Remus folk tales popularized by folklorist Joel Chandler Harris,[10] which recount the adventures of Br'er Rabbit and his adversarial briar patch brethren. James Baskett plays the live-action Uncle Remus, who introduces animated segments each time he tells a story to young Johnny, played by Bobby Driscoll (the first actor to enter into a long-term contract with Disney, the future voice of Peter Pan, and a tragic case of a child star fading into drug-ridden anonymity).

The film was a box office success and landed two Oscars, including a special award given to James Baskett, making him the first black actor to win an Academy Award. Also starring in the movie is Hattie McDaniel, who just a few years earlier became the first black actress to take home an Oscar, having won the Best Supporting Actress honor for *Gone with the Wind*. Under other circumstances, one might expect those milestones to be celebrated today as major accomplishments for black artists at a time when segregation was alive and well (Baskett couldn't attend the world premiere of his own film, held in Jim Crow-era Atlanta). Instead, *Song of the South* is entirely unavailable on U.S. home video and hasn't seen a public release since its 1986 theatrical reissue.

The prohibition on the film is self-imposed by Disney. Contrary to popular belief and urban legend, the movie isn't "banned." There's no legal action preventing its distribution. Bill Cosby did not buy the rights to block its release. And while the NAACP did register some criticism of the film at the time of its release, the organization takes no position on it today.

Then why is this in-demand classic so hard to find? The controversy stems from Uncle Remus's portrayal as an indisputably happy guy in the film, brimming with whistling, song-singing cheeriness — all this despite the fact that he's a black man living and working on a white-owned plantation in the American Deep South sometime after the Civil War. While he isn't a slave, he is living in conditions that probably didn't elicit the same gleeful contentment from most who were leading that life.[11]

Despite that uncomfortable notion, numerous film critics have called for *Song*'s release, including noted Disney historian Leonard Maltin. But then, the late Roger Ebert (probably history's most famous film critic) famously opined that it should be made available to adult audiences only, given that children are prone to literal readings of stereotypes. In Europe, where the movie has been released on VHS, many who see it are underwhelmed by its relative lack of shock value after their expectations were set so high by the decades of hype — *The Birth of a Nation* this is not. Having been out of the public eye for so long, the prevailing obstacle to a wide release probably has more to do with the *perception* that the movie is offensive as opposed to whether or not the content *actually* is. (Truth be told, most people today don't have an opinion as to whether it is or isn't, as they haven't been able to see it.) That leaves Disney with a tough choice from a public relations standpoint — release it, hope no one gets too mad, and make some money on the Blu-ray sales, or keep it in the vault while the stigma grows with the passage of time and shareholders complain about lost revenue from shelving an in-demand property. (The company reevaluates its stance every few years, but so far it's opted for the latter position. Unofficial sources suggest that won't change with the launch of Disney+.) Uncle Remus contemplated just such a scenario in *Song of the South*'s famous "tar baby" sequence: a sticky situation that just gets stickier the further in you go. In essence, Disney is battling a tar baby all its own.

The tension surrounding the movie hasn't kept it from living on as one of the company's most valuable properties. Take, for instance, the soundtrack's Oscar-winning number, "Zip-a-Dee-Doo-Dah." There is perhaps no song better known in the whole Disney repertoire, no anthem more quintessential to the Disney legacy. Louis Armstrong, Rosemary Clooney, The Jackson 5, Miley Cyrus, Paula Abdul, and Doris Day are among the many who have recorded cover versions. One of the best-known movie songs of all time, it has clearly taken its place in the Great American Songbook. Yet despite knowing the tune by heart, few likely know its origin. The song's source often goes uncredited, as if the composition magically appeared in the Disney songbook one day. Tourists without a sound sense of history are apt to conclude the song comes from Splash Mountain itself.

That's because Splash is a rather faithful adaptation of *Song of the South*, incorporating the Br'er characters, the catchy songs, and the memorable stories — everything except Uncle Remus. *South*'s main character and narrator is nowhere to be found in the dips and recesses of the enormous, thorny mountain. Of course, Johnny and all the other live-action characters are missing too. Remus isn't just absent, though; he's *replaced*. In his stead is Br'er Frog, a minor character from the movie who plays a big part in Splash Mountain, where he serves as recurring story guide. Whether that's a good or bad thing is up for debate, but more interesting than that surface-level question would be a study of what Remus's absence means in Splash Mountain's context as an adaptation of literature.

Many of the same criticisms leveled against Walt's film were leveled against Joel Chandler Harris's original stories too, and today, that written work is often kept as far away from school libraries as Disney keeps the movie from store shelves. Children's literature has historically welcomed racial tensions like those found in Mark Twain's *Adventures of Huckleberry Finn*, but Splash Mountain offers an adaptation of the Uncle Remus stories (traditionally considered works of children's literature) that eliminates their title character and the racist stigma attached to him. What kind of history does the attraction then represent? What are we to make of its literary origins? What does it say about our understanding of children's literature and the way new generations of young people should approach it? Is this social responsibility or misleading dilution? These questions cry out for critical thought and study about this important piece of culture.[12]

In Splash Mountain, we find a perfect illustration of why theme park attractions are as deserving of careful scholarly examination as any other significant cultural artifact. We will return to the relationship between Disney rides and children's literature when we take a look at Fantasyland in a later chapter.

Fortunately, neither familiarity with nor a favorable opinion of *Song of the South* is required to appreciate the grand spectacle that is a ride through Splash Mountain. The attraction first opened in Disneyland in 1989, part of the Eisner/Wells revolution[13] that took the Mouse House to new heights that year. *The Little Mermaid* and *Honey, I Shrunk the Kids* were topping the box office. Walt Disney World dropped the rope on Disney-MGM Studios and Typhoon Lagoon. Disney television had two new hits in "Chip 'n Dale Rescue Rangers" and a "Mickey Mouse Club" relaunch. Their Touchstone[14] subsidiary even had a big success with *Dead Poets Society*. Suddenly, Disney was on top of the entertainment game for the first time since Walt's death.

At a reported cost of $75 million, the Splash Mountain project was the big headline in Disneyland that year. It borrowed Audio-Animatronics from the just-closed America Sings attraction to populate its many scenes. Soon after, in the fall of 1992 (another big year for Disney), slightly different versions opened at both Tokyo Disneyland and Walt Disney World.

The ride is designed with a deliberate fear factor in mind and the psych-out begins before you even get in the line. Splash Mountain is one of Magic Kingdom's key "weenies," meaning a massive landmark that draws big crowds from far away. The Frontierland path leads directly to the foot of the mountain, a journey set to the far-reaching sound of screams as one log full of guests after another drops 52 feet at a 45-degree angle before your very eyes. There's no hint in that spectacle of the epic ten-minute ride that precedes the terrifying plummet, and therein lies the little surprise that makes Splash Mountain the absolute favorite of so many parkgoers.

Before boarding the log that will be our mountain vessel, we wander through a long and winding queue that is appropriately lined with rock and knotted wood, dark corners, and discomforting signs warning of a waterfall ahead. Given the long waits that quickly accumulate at this perennial favorite, the queue is the ideal breeding ground for anxiety. Finally, at the loading zone, we find a freshly soaked seat opening up for us and a dark entrance directly ahead. Two questions become of pressing importance at that moment: "How wet will I get?" and "When do I drop?" First-timers have no reason to expect the stomach-turning uncertainty that will prolong the answers to those questions as they are treated to an unforeseen, ride-along narrative.

Disney doesn't cut to the chase, opting instead to take its guests through the trials and tribulations of Br'er Rabbit as he runs from and outwits Br'er Fox and Br'er Bear. The scenes here are lengthier and more elaborate than anything found in the dark rides of Fantasyland. Initially, the atmosphere is one of levity. Animals laugh and sing along to peppy music that has the whole log toe tapping. Br'er Rabbit cracks wise as his would-be captors fail and Br'er Bear amuses with his propensity for putting his posterior on display. Having seen the big splash that is coming sooner or later, this happiness has a kind of sick irony to it, but the good mood is irresistible. As the ride progresses, it becomes increasingly foreboding. The path takes dips and turns that each look like they must be "the big one" and stomachs are already halfway up nervous guests' throats before they realize a still steeper fall awaits them. Disney makes an art of the classic fake-out. And all the while, you either find yourself getting wetter or casting looks of relief at those around you who didn't share in your narrow escape from a random splash.

As chatter about a mysterious and not altogether funny-sounding "laughing place" increases, the music takes an eerie turn. The click-clack of an inclined track can be heard in the distance. Thunder booms above. At last, vultures appear (yes, vultures — Disney really goes for the gut). In a sinister voice, they advise you to turn around. The joke's on you, I'm afraid, because you can't. That must be why they call this "the laughing place" but, as the vultures are only too happy to point out, you aren't laughing anymore. As your log makes the slow climb to the tip-top of the mountain, you're treated to just a moment's pause in which you can take in the thick and thorny briar patch that awaits you below — far below — and the absence of any steadily declining ramp to get you there. And then, at long last, just as you're praying it won't, the log drops. Fast. With you in it.

Splash Mountain absolutely revels in suspense. On the one hand, the whole experience is a series of teases. On the other, it's an epic three-dimensional incarnation of truly entertaining stories. On both counts, chances are good that you'll end up wet and delighted at the end. But just as there was more to the attraction's beginning than met the eye, there's more to its ending than anticipated, too. It just so happens that the grand finale is not the plunge, but a grand pageant of Animatronic animals making a gospel revival out of "Zip-a-Dee-Doo-Dah." The uplifting finish serves as soothing relief to jangled nerves still aflutter from the hyped-up drop.

After emerging from the log and seeing apprehensive guests on the other side eye your drenched T-shirt nervously as they sit down for their first ride, it becomes easy to appreciate the grandeur of what you've just experienced. This is Disney showmanship at its very finest, delivering on the promise of "Zip-A-Dee-Doo-Dah": a "wonderful feeling" for a "wonderful day." That's when you realize that you found your laughing place inside the mountain after all — and you can't wait to go back.

WATCH THIS - Mary Poppins (1964)

Mary Poppins isn't the first movie that comes to mind when you ride Splash Mountain, but Walt's most enduring live-action classic has a lot in common with *Song of the South*. Uncle Remus's role in his movie is not unlike Mary Poppins's in hers. Both are mysterious guardian types who tend to make the best of a child's despair, and they share an uncanny ability to summon animation out of live-action's thin air. While Disney keeps *Song of the South* in the farthest corner of their vault for the time being, simply understanding the Mary Poppins character can at least help modern audiences appreciate Uncle Remus's value to the story.

Tom Sawyer Island

Type: Walk-through environment
Duration: Self-paced
Height Restriction: None
Popularity/Crowds: Low, but the rafts have very limited capacity
FastPass+: No
Fear Factor: 1.5 out of 5 (optional dark caves; optional gun play)
Wet Factor: None
Preshow: None
Boarding Speed: Slow (due to limited raft capacity)
Best Time to Visit: Anytime, but the island closes by dusk.
Special Comments: Plan on a bare minimum of 20 minutes to get there, see it, and travel back (30 to 40 or more if you really want to explore).

Tom Sawyer Island is marketed as a place to kick back and put up your feet. If you happen to visit Walt Disney World in the dead of winter, that might not be a bad idea. During the rest of the year, relaxation is the last thing you'll find there. Sure, you'll be putting your feet up — onto stairs, bridges, and hills. Hoping to settle down in a rocking chair? You'll have to beat the crowd to snag one of the very few available on the island, though there are plenty of rocks for you to walk across if you don't. Looking for shade? Crawl inside a dark cave and it's all yours! Just beware the droppings of children who mistook the space for a bathroom (not kidding).

Truth be told, there's a lot to get out of Tom Sawyer Island. Good ole "R&R" just isn't part of the package. That's because the island, billed as an attraction, boils down to a playground. Being part of Disney, of course, it's a vast and elaborate playground themed to a great work of literature — but far from a haven for relaxation, it's probably the most exhausting experience in the whole resort.

For starters, the entire attraction is outdoors. For those who struggled in Geography and need a refresher, Florida is hot. And humid. Tom Sawyer Island also happens to be... an *island*, which means (again for the geographically challenged) it's surrounded by water, which doesn't help the whole humidity thing one bit. It's fair to say, then, that the place is pretty stuffy for most of the year. The only way to get there is on a log raft, the line for which forms in Frontierland and stays put until the next raft moseys back to the shore. On crowded days, you could put a dent in

The Adventures of Tom Sawyer while waiting. When the raft finally arrives, you'll be packed onboard nice and tight as one island seeker after another follows. With the sun beating down, you'll wonder how it could take so long to travel across the seemingly narrow Rivers of America that separate the attraction from the rest of the park.

Once there, you'll have the whole island to yourself (well, you and everyone else). You can travel its great length by crossing rope bridges, climbing stairs, and tunneling through caves until you reach a two-story gun outpost at the end. There *is* the scenic Aunt Polly's Dockside Inn, a covered spot for modest meals with a stunning view of Haunted Mansion across the water. In theory, parents could relax there while their kids romp about, but the restaurant is seldom open and Tom Sawyer Island is simply too big to let children wander far out of sight. In short, the attraction is best visited in the morning hours (nighttime won't do, as safety requires the island to close at dusk). Then, with the right expectations in mind, the grounds actually offer a rewarding escape into a fully realized literary universe.

Disneyland's island was in place at the park in 1955 but it wasn't open to guests until officially debuting as Tom Sawyer Island in 1956. Likewise, Magic Kingdom's version was there in 1971 but rafts didn't run to it until 1973. The islands at both parks are substantially similar. Walt Disney World originally named its pioneer outpost Fort Sam Clemens in honor of Mark Twain's real name, while Disneyland's was simply titled Fort Wilderness. After the box office success of *Tom and Huck* (1995), Magic Kingdom in 1997 redubbed its outpost Fort Langhorne, which appears in the movie and was inspired by Twain's actual middle name. Disneyland's Fort Wilderness was demolished in 2007 and the island there largely abandoned its Tom Sawyer theme for a *Pirates of the Caribbean* overlay. That makes Florida's Magic Kingdom and Tokyo Disneyland the only two parks to retain a true Sawyer Island (Paris and Hong Kong have radically different themes for theirs).

The attraction is right at home in Frontierland, one of three Magic Kingdom sections set in historic United States of America. The inspiration here comes from Mark Twain's *The Adventures of Tom Sawyer*, one of the most enduring American adventure stories every written. Twain's sequel, *The Adventures of Huckleberry Finn*, is widely accepted as one of the "Great American Novels," a work so influential (and controversial) that it birthed a national literary identity. That such a cornerstone of Americana would get a big plot of land all its own inside this recreation of The American Frontier is fitting. It's also surprising. While most Disney attractions are either original creations or inspired by the studio's own films, Disney didn't attempt a movie adaptation of Twain's most famous adventure stories until 1993's *The Adventures of Huck Finn*; Tom Sawyer wasn't tapped until 1995's *Tom and Huck* — both of them made long after Tom Sawyer Island had already opened in three Disney parks. Like Abraham Lincoln and Charlie Chaplin, though, Mark Twain was a personal hero for Walt Disney. The real surprise isn't that Walt wanted a Tom Sawyer attraction in his parks; it's that he didn't make a major motion picture to go along with it.

Tom Sawyer is one of the more famous fictional explorers, his adventuring carried out along the mid-1800s Mississippi River in St. Petersburg, Missouri. The attraction seizes upon that spirit of adventure and wide-eyed wonder, wherein one finds the magic in this woodsy excursion. Walt Disney World is generally a rigidly controlled environment. Guests walk along the paths paved for them, go in and out the doors they are directed to, and wait for a cast member's okay to board the next ride vehicle. Tom Sawyer Island is a fascinating exception to those rules. While you can rest assured you won't find anything on the island that you aren't meant to find (the aforementioned child poo notwithstanding), the direction and duration of your visit is entirely up to you. Any number of paths will take you from the front of the island to the back, and you can even jump from one trail to the next along the way. If you want to see *everything* the island has to offer, you'll have to, and you'll need to devote plenty of time to doing so. Without a map to guide you, it's easy to get lost and if you find yourself moving in circles, you won't be the first. Caves, buildings, and an occasional homage to the source material are hidden around rocky bends, and some of the doors actually open and invite you inside.

That sprawling and intricate design creates an irresistible invitation to exploration, a delightful contrast to the otherwise prescribed nature of your vacation. You're not just exploring any old island, either — you're exploring a familiar and beloved storybook world brought to life. There's nothing more gratifying to a Mark Twain fan than walking down a path along the river and stumbling upon a half-painted fence, a nod to one of Sawyer's more entertaining scams.

The invitation to look around also makes this one of Disney's most interactive creations. The island offers no shortage of hands-on opportunities. Fort Langhorn is particularly engaging, with opportunites to climb up some stairs and catch a grand view of the island and Big Thunder across the river. Inside the outlook are guns that fire audible blanks, a real treat for kids and excitable adults alike. There's even a secret passageway!

Tom Sawyer Island is a unique treasure of the Magic Kingdom. Like any great book, it requires a time commitment and an open and alert mind to appreciate. With your sleeves rolled up and breathing room in your touring schedule, you'll find it's surprisingly fulfilling. Just make sure you get there before the sun hits its peak.

WATCH THIS - Tom Sawyer (1973)

Disney's *Tom and Huck* might be the most exciting adaptation of Twain's *Tom Sawyer* ever put on film, but there's an older movie even more in tune with Tom Sawyer Island: 1973's Oscar-nominated musical, *Tom Sawyer*. It was produced by *Reader's Digest*, distributed by United Artists, and brought to home video by MGM. That's a lot of companies for one movie, and you'll note that Disney isn't one of them. With nine songs and a screenplay written by Disney's legendary Sherman Brothers, the movie sure feels like a Disney production, even if it isn't one. The cast, too, features a slew of Disney film veterans, with young Jodie Foster and Johnny Whitaker ("Family Affair") in the lead. Music phenom John Williams collaborated with the Shermans on the film score, earning them an Oscar nomination and a Golden Globe. I could throw more big names your way, but the movie's stunning assemblage of talent isn't even the most important reason to see it.

The adventuresome film sets are positively overflowing with Frontierland flavor. The movie plays up the same story scenes emphasized on Tom Sawyer Island, and there are times you'd swear it was filmed inside Magic Kingdom — especially when a big white riverboat goes steaming by Huck Finn's fort.

If that's not enough of a connection for you, consider the timing. *Tom Sawyer* hit theaters less than two months before Tom Sawyer Island opened in Magic Kingdom. The movie is a contemporaneous take on Twain's tale in 1970s style. It's entirely possible that some guests saw the movie in theaters and attended Tom Sawyer Island's grand opening on the very same day.

Chapter 3

Liberty Square

"Past this gateway stirs a new nation waiting to be born. Thirteen separate colonies have banded together to declare their independence from the bonds of tyranny. It is a time when silversmiths put away their tools and march to the drums of a revolution, a time when gentlemen planters leave their farms to become generals, a time when tradesmen leave the safety of home to become heroes. Welcome to Liberty Square!"

Plaque at Liberty Square

Unlike the other five lands in Magic Kingdom, Liberty Square is exclusive to Walt Disney World. Because it wasn't part of Disneyland, Walt obviously didn't prepare a dedication for this area as he did with the others. No matter... the Imagineers created this inscription themselves and engraved it on a plaque at the land's brick-paved entryway.

Liberty Square and Frontierland are really one in the same. Disney counts them as separate entities and to be sure, each exhibits a distinctive ambiance. There is a reason, however, that the two lands sit side by side. They are bound together by history, and determining just where one ends and the next begins can be a challenge if we're to accept that each of Magic Kingdom's six lands is a world unto itself.

To walk from the beginning of Liberty Square to the end of Frontierland[1] is to take a stroll through American history. We cross the bridge from the Cinderella Castle hub into Liberty Square and enter Colonial America, just on the cusp of the Revolution. The house number on each building is said to coincide with the year of its construction, signaling the passage of time through the Declaration of Independence, the war, the Articles of Confederation, and finally, the Constitution. Our next steps take us into the next chapter of history, The American Frontier. The dating of buildings continues in Frontierland, beginning in the early 1800s and moving through the nineteenth century.

More of an intersection than a square, the Magic Kingdom's smallest area is still as intricately themed as any other. Cast members sport Colonial garb with tricorn hats and bonnets. Replicas of the Liberty Bell and the Liberty Tree serve as centerpieces, and not far from them are the stocks, where you can be locked up and humiliated for taking flash pictures on that ride when they *told* you not to.

Liberty Square has a delicious personality all its own... and I do mean literally delicious, provided you pay Ichabod Crane a visit and scarf down a warm funnel cake or waffle sandwich from Sleepy Hollow Refreshments. There are only four attractions here, but they're among the park's most thought-provoking — Liberty Square Riverboat, The Muppets Present... Great Moments in American History, The Hall of Presidents, and Haunted Mansion. In between them, we hear fifes and drums and feel like we're on the brink of battles for freedom, as though Paul Revere might come riding through at any time. Sure enough, his "two if by sea" lamps are hanging in one of the windows. You've come by land, though, because that's the only way to get to Liberty Square, and that fact is of some importance to our first attraction here...

Liberty Square Riverboat

Type: Boat ride
Duration: 16 to 18 minutes
Height Restriction: None
Popularity/Crowds: Low
FastPass+: No
Fear Factor: None
Wet Factor: None
Preshow: None
Boarding Speed: Boards quickly, but only once every 30 minutes (usually on the half-hour and hour)
Best Time to Visit: Anytime, but the boat sometimes closes at dusk.

The Liberty Square Riverboat encapsulates the identity crisis that exists on the border between Liberty Square and Frontierland. It's very much an open border, and the *Liberty Belle* crosses it freely.

This beautiful triple-decker paddle steamer travels the Rivers of America, a body of water encircling Tom Sawyer Island. We're able to roam as we wish about the slow-moving ship while the voice of Mark Twain narrates our journey. Highlights include hard-to-come-by views of Big Thunder Mountain Railroad, Haunted Mansion, and the island itself. There's not much here we couldn't get from a walk through Frontierland and a half-hour on Tom Sawyer Island, but the photo-ops and serenity the ride can provide on a nice day make it well worth the trip. There are even a few sights visible only from the Riverboat and the Walt Disney World Railroad — frontier settlers' cabins, grazing Animatronic animals, and a Native American village, for example.

If that description sounds a lot like the Old West, you won't be surprised to learn that the "Liberty Square" Riverboat actually has its origins in Frontierland. Disneyland had something just like it in 1955 — the Mark Twain Steamboat — and it's still there. That one circles Tom Sawyer Island along the Rivers of America, too, but it's officially a Frontierland attraction — there is no Liberty Square in Disneyland.

The Magic Kingdom counterpart opened on the park's second day and was a Liberty Square attraction from the get-go. The original riverboat was named the *Admiral Joe Fowler*. That was later replaced by a second boat, the *Richard F. Irvine*, which ran alongside the *Fowler* for several years before the attraction returned to a one-ship operation in 1980. The *Irvine* is still sailing today, though Disney rechristened it *The Liberty Belle* in 1996, as if to say, "See, this does belong in Liberty Square — just look at the name!" So as it stands now, the Liberty Square Riverboat is the attraction that hosts the *Liberty Belle* paddle steamer, which has its entrance in Liberty Square even though its themes have little to do with "liberty." The fact that paddle steamers were icons of Mississippi River travel in the nineteenth century, coupled with the Mark Twain narration, means we're in the middle of the 1800s once it's underway. In that sense, the *Belle* embarks in Liberty Square and then sails into the future. Steamboats were around in the late eighteenth century, even though we don't associate them with that era now, so it isn't really improbable that we board our cruise at the very beginning of Constitutional America. That reading does require us to ignore the fact that the ride ultimately drops us right back off in Liberty Square, but then life's about the journey and not the destination, right?

The Riverboat is a case study of the narrative hodgepodge that is intrinsic to Magic Kingdom. The park aims to bring historical fact and fantastical fiction equally to life within the same experience. By popular consensus, it succeeds. The resort's success comes from its storytelling but unlike the source fables it adapts, the stories here zig and zag from one time period and plot line to another. The favorable response to this jumbled presentation surely says something about how different cultural narratives work together to create our American identity. Narratives of patriotism, national history, and exploring new territory can coexist for us in a theme park because they coexist for us in our cultural subconscious. We embrace the idea that exploration (one might even say conquest) is patriotic because our nation was founded upon it. So the whole idea of receiving a history lesson as we move from a tribute to our nation's founding into a tribute to our nation's expansion doesn't seem particularly weird.

It can be argued that this interwoven experience is "postmodern." If the murky and contested idea of postmodernism is essentially about genre bending, blended narratives, and disrupted continuity, then Walt Disney World is about as postmodern as you can get. And if you buy into the academic argument that we live in a "postmodern era," those very qualities might explain why Walt Disney World continues to resonate with millions of people each year — it's a form of entertainment that appeals to our disjointed sensibilities.

On the other hand, postmodernism is also supposed to challenge the basic idea of historical truth and, on that score, the Magic Kingdom begs to differ. As jumbled as its stories and lands may be, the park holds fast to historical orthodoxy and stands in proud and patriotic defense of its reverent vision of America. Then again, as we will see, The Muppets are here and are *not* quite so reverent. We'll also walk through the changes made at The Hall of Presidents and find that the park has, at times, adopted slightly different perspectives on the past.

If you're able to set such academic quibbles aside long enough to enjoy a 15-minute boat ride (and I suspect we all are), you'll find plenty else onboard to stimulate you. The *Belle*'s charm stems from many of the same attributes that bring Tom Sawyer Island to life. Like that sprawling playground of adventure, this attraction invites guests to explore. The freedom to move about the vessel, discover almost-hidden compartments, and get a bird's-eye view of the massive paddle wheel at the stern makes for entertainment all its own. The ship appears remarkably authentic, having all the outward markings of the real deal. Many guests likely exit still believing the boat is free-floating, self-propelled, and manually steered. They're partly right — the *Belle* is a fully functioning steam-powered vessel — but it moves along an underwater track. A cast member controls the ride from up inside the pilothouse, but there's not a captain in the traditional sense.

Seating is hard to come by on the Riverboat, but even without it, the experience is a relaxing one. That's doubly true if you catch a cool breeze while you're aboard. Here guests can find the quick refuge from hustle and bustle that they might have mistakenly hoped to discover on Tom Sawyer Island. Just know that if you plan to keep an eye open for Frontierland's intermingling with Liberty Square, your mind won't get as big a break as your body.

WATCH THIS – A Kid in King Arthur's Court (1995)

This is the second of Disney's three feature-length adaptations of Mark Twain's *A Connecticut Yankee in King Arthur's Court*, following 1979's *Unidentified Flying Oddball*. (We'll discuss the third, 1998's *A Knight in Camelot*, in *Chapter Four*.) Awkward teen Calvin Fuller (Thomas Ian Nicholas) is playing baseball in 1995 when an earthquake hits and he falls through the middle of the Earth, suddenly finding himself thrust into Camelot during the days of King Arthur and his round table. Dazzled by Calvin's portable CD player and other modern gadgetry, the locals are soon convinced that he's a wizard of great power.

This very fun (and admittedly dated) movie doesn't exactly have a Liberty Square tone to it, but the collision of timelines and national origins mirrors to some extent the tensions we find aboard *The Liberty Belle*. The movie also marks just one of many intersections between the Disney legacy and that of the ride's purported narrator, Mark Twain.

The Muppets Present...
Great Moments in American History
Type: Outdoor theater show
Duration: 11 minutes ("The Declaration of Independence") or 8 minutes ("The Midnight Ride of Paul Revere")
Height Restriction: None
Popularity/Crowds: Moderate
FastPass+: No
Fear Factor: None
Wet Factor: None
Preshow: None
Boarding Speed: Anytime
Best Time to Visit: The Muppets alternate between two different shows throughout the day. The daily times guide and MDX app list the showtimes but do not specify which performance is which. If you want to catch a particular show, ask a Liberty Square cast member for the time. All performances can be viewed from anywhere around The Hall of Presidents, so showing up just a few minutes early will suffice on all but the busiest days.

The *Muppets* are going in... *Liberty Square*?

Look, I love the Muppets, but is this really the best place for them? Aren't they more 1976 than 1776? More hysterical than historical? More pig than Whig?

These were the questions I asked myself when Walt Disney World — ever unsure of what to do with the Muppets[2] but nevertheless determined to do *something* with them — announced that The Muppets Present... Great Moments in American History would open as the newest attraction in Magic Kingdom's smallest land. Sam the Eagle would take residency at the top of The Hall of Presidents, regaling guests on the streets below with tales of national pride... and where Sam goes, the rest of the Muppets and their tomfoolery are sure to follow.

I was wrong to doubt them. After all, the Muppets (and Jim Henson[3], the man who created them) have been described as "revolutionary,"[4] so why not welcome them into Revolutionary America, where their trademark irreverence can shake up the solemnity of Liberty Square and can give American history the sendup it sorely needs in these take-ourselves-too-seriously times? These are the same Muppets who burst onto the Disney scene in 1990 with an NBC special in which the Muppets spent a most irreverent afternoon in Magic Kingdom (fourteen years before Disney bought the Muppets and six years before buying ABC). Now they're dropping anchor in the heart of that same park, taking their seats as rightful heirs to the Disney dynasty.[5]

You know, Sam the Eagle *would* live in the rafters over The Hall of Presidents.

Oh you remember Sam, the Muppets' moral warrior and self-appointed censor, the patron puppet of patriotism. He is the American spirit in felt, puritanical and with the confidence of Manifest Destiny.[6] One part Bill O'Reilly, one part Eugene Levy, he's the bald-eagle blowhard whose eyebrows say "judging you" without saying anything at all. He's here to make sure Americans conduct themselves with decency… and that all non-Americans understand that they count just a little bit less. It's the reason he heads over to Hollywood Studios every day for a "Salute to All Nations, But Mostly America"[7] and why he's now taking up residency in Magic Kingdom as the official historian of Liberty Square.

It matters very much to Sam that the guests of Walt Disney World appreciate their heritage. Reluctantly, then, he has enlisted Gonzo, Fozzie Bear, Miss Piggy, and Kermit the Frog (all of them weirdos in his estimation) to reenact great moments from American history on the streets of Liberty Square — or in the windows overlooking it, rather — each and every afternoon. Together, they recount two historical tales the only way the Muppets know how: *sorta*.

First up is "The Midnight Ride of Paul Revere," an adaptation of Henry Wadsworth Longfellow's famous 1860 poem, "Paul Revere's Ride," with additional dialogue by Sam himself.[8] Kermit takes the title role, while Fozzie waits for his cue to hang lanterns when the British arrive (one if by land, two if by sea, "three if by monorail").[9] Miss Piggy wants to play the part of "Paula Revere" but storms away when she learns there's no role for a woman here, turning up later as a *fabulous* Redcoat instead.

Historians have long derided Longfellow's poem for keeping key players out of the story, among them: John Hancock, John Adams, and Samuel Adams. In what is surely an intentional effort to right that historical wrong, Fozzie goes out of his way to mention all three here, which goes to show that learning history by way of Muppet can sometimes teach you more than history by way of history itself. Don't worry, though; this is no by-the-book stage play. No sooner do the British come by sea than does Gonzo come with chickens, and both those things usually mean bad news. The story crumbles in hysterics, and we're treated to a closing-credits version of the show's theme song: "Great moments in history... but just the American parts." (You're welcome to analyze that particular phrase in light of the fact that the Audio-Animatronic likeness of Donald Trump is delivering a Presidential address not ten feet below them at the same time and come to your own conclusions.[10] But more on that later in this chapter.)

When they aren't recounting Paul Revere's ride, they tell the story of The Declaration of Independence, with Gonzo in the role of John Adams, Fozzie as Ben Franklin, and Kermit as Thomas Jefferson. "This is about the founding *fathers*," Kermit tells Piggy in an oh so of-the-moment exchange; "there's no part for you." When she turns up as King George later, Kermit frogsplains that women aren't kings but queens, prompting Piggy to declare herself Queen Georgette — a *Hamilton*-era counterpart to King George and a declaration of independence all her own. Like the Schulyer Sisters before her, she's compelling Thomas Jefferson to "include women in the sequel." (Work!) Too revisionist for your taste? "You've got a bear playing Ben Franklin," she reminds us. Touché.

In this latter performance, the Muppets are accompanied by James Jefferson (J.J., they call him), the official town crier of Liberty Square. He fulfills a few traditions, first and foremost that of 'Henson's human.' Whether it's with Julie Andrews on "The Muppet Show" or Michael Caine as Scrooge, Henson's kooky characters are often at their best when they can riff off real-life flesh and blood. In that sense, J.J. enters the encyclopedia as both an original Disney Parks character and a Muppets one. He also brings back to Magic Kingdom the barker bird — well, Sam's the bird, but it's J.J. who does the barking, calling guests from all around to attend his attraction in much the same way that barker birds used to summon guests to the Enchanted Tiki Room and Pirates of the Caribbean in the Magic Kingdom of the 1970s (incidentally the decade that introduced us to both "The Muppet Show" and this theme park for the first time).

You have to wonder how we've gone this long without any town criers in Liberty Square. They were an important part of Colonial America, having carried over from the English tradition of criers (officers of the court responsible for reading criminal charges and reporting the news)[11] and town waits (instrumental bands that travelled by foot on the government's behalf, sometimes in a law enforcement capacity, responsible for welcoming visitors and for using their horns to wake up the townsfolk each morning). They were still around in Walt's days too, several large U.S. cities having kept criers on the payroll through the early 20th century.[12] Criers and waits were known to sometimes sing to townsfolk as part of their duties, and J.J. does the same.

Great Moments in American History premiered in Magic Kingdom on October 2, 2016. I've had the chance to see it numerous times since then, and I like watching the crowd as much as the show. What's remarkable is how genuinely delighted people seem to be each time, most of them presumably casual Muppets fans, their fondness for these characters falling somewhere on a scale of Walter to Waldorf (the former a doting devotee in the new movies and the latter an inveterate heckler). It's remarkable because the Muppets have struggled to put these kinds of smiles on the average American face for some time now. When the Walt Disney Company acquired the property in 2004, many doubted Disney's ability to revitalize the already-languishing brand, still smarting from the ice-cold reception to things like *Muppets from Space*. There have been hits and misses in the fifteen years since. For every *The Muppets* (the acclaimed Jason Segel feature of 2011), there's been "The Muppets" (the quickly cancelled ABC series of 2015). For every "Muppet Babies" (the hit 2018 reboot of the 1984 kids' cartoon), there's been a *Muppets' Wizard of Oz* (the tornadic mess of a TV movie from 2005). Part of the problem is that at least three generations lay claim to these characters, and none of them quite agree on who the Muppets ought to be. And yet, standing here in Liberty Square, there seems to be a consensus of approval more pronounced than any we've seen in at least twenty-five years.

It leads me to wonder what we like about the Muppets, detached from any nostalgic associations we might individually have with whatever era we first met them in. Beyond the debate about whether Kermit should have been retired after Jim Henson died or whether Pepé the King Prawn (absent from Magic Kingdom, by the way) is an abomination to Henson's legacy, I'm interested in *why we care* about who voices Kermit or whether Henson's legacy gets honored in the first place. We don't love the Muppets for no reason, and we probably don't each love the Muppets for wildly different reasons, so what *is* the reason? Maybe we should start at the very beginning because, as the aforementioned Andrews once told us, it's a very good place to start.

"The Muppet Show" hit the airwaves in the mid-1970s as a variety show at a time when variety shows like "Hee Haw," Glen Campbell's, and Carol Burnett's were a television mainstay. But "The Muppet Show" was never *really* a variety show.[13] It was a show about trying to put on a variety show and very rarely succeeding. The cameras spent as much time backstage with Kermit & Co. in crisis as it did on stage with the week's featured acts, a formula we'd see emulated on "30 Rock" thirty years later (Tina Fey acknowledges "The Muppet Show" as its forebear).

If there's one thing the Muppets' most celebrated works have in common, it is this: the earnestness of a failed effort. Specifically, a *community* effort. I think it speaks to two of our fundamental needs at the same time: our need for companionship and our need to push ourselves to be more than we are. I love the Muppets for the same reason I find myself drawn to singers with imperfect voices. Nothing is more honest or relatable in an artist than imperfection — doing the best you can with what you've got, striving for even a little bit more than that, and laying the effort bare. Vocals are rarely as moving as when we hear this modest little frog sing about the color of his skin, and he does it with a lump in his throat that wouldn't make it past Hollywood Week on "American Idol." The Muppets' efforts are diligent and passionate if hilariously hopeless but — this is key — never hidden away from us or masked with pretense. Vulnerability is so appealing because we recognize it in ourselves. We like to see the Muppets try and fail because we see in them our own scrappy ambitions and inherent limitations. If *they* can try and mostly fail and still be okay, so can we.

Great Moments in American History isn't complicated. It's just a bunch of motley Muppets talking to a small group of townsfolk in the Colonial gathering spot that is Liberty Square. Yes, *actual* Muppets — the ones we never thought we'd get to see performing *right in front of us* — in the second-story windows of Liberty Square, which now suddenly seem so real and lived in.[14] Here, as in their best work, they're trying their hardest to pull off a show. And they're doing it together, with genuine affection for one another despite all their differences and flaws. Theirs is the magic of "Parks and Recreation," "The Golden Girls," and "Friends" — all series that work by creating a circle of belonging we want to emulate in our own lives.

Inclusivity was a hallmark of Henson's work. His mission with "Sesame Street" was to level the playing field and make high-quality edutainment available to people of every economic background, even those who can't afford cable. His mission in "The Muppet Show" was to create a culture where characters of all kinds worked together toward a common good: the Type As and the agents of chaos… the timid and the self-obsessed… the hippies and the conservatives… the humans, the animals, the monsters, and the whatever Gonzo is. And maybe that's precisely why they hit their stride in Liberty Square.

The Muppets are ultimately about the notion that every individual, whether outcast or oddball, can coexist and build something of value together — messy as it might be — all while striving to hit it big. Their message is an echo of one familiar to us from the Statue of Liberty. Give me your tired, your weak, your weirdos, your big noses, your bad jokes, your neuroses, your inflated sense of self... Indeed, the Muppets stand as nothing less than a silly little microcosm of America.

WATCH THIS - I Love Liberty (1982)

In 1982, The Henson Company partnered with Norman Lear's People for the American Way as part of a two-hour, all-star variety special celebrating the 250th anniversary of George Washington's birthday. Live performers included Frank Sinatra, Barbra Streisand, Robin Williams, Helen Reddy, and many more, but the biggest star of all was Big Bird, who arrived at the Los Angeles Sports Arena to diffuse political tensions with a pre-taped segment starring the Muppets.

If you want to see the entire special, you'll need to travel to the Paley Center for Media archives in New York or L.A. Happily, however, People for the American Way offers "The Muppets Reenact the Continental Congress" as a stand-alone feature on YouTube, free of charge. In it, Kermit and the gang are getting ready to stage their own production of the Broadway musical *1776*. As in Liberty Square, Kermit is cast as Thomas Jefferson and Miss Piggy wants to know why there aren't any roles for women. Fozzie stars as John Adams, Gonzo as John Dickinson, Scooter as John Hancock, Floyd Pepper as Ben Franklin, and Rizzo the Rat as Charles Thomson. Sam the

Eagle is around too, part of the Second Continental Congress. The eight-minute skit is thoroughly enjoyable and strikingly similar to Great Moments in American History... so much so that you have to wonder if it served as a template for the Magic Kingdom show writers. It's a testament to just how well in tune this new show is with what the Muppets were in the Jim Henson days.

The Hall of Presidents
Type: Theater show
Duration: 23 minutes
Height Restriction: None
Popularity/Crowds: Moderate
FastPass+: No
Fear Factor: None
Wet Factor: None
Preshow: None
Best Time to Visit: Anytime
Special Comments: Giant theater usually means long lines aren't an issue.

Deep inside Liberty Square, there is a sprawling chamber haunted by the ghosts of dead men. Their voices call out from the grave to remind us of their stories. Never resting, they constantly search among the living for a new soul to join them. Every four to eight years, they find one. No, they aren't the ghouls of the Haunted Mansion. These illustrious spirits (and their surviving successors) hail from a different mansion instead. I'm talking, of course, about the Presidents of the United States.

The Hall of Presidents has been a part of Magic Kingdom — and *only* Magic Kingdom — since the very beginning. It opens with an overview of American history, presented as a feature film in widescreen so wide the screen gets *wider* as the nation expands. But once the story of presidential succession catches up to current events, a curtain rises to reveal the 44 Presidents themselves, each poised with pride before guests' very eyes.[15] Blinking and breathing, or at least appearing to, they all nod in turn at the call of their names. Washington and Lincoln even give stirring speeches from beyond death's door, culminating in a showy finale with words from the current Commander-in-Chief.

Walt Disney originally wanted to put The Hall of Presidents on Disneyland's Liberty Street, an offshoot of Main Street that would have recreated revolutionary life in much the same way that he had just done on the set of 1957's *Johnny Tremain* (a charming period piece that was in production at the same time).[16] Having expressed some concern about Americans losing sight of their own history and heritage, he wanted to remind us what it must have felt like to live in a country that was setting up its own rule — how urgent it must have seemed for America's early citizens to get it right. "The Hall of The Presidents of the United States" would have been the counterpart to "The Hall of the Declaration of Independence," both of them to sit inside the cul-de-sac at the end of Liberty Street and present stories about America's history using wax figures, dramatic narration, and painted tableaus.

Alas, those were busy days for Disneyland, with new attractions popping up all over the park. Liberty Street kept getting pushed back as plans changed. Eventually, Walt got a taste for what Audio-Animatronics could do, and once he'd seen his Tiki Birds flap their wings, wax dummies wouldn't do. No, The Hall of Presidents would need Audio-Animatronics, and those would be expensive. Fortunately, the year was 1963, and Walt had major companies knocking down his door to build spare-no-expense attractions for the 1964 New York World's Fair. Here is where he could get the funding he'd need to build something bigger than a bird.

Hoping to really catch a sponsor's eye, the Imagineers merged those dual "Hall of" shows into a singular presentation called One Nation Under God, a big-budget Audio-Animatronic cavalcade coupled with a dramatic presentation about America's earliest trials and challenges. "We love it!" the sponsors said, "...but it's too expensive, and what's it got to do with us?" Unless Thomas Jefferson could write the Declaration on a Hallmark card or George Washington could open up a can of Coke, corporate leaders couldn't find a rationale.

Walt resigned to getting only enough money to make *one* president. There was no question about who that would be. He felt a great personal fondness for Lincoln, speaking often of his admiration for him as one of the great heroes of history. So even though he had no idea which sponsor might sign on, he decided to go ahead and build himself an Honest

Abe on the assumption that *somebody* would see the thing and pay for it. There just wasn't enough time to wait for a green light in advance. "Well," Walt said then, "we couldn't get the entire Hall of Presidents together in time... but we might be able to finish Lincoln."[17]

As legend has it, the Fair's organizer, Robert Moses, walked into Disney's workshop one day and went to shake hands with the actor posing as Abe Lincoln's model, only to realize that this was no actor at all: it was an Audio-Animatronic. (Years later, when the same figure made its way to Disneyland, there were countless reports of guests having no idea he wasn't a real human being.) Moses was bound and determined that this thing be a part of the Fair, and he went to hunt up a sponsor. He found one in the State of Illinois, whose legislature had just approved a hefty chunk of change so that the state could somehow honor Abraham Lincoln's legacy as part of the Fair.[18] Talk about fortuosity! Well, the public didn't think so. The idea of turning a revered president into a robot struck many as disrespectful or downright creepy... until they saw it. Like everything else Walt touched at that Fair, it was a sensation in the end.

When the Fair wrapped, Walt still didn't have the funding he needed to make The Hall of Presidents a reality. But people loved Lincoln as he was, so a version of that show came to Disneyland: Great Moments with Mr. Lincoln, still running there today and sitting just catty corner to where Liberty Street would have been built behind it.[19] Walt died not long after, but time has a way of altering analysis, and by the time the 1970s rolled around, the Hall of Presidents looked like a sound financial prospect for Magic Kingdom. Executives figured the park needed something like New Orleans Square, only *not* New Orleans because that's too close to Florida. "Well, what do you know?" they thought. "We have the blueprints for a *Liberty* Square all ready to go!" The land would need an enticing attraction or two to anchor it anyway, so there would be money on the table for something impressive. The Hall of Presidents fit that bill and became one of 23 opening-day attractions in 1971.

The Hall of Presidents had the same basic structure then as it has today: a film followed by a Presidential roll call, only it ended with little more than a wave from then-President Richard Nixon, not yet a speech. At the time, Lincoln was the only President to address the audience directly, approximating his message from the World's Fair. Ford, Carter,

Reagan, and Bush were added in turn, their Animatronic likenesses joining the assembly upon each new President's election. When Bill Clinton took office, the attraction underwent its first major overhaul with a new script narrated by Maya Angelou[20] and a bonus show component: the incumbent President's address. Clinton became the first of America's leaders to record his own speech for the attraction, a tradition that has continued on with George W. Bush, Barack Obama, and now Donald Trump.

Think about that — so important has Walt Disney World become to our national consciousness that one of the earliest acts a new President must undertake is recording their Hall of Presidents address. The speech will be one of their first as President and is likely to rank among their most frequently heard.

There was much speculation upon Donald Trump's election that this newly established tradition might end with him. *All* bets were off with Trump, it seemed, and no one quite knew *what* he would do — or what Disney might do, given the intensive division surrounding his election and the various petitions imploring CEO Bob Iger to deny Trump a spot on that stage. Suddenly, and briefly, The Hall of Presidents became an early test of how one of the most visible gatekeepers of history — the Walt Disney Company — would respond to a presidential election that seemed to upend every assumption Americans had once made about their political system and its realm of possibilities.

As months went by and the Hall of Presidents remained closed for refurbishment, fans and journalists — and the public at large — got worked into a full-fledged frenzy. Headlining nighttime newscasts and talk shows, it seemed almost a foregone conclusion that while Trump's Animatronic would definitely appear within the attraction — a fact Disney had confirmed even before he was elected — he almost certainly would not speak in the show. Whether you thought that was Trump's decision or Disney's probably had a lot do with who you voted for. Speculation from *both* sides suggested that the Imagineers might secretly have built a Hillary Clinton Animatronic on the assumption she would win, and now they were scrambling to sculpt someone new (or to put all that plaster in a tanning salon).[21]

Adding fuel to the fire was an article in May from *Vice.com*, which claimed to have sources from inside Imagineering confirming that

Trump wouldn't speak, and that his very installation in the attraction was causing a near-meltdown within the hallowed halls of Imagineering. Alas, it turned out to be "fake news" at a time when that term still seemed relatively new. The sources were bogus, the article went offline, and *Vice* issued a formal retraction.[22]

Around that same time, Bob Iger reluctantly granted an interview in response to the controversy, confirming that Trump *would* speak in the attraction like the three presidents before him, but the process would take a little longer this time.[23] Disney's PR department doubled down soon after, sending out an official statement to media outlets confirming Trump's speaking role and moving the timeline up to late 2017. And then the official *Disney Parks Blog* tripled down with additional confirmation of the same. This time, they explained why the conversion was taking so long:

> *The Hall of Presidents is getting a new show, and a complete theater upgrade including a new sound system, lighting and high-definition projection system. The multi-screen viewing experience you may have seen in prior versions of the attraction is returning with an even wider vantage point of our country's history.*[24]

In all, the process took *eleven months*. One has a hard time believing that no part of it was to allow for a "cooling off" period. Recent reports have suggested that Disney and Trump couldn't agree on whether Trump could credit America with inventing skyscrapers in his speech and then make the following aside: "which, of course, I know a thing or two about, right?".[25] But there's almost certainly more to it than that.

It took roughly a month to add Bill Clinton in 1993, and not much longer than that to add George W. Bush in 2001. While the narrator changed for each of those conversions, the show stayed largely the same. In fact, when Bush took over, the Imagineers just stripped down Bill Clinton's Animatronic and rebuilt him as George W. Bush! (Then they made a *new* Clinton using less sophisticated Audio-Animatronics technology since he wouldn't need to do as much in the show anymore.) All of this was to save time and money.

When Obama came in, the attraction closed for *eight months*, not only to allow for new, state-of-the-art Animatronic design but also for a significant revamping of the show, including a new speech from George Washington, who'd never had a speaking part before.

Trump's installation brought with it even bigger change: a whole new movie, security officers inside the theater, a physical barrier to keep guests away from the stage, and all those techy improvements the *Parks Blog* promised. Whether those extras were enough to account for eleven months of transition — three more than Obama's required — is a question for you and your cable news channel of choice. But if it seemed like even longer than it was, consider this: there was a wrinkle in the timelines that makes them difficult to compare. Magic Kingdom started the Obama-era conversion in October 2008 (before the election was even held), whereas the Trump changes didn't begin until January 2017 (well after the election and just three days prior to Trump's inauguration).

For all the recent rancor over the roll call part of the show, it is the first act — the movie — that has earned the lion's share of disparagement over the years. The original, narrated by Lawrence Dobkin (the show's first and only non-minority narrator), came under fire for not paying enough attention to America's ugly history with racism and slavery. The next version, narrated by Maya Angelou, was an improvement, but it went so far in the other direction that one got the impression our founding fathers spent most of their time in the Continental Congress lamenting slavery. (Sadly, they did not.)

With the election of George W. Bush came new narration from J.D. Hall[26], who still read from the same script. As scholar Stephen M. Fjellman pointed out, the Angelou/Hall version was curiously defensive of exercising executive power against the will of the people.[27] When current-day controversies would tap into that same theme, whether it was Waco and Elian Gonzalez or enhanced interrogations and the Patriot Act, it was all too easy to read the show as politically interested. So Disney decided to try all over again when Barack Obama took office.[28]

That version, stirringly narrated by Morgan Freeman[29], glorified populism, even going so far as to dedicate several minutes to a glowing review of Andrew Jackson as "one of us." It made for an odd complement to Obama, who would often warn the public about populism, especially in his later years in office, even if he occasionally waded into those campaign waters himself.[30]

Probably because populism is the last subject Disney wanted to touch on the heels of Trump's unexpected populist victory — and because the first major-party female candidate had just lost — 2017 brought yet another new film to The Hall of Presidents, this time narrated by African-American actress Joy Vandervort-Cobb.[31] [32]

This latest version of the show makes for an interesting read in the era of Trump. On the one hand, it speaks approvingly of "a progressive movement" in the early 20th century (using those very words) and links immigration to economic prosperity — probably not Trump's favorite part of the show. And the section on Andrew Jackson, who Trump frequently singles out as his favorite president, is gone. But on the other hand, this version praises Teddy Roosevelt as "a knight on a crusade" who "speaks with force and vitality in clear terms that make colorful headlines at a time when mass-market newspapers have become the new media." Change that to "social media" and it reads like the introduction at a MAGA rally.

"Elections are often bitter," Vandervort-Cobb tells us, soothingly. "Each president stands at that fiery intersection where personal character meets the challenges of the times." Read into that what you like. Of course, it's quite possible that *I'm* reading too much into all of this. Then again, given the temperature of discourse these days, perhaps not. Or maybe Disney is just trying ever so hard to make everyone happy. To that end, the show now opens with an uncredited male announcer emphasizing that the attraction was *Walt's* idea, almost as if to say, "Hey, don't blame us."

Make what you will of the script, but you can't deny Vandervort-Cobb this: she reads the hell out of it. For the first time, The Hall of Presidents' first act doesn't sound like a video your teacher turned on in class. It makes history sound real, crisp, and alive. Her recitation is elegant and striking, reinforced by heady new on-screen titles that appear over amber-colored bokeh, giving the whole proceeding a modern and cinematic flair. The Hall of Presidents has never looked nor sounded so good. And those few curious comments notwithstanding, the new script redirects its focus away from issues and instead toward the very personal and human challenges that any president must endure — a more universal and overall less controversial approach. The whole thing has the air of an episode of "Downton Abbey."

Lincoln's remarks come in the middle of the movie, reciting the Gettysburg Address verbatim.[33] His delivery of that speech comes on the heels of an enthralling, on-screen portrayal of the Battle of Gettysburg. The juxtaposition puts Lincoln's address, one of the most famous ever given, into its gripping context. It's a lot like Walt's plans for a scene where "artillery.... would fire from one screen across to the enemy on a screen on the other side."[34] But it's when all the presidents appear together that the show really shines.

Today, the stage is occupied by 44 of the most important people who ever lived — eleven more than had held the office when Walt first imagined this. Their assemblage is a stunning sight that almost always elicits an audible gasp from the audience when the curtain is raised. In that moment, the show brings new meaning to the idea of "living history."

But gasps aren't the only things you'll hear from the audience inside The Hall of Presidents. There's sometimes cheering, booing, scoffing, and almost always snoring. The whole affair is a reflection of the political process — engaging, divisive, and occasionally tiring.

By the time the Presidents take the stage, the audience members — especially those who are U.S. citizens and politically inclined — are swept up in feelings of pride and conviction as the roll call begins. The room remains fairly tranquil, even reverential, while the first three dozen names (give or take a few) are called. At some point, though — and it's usually right around Richard Nixon — there's an unmistakable change in the atmosphere, as if you could hear the sound of several hundred people's facial muscles scrunching into either a smile or a frown.

By the time Ronald Reagan is named, someone in the audience has usually made some kind of audible noise. And everyone else in the audience has noticed. And a few of them have reacted. For every Republican who cheers for Reagan, a Democrat defiantly cheers for Clinton, prompting a mix of booing and applause for George W. Bush and another round of the same for Obama, with all sides reserving their biggest fuss for Trump. Hissing begins and it's not until the speeches drown it out that order is restored.

Despite the politically charged state of the national discourse, the audience manages to keep its cool, that brief battle of boos and bravos notwithstanding.[35] Still, when the show closed for the addition of President Obama's Animatronic, some speculated that it would be changed to remove all of the Presidential speeches and the audience's outspokenness along with them. As we've already seen, calls for its closure reached a fever pitch in 2017. But I think that would be a shame.

A common criticism of The Hall of Presidents is that it's the one part of Magic Kingdom that doesn't transport guests away from reality, at least not completely. On the contrary, I'd argue that its engagement with reality puts us into the story Walt was trying to tell. The attraction serves as Walt Disney World's town hall meeting, a quintessential function of democratic self-governance. How appropriate that such a convention unfolds inside Liberty Square, a land dedicated to the early, small-town exercise of American freedom. By confronting their own political identities and the opposing stances of those sharing the same room, guests play an important role in the Liberty Square narrative: that of the concerned townsperson. Inside the theater, they're given a chance to take a side when the emotional stakes are high, just as the folks living in the late eighteenth century might have done.

As the heart of Liberty Square, the attraction is a glimmering example of a Disney illusion made real — in a way, guests become citizens of Liberty Square's fictional colonial town by taking an interest in its affairs. Sure, the present-day issues may be the ones stirring their passions, but the themes of discourse and free assembly are universal and span the centuries.

The Hall of Presidents, and all of Liberty Square along with it, abounds with First Amendment optimism. This is the very thing Walt wanted out of One Nation Under God — a way to reconnect his guests with their heritage. Thinking about his original plans for the attraction calls to mind yet another great speech — not from a President, but the one Walt himself gave on Disneyland's opening day. In it, he dedicated his park "to the ideals, the dreams, and the hard facts that have created America." The Hall of Presidents consecrates those very ideals, dreams, and hard facts within the Magic Kingdom, ensuring the park continues its creator's vision and works toward achieving his goals. Presidents come and go. Let's hope The Hall of Presidents never will.

WATCH THIS –
The One and Only, Genuine, Original Family Band (1968)

Set during the 1888 U.S. Presidential Election, this Sherman Brothers musical is probably Disney's most political movie, but also one of its lightest and most charming. The eponymous family is mostly made up of hardcore Democrats and supporters of President Grover Cleveland, currently seeking reelection. When they move to the Dakota Territory, they spar with the largely Republican populace, which hopes to see the territory admitted as two separate states — North Dakota and South Dakota — so that they can send four Republican Senators to Congress instead of just two.

Among the many great songs in this movie are two relatively popular numbers, "'Bout Time" and "Ten Feet off the Ground," both famously covered by Louis Armstrong. The cast is one of film history's most interesting. In a very small role, Goldie Hawn makes her film debut here as a young girl, starring alongside a boy who would grow up to be the father of her children, Kurt Russell. The movie is also the second theatrical outing for both Lesley Ann Warren and John Davidson, who had made their film debuts one year earlier in Disney's *The Happiest Millionaire*. They played one another's love interest in both films before going on to enjoy long and vibrant entertainment careers. The all-star cast also includes legendary actors Walter Brennan and Buddy Ebsen, who both worked on other high-profile Disney projects during their careers.

The movie's political bantering does start to get a mite tedious before it ends, but the town square discourse and the rarely explored historical setting make the film extremely interesting, even unique. The local fervor for the political process depicted so memorably in the movie mirrors the atmosphere in The Hall of Presidents.

Haunted Mansion

Type: Dark ride
Duration: 9 minutes
Height Restriction: None
Popularity/Crowds: Moderate to High
FastPass+: Yes; medium priority
Fear Factor: 2.5 out of 5 (darkness; spooky effects; some dramatic intensity)
Wet Factor: None
Preshow: A graveyard queue (usually inaccessible for those using FastPass+) acts as a sort of preshow. All guests then proceed on foot through a foyer and the famous elevator scene before boarding the ride vehicles.
Boarding Speed: Very fast
Best Time to Visit without FastPass+: Wait times tend to be relatively moderate throughout the day except during peak attendance, but mornings and late evenings usually have the lowest waits.
Special Comments: One of the best, yet least scary, haunted houses you'll find

There's a perverse joy we find in scaring ourselves, and theme parks specialize in the kind of fear that puts a smile on your face. You need look no further than the top of an impending roller coaster plunge to find pearly whites on wide display. If you've ever exchanged gleefully nervous looks with a friend in the moments before some serious G-force comes your way, you know just the kind of smile I'm talking about. We might call this involuntary response "grim grinning," which is how Disney describes the 999 ghosts dwelling inside the Haunted Mansion. This slow-paced open house tour through the lifestyles of the rich and departed plays on the same sick satisfaction we get from thrill rides, except that the thrills here come from poltergeists not plummets.

The Mansion tour begins inside a doorless chamber, where pale-faced ushers herd us into the "dead center" of the room. Standing inside that small space with seemingly no way out, claustrophobia might start creeping in. Before that happens, the enclosure suddenly starts to grow. While the bone-chilling voice of Disney legend Paul Frees[36] delivers an unforgettable welcoming speech to his helpless guests ("Your cadaverous pallor betrays an aura of foreboding" might be the best sentence ever constructed), the room begins to expand as the portraits crawl toward the ceiling, revealing a surprising bottom half to each painting and a lot more wall than there seemed to be before. As the self-appointed Ghost Host, Frees mocks his mortal prisoners. "It's almost as though you sense a disquieting metamorphosis," he says, and then asks tauntingly, "Is this room actually stretching or is it your imagination?"

When the chamber comes to a halt, the host shows the captives exactly how he crossed over to his ghostly state. The lights go out and high above us, we see a hanging corpse and hear a blood-curdling scream. When the lights return, the once impenetrable walls have given way to a long hallway, at the end of which ever-moving "Doom Buggies" are ready to whisk us deeper into the hereafter.

That lengthy proceeding is but the introduction to Haunted Mansion, one of Walt Disney World's most cherished attractions, and at times, one of the bleakest. Frees's morbid narration, the sense of helplessness guests experience, and the gruesome display in the rafters all add up to one of the darkest sequences in the usually cheery Magic Kingdom. The ride that follows, though, is more comedy than horror as the tone grows increasingly playful and the spirits get sent up for laughs.

This friction between haunt and hilarity stems from tension between two of the ride's designers. Background painter and concept artist Claude Coats[37] wanted to stage something truly spooky, while classic Disney character guy Marc Davis[38] wanted to infuse more of the studio's signature whimsy. They both won in the end. The attraction had been conceived of as a walk-through tour and eatery; the Mansion we know today didn't materialize (no pun intended) until 1969, nearly four years after Walt Disney's death. By the time the doors formally opened to Disneyland guests, Imagineering legend X Atencio[39] had masterfully scripted a ride-through incorporating both Coats's unsettling sense of the supernatural and an abundance of Davis's comic relief. Two years later, Walt Disney World's version opened along with the Magic Kingdom itself on October 1, 1971. Since then, Haunted Mansion has made its way to Tokyo, Hong Kong, and Paris too. It is the only Disney attraction to exist in a different themed land within each of those five resorts.[40]

At Magic Kingdom, we find it in Liberty Square. The building is arresting both in its ornate beauty and its eerie aura. The Gothic architecture is inspired by nineteenth century homes along the Hudson River, which supposedly makes Liberty Square an ideal setting. While that may be true, there's no getting around the fact that the mansion has very little in common with the other buildings in that land, or that a haunted house bears no immediate relevance to Colonial America. Consider also that while Disneyland built a Southern antebellum manor for its Haunted Mansion in New Orleans Square and Disneyland Paris went with an abandoned estate in Frontierland, the Fantasyland mansion in Tokyo Disneyland looks exactly the same as the one in Magic Kingdom's Liberty Square.

Thematically, there seems little question that Fantasyland would make a better fit for Haunted Mansion than does its current home, Liberty Square. Hauntings are inherently fantastical and there's a whole lineage of Disney cartoon shorts — like those that have inspired other Fantasyland attractions — that address ghosts with the same levity as Haunted Mansion (see *Lonesome Ghosts* and *The Skeleton Dance* for examples). The darker elements would feel right at home in Fantasyland, where edgy entertainment born from the terrifying traditions of children's literature is the order of the day. Why Liberty Square, then? The most honest answer is probably that this little land needed to claim as many attractions as it could, and the Imagineers figured Haunted Mansion was close enough to fit the bill.

Given that Fantasyland is unlikely to annex the attraction anytime soon, the mansions of the Hudson River will have to suffice as the thematic connection, but that little nugget is not to be dismissed — that Disney cares enough about storytelling to ensure that the ride's placement is credible is part of what makes their parks so stimulating. There might also be something to the notion of housing the Magic Kingdom's most noteworthy nod to the afterlife in an area dedicated to national heritage, given that belief in the supernatural has historically been an integral part of the American experience.

Whether the attraction jells with Liberty Square narratively is hard to say. Touring the mansion, one does get the idea that there's a backstory at play. We see that our Ghost Host hanged himself. Later, we ride by what looks like an abandoned funeral. There are lots of discarded wedding portraits as we enter the attic and, at the tip-top of the house, we find one very violent ghost bride waiting for us to round the corner. Exactly how those pieces fit together is never really made clear, though there have been many attempts to craft a definitive storyline (most involving Mr. Gracey, the apparent master of the home, his young bride, and one of those two killing the other and/or themselves). While X Atencio could have scripted a bit of narration to clear up these details, all we're told instead is that the mansion is now inhabited by 999 ghosts who are looking for one more to join them ("any volunteers?"). In some ways, Haunted Mansion is, like Pirates of the Caribbean, less a navigable story and more a story world. And yet it clearly puts enough plot points in place to suggest that there is one series of events that connects the dots — we, the audience, just don't know what those events were.[41]

Like true explorers, we find only the aftermath when we enter these ruins a century (or more) later, and it's up to our imaginations and powers of observation to figure out exactly what happened. Like the greatest works of art, Haunted Mansion is enduringly ambiguous. The effect of that uncertainty is twofold. First, it generates a need to go back inside again. As with cryptic films and novels, we feel compelled to take another look to see how much more we can figure out, especially since the time-controlled tour allows no more than a fleeting glance at any of the many clues. Second, the mystery produces a fear of the unknown. The suggestion that more has gone on inside the mansion than we understand, things nefarious and otherworldly, creates suspense and uneasiness just as that same device — teasing the audience with the unknown — has in mystery novels for ages.

Lavish detailing inside the ride accentuates this sense of paranormal investigation. While the ominous façade visible from Liberty Square has, in actuality, nothing to do with the real building guests ride through once they're inside, the disconnect is never apparent. The designers have gone to great lengths to preserve the premise of an open-house tour. The Doom Buggies begin their tour by ascending a staircase, then moving through actual hallways while peering down others (including one that never ends). The Buggies wind from room to room, through all the spaces one might expect to find in an extravagant home — a library, a conservatory, a ballroom, and even a cluttered attic. Along the way, little details like wall paintings (most of them possessed) and pieces of furniture add to the illusion that this is a once-lived-in home.

For the ride's finale, the Doom Buggies enter the graveyard outside the house and the perceptive passenger will note that they fly out of a window and descend through the nighttime air to the haunted grounds below, where a recreated exterior of the mansion they've just supposedly exited can be seen behind them.[42] Again, the attention to detail bolsters the idea that the house really might have once been a home for this unfortunate family.

The ride stands out for its special effects, which add to the believability and crank up the creep factor. A hovering candelabra, a disembodied head calling out incantations from inside a floating crystal ball, and footsteps that walk in all directions through a seemingly unending series of stairways are all part of the "how'd they do that?" awe that the attraction so skillfully inspires. These latter two effects are the results of more recent enhancements to the attraction, but Haunted Mansion's most remarkable special effect has been part of the attraction since it opened: the dancing apparitions in the ballroom scene that materialize before our very eyes and have the fully animated and transparent appearance of actual ghosts.

The music works both to enhance the chilling mood created by the special effects and to counter it with the lightheartedness that emerges as the attraction's prevailing sentiment. That's thanks to "Grim Grinning Ghosts," the theme song that appears in one form or another throughout most of the ride. Sometimes it's played on a slow and haunting organ, other times it sounds like a merry little jingle with lyrics performed by "happy haunts" and a barbershop quartet.

The term "grim-grinning ghost" originated in Shakespeare's poem *Venus and Adonis*,[43] but the rest of those funny, very clever lyrics were written by none other than X Atencio himself, having tried his hand at songwriting after Walt Disney encouraged him to do so. Among the voices singing the song is Thurl Ravenscroft[44] (the voice of Kellogg's Tony the Tiger and the deep baritone responsible for "You're a Mean One, Mr. Grinch"), who leads the quartet of singing busts in the graveyard.

Yet for all its frivolity, Haunted Mansion remains undeniably eerie. If Disney would allow it, I'd challenge those who say otherwise to take a stroll through the mansion alone, on foot, during the night. In *Hocus Pocus in Focus*, my book about Disney's kooky-spooky witch comedy, I argue that the things that scare us as kids often bond us to them.[45] I think that's a big part of why *Hocus Pocus* has a hold on whole generations, and maybe the same kind of effect is at work in the Haunted Mansion. That would explain the hordes of zealous fans and the endless urban legends that have cropped up over the years. You need look no further than online communities like DoomBuggies.com to find evidence that the attraction has taken on an (after)life of its own. Rumors range from wedding rings buried in the cement outside the mansion[46] to the actual ghosts of children whose ashes were spread inside the ride by parents seeking to carry out their last wishes. Search the internet and you'll find some unsettling night vision photographs.[47]

Haunted Mansion has cultivated a mythos all its own, made possible by its exquisite artistry. As a kid, it's scary but irresistible; riding it feels brave. As an adult, you aren't so much scared as scared silly. Here at the Haunted Mansion, the grins are always grim, but unlike the happy haunts inside, they never disappear.

WATCH THIS - Candleshoe (1977)

Naturally, *The Haunted Mansion* (2003) starring Eddie Murphy is a good place to start... or maybe not so good, given its critical reception. It was a modest box office success, however, and in all fairness, what the movie lacks in most other areas, it makes up for (a little) in set design and atmosphere. In 2010, Disney announced that yet another *Haunted Mansion* movie is on the way, this time produced, written, and likely directed by the visually emphatic Guillermo del Toro (*Pan's Labyrinth*). The new film will be darker in tone than the Murphy vehicle and will establish itself as a reboot rather than a sequel (and may even cross over with the supposedly upcoming *Magic Kingdom* film, which is discussed in *Chapter Six*). As this book goes to press, work on the screenplay reportedly continues, but production and release are likely much farther down the road. In the meantime, let's look at a forgotten classic from Disney's live-action stable: *Candleshoe*.

A teenage Jodie Foster stars as Casey Brown, a street-smart American girl picked up by a couple of con artists who plan to pass her off as the long-lost granddaughter of Lady St. Edmund (Helen Hayes, in her final big-screen appearance). The scammers aren't after the St. Edmund fortune, though — as we soon learn, that disappeared a long time ago. No, they want to crack a code that will lead them to an ancient treasure they believe to have been concealed inside Lady St. Edmund's Candleshoe estate. They have one clue to start with: "For the sunrise student, there is treasure among books." Once they get Casey inside Candleshoe, she'll search for the next clue in hopes of finding the hidden gold.

Disney used the real-life Compton Wynyates manor in Warwickshire, England as Candleshoe in the movie. The beautiful Tudor home is made of red brick with numerous gables and turret-like chimney stacks and bears an immediate resemblance to Walt Disney World's Haunted Mansion. The house isn't haunted but Casey's search for clues does lend the massive home a sense of mystery, appealing to our curiosity in much the same way that Haunted Mansion does.

Chapter 4

Fantasyland

"Here is a world of imagination, hopes, and dreams. In this timeless land of enchantment, the age of chivalry, magic, and make-believe are reborn, and fairy tales come true. Fantasyland is dedicated to the young and the young in heart, to those who believe that when you wish upon a star, your dreams do come true."

Walt Disney, "Dateline: Disneyland," *July 17, 1955*

That was the final dedication that Walt read out in his live-from-Disneyland telecast at the park's grand opening. With a beautiful, instrumental version of "When You Wish Upon a Star" playing behind him, the words sounded even more poignant than they do on paper... or would have been in stone had they been engraved, as this is another plaque that was never planted.

Fantasyland is the centerpiece, pinnacle, and shining star of Magic Kingdom. It is home to one of the most famous sites in the world, Cinderella Castle, and is the dwelling place of the Disney Company's cornerstone creations — its magical fantasy films. One of the resort's most powerful fantasies is that of a return to childhood, the idea that here is a place where kids can be kids... and adults can, too. The bright colors, the calliope music, the open-hearted embrace of stories so central to our upbringing, and the sheer number of attractions here all make this feel like the park's most special land, and it's the indulgence in unadulterated escapism that really seals the deal.

Between 2010 and 2014, Magic Kingdom undertook a massive expansion project known as "New Fantasyland," more than doubling the land's acreage and bringing more rides and shows to Fantasyland than any other part of the park by far.

Today's Fantasyland consists of four primary "boroughs" (my term, not an official one) — the Castle Courtyard, the Enchanted Forest, Storybook Circus, and "Tangledtown."

The Castle Courtyard includes most of "old" Fantasyland, including Peter Pan's Flight; It's a Small World; Prince Charming Regal Carrousel; and Mickey's Philharmagic.

The Enchanted Forest is home to five attractions — Enchanted Tales with Belle; Under the Sea ~ Journey of the Little Mermaid; Seven Dwarfs Mine Train; The Many Adventures of Winnie the Pooh; and Mad Tea Party. It's also where we find two new hot spots for dining. Be Our Guest Restaurant is situated inside the *Beauty and the Beast* castle, while next door, Gaston's Tavern serves its own signature beverage, LeFou's Brew, an apple-marshmallow-mango concoction that endeavors to rival the delicious Butterbeer beverage at Universal Orlando's Wizarding World of Harry Potter.

Storybook Circus stands in the area previously occupied by Mickey's Toontown Fair, no longer considered a separate land. Its attractions include Dumbo the Flying Elephant and The Barnstormer featuring Goofy as the Great Goofini.

Finally, Tangledtown doesn't have a proper name, but hey, we have to call it something. Truth be told, it's barely a "borough" at all, home to just one thing: the restroom. But it's the most elaborate restroom you'll ever see. Approaching it, you'll feel certain that there must be a ride in it somewhere, so grand is its entryway. But alas, it's just a serene little courtyard with resting stools, smartphone charging stations, and the restrooms themselves, all themed to 2010's Rapunzel flick, *Tangled*. Beautifully lit, exquisitely decorated, and even featuring its own background music loop, Tangledtown is undeniably nice to wander through, so much so that you hope they find a way to fit an attraction in here someday.

Fantasyland's power is in its survey of archetypal narratives. With the exception of It's a Small World and The Barnstormer, the land's rides and shows are adaptations of classic short stories, fairy tales, and literary greats. Their corporeal interaction with the written word allows them to tap into morals and fables that have been a part of our cultural fiber since birth.

From *Snow White* on, "Disney magic" has always been tethered to literature and fantasy. Fantasyland is where this ethereal "magic" lives — and it is where the Magic Kingdom's heart beats.

Peter Pan's Flight

Type: Dark ride
Duration: 3 to 4 minutes
Height Restriction: None
Popularity/Crowds: High, verging on E-ticket
FastPass+: Yes; a top priority
Fear Factor: 0.5 out of 5 (moderate heights)
Wet Factor: None
Preshow: The newly interactive queue offers a tour through the Darling family's nursery (never mind that it's different from the nursery we later see in the ride).
Boarding Speed: Slow
Best Time to Visit without FastPass+: Very first thing in the morning or very end of the night
Special Comments: An absolute must, despite the long waits

"You can fly! You can fly! You can fly!" So goes the touchstone lyric in 1953's *Peter Pan*. There are few super powers as invigorating to the imagination as that of flight, probably because it is so thoroughly unachievable. To fly is to breach the realm of possibility, and yet Walt Disney famously quipped that "it's kind of fun to do the impossible." That, in a nutshell, is the allure of Peter Pan's Flight — having fun while doing the impossible.

We begin aboard a flying pirate ship, propelled by pixie dust into the Darling family nursery, where we meet Wendy, John, and Michael.[1] The eldest is telling a story when Peter Pan interrupts her with the words we really want to hear — "Off to Neverland!" Then, in a subtle scene change, our ship glides out of the nursery window and into what looks like the open evening air. Our vessel is suspended from the ceiling, moving along a track above us, and we find ourselves peering down on a tiny-looking London far below. Traffic moves in grids, lights twinkle from bedroom windows, and Big Ben glows in the distance. Car horns are audible, as are anxious barks from Nana, the Darlings' matronly pet dog, and the film's gorgeous score.

We head toward the moon and see the shadows of our companions in flight (Peter and the children). A right turn two stars later and we've made our way into the hidden realm of Neverland. The mermaids, the crocodile, Tiger Lily's tribe — they're all here. And so is Captain Hook. He, Smee, and his band of pirates cross swords with Pan and the Lost Boys aboard the *Jolly Roger*, all just below the bow.

I don't have any empirical studies to support it, but it seems to me that Pan's Flight holds a special place in people's hearts, one that even the park's busier classics can't quite claim. Certainly, it is the only original dark ride[2] still running in its (more or less) original form at both U.S. resorts. In Magic Kingdom, even after all the new attractions, it remains one of Fantasyland's most popular. There's also the incalculable "awww" factor. Bring the ride up in conversation and it's like you pulled out a puppy. That reaction probably has something to do with the pure and unmitigated fantasy that people discover in their flight over Neverland.

Inspired by J.M. Barrie's 1904 stage play, *Peter Pan* is more fantasy-laden than any of Walt Disney's other animated movies.[3] Created in the aftermath of World War II, the film's journey from London to a magical world where people never grow up resonated with an audience in need of escape. And following a decade of turmoil in his company, Walt needed escape too. *Pinocchio*, *Fantasia*, and *Bambi* had all been box office disappointments; his animators had gone on strike; and the government had essentially commandeered his studios to produce propaganda films. *Dumbo* did manage to turn a profit in 1941, but mostly because he'd been forced to make it on the cheap. In the years immediately following the war, he was resigned to producing "package features" — films that barely qualified as full-length, comprised as they were of disjointed cartoons stitched together. They brought in just enough money to keep the company afloat. All the while, Mickey Mouse's star was fading.

Despite having produced four of what we now consider to be the greatest animated movies ever made, the 1940s weren't kind to Walt. We shouldn't be surprised, then, that he kicked off 1950 with something as lavishly imaginative as *Cinderella*, introducing his audience to an era of fantasy that would define the rest of that decade. *Peter Pan* was the third release in what we might now call the Second Golden Age of Disney Animation,[4] and it kicked the magic into higher gear. The film's spirit of fantasy and adventure is pervasive and drives its theme park ride, too.

Wendy, John, and Michael are whisked away from their boring nursery to a place where youth is eternal and adventure abounds. Children live alone, take up arms, and have little responsibility beyond fending off grown-up pirates. Naturally, Hook and his crew fear the children and consider them their greatest adversaries. Like the most enduring children's entertainment, the film (and Barrie's original play) empowers children by making them formidable and front-and-center. That's especially true for boys.

Peter Pan is a male fantasy. The young protagonist crows in dominance as mermaids fawn over him, Wendy and Tinker Bell spar jealously for his affection, and the Lost Boys revere him as a sword-wielding action hero and their leader. His is an idyllic boyhood that lasts forever.

Scholars have written at length about Barrie's fixation on masculinity and its impact on Pan.[5] He might as well have dipped his quill in testosterone. Perhaps inevitably, that same tenor makes its way into Disney's adaptations.

Wendy is not altogether denied agency, but the female adventure in this story is relayed through an exclusively masculine prism — Peter's. And yet the story has proven fiercely compelling to readers and viewers of any age or gender. What are we to make, then, of a story that is near-universally beloved by both men and women, even as it defines its female characters wholly in terms of their obsession with a boy?

The gender dynamics in *Peter Pan* are complex, and even more so in Fantasyland, where gender roles are already ripe for study. Peter Pan's Flight happens to be the only ride widely regarded as "masculine" in an otherwise "feminine" Fantasyland, Cinderella's backyard. Where Adventureland is interested principally in piratedom and calamity, Fantasyland looks and feels like a royal soiree. One might argue that Pan's Flight represents a hybrid of the two — one part cannonball, one part pixie dust. But the ride is often talked of as a high-flying pirate parade capable of keeping young boys interested in Fantasyland where "girly" princesses and fairies otherwise rule the roost. Is it really so clear, though, that boys aren't compelled by fairy tales or that girls aren't compelled by action? Hardly. And yet conventional wisdom insists that Fantasyland target the two separately.

The long lines for Pan are thoroughly coed, and the families queuing up here are the same who just saw Merida, the ardent feminist of *Brave*, "shooting for her own hand" at a meet-and-greet around the corner. If they love both, how are we to draw a clean line between them? Merchandise sales apparently do break down along these lines, but how useful an indicator is that of anything? There may be a paucity of boys buying princess dresses, but does that mean they're any less enraptured by *Sleeping Beauty*? Is *Peter Pan* "for boys" if it doesn't sell swords to girls? Nobody working in Fantasyland is going to ask you these questions, but they're there nonetheless, floating around in the air between "second star to the right" and "someday my prince will come."

As if this weren't all multifaceted enough already, let's not forget that until the Disney movie, boys'-boy Peter was always played by a girl. That fact has only added to scholars' perplexity over *Pan*. How is it that a play long noted for privileging the masculine ego has unfailingly cast a woman as its leading man?[6]

Disney's *Pan* raises a lot of questions that aren't easy to answer, but they absolutely beg for academic attention, especially given all the gender tension boiling just under Fantasyland's surface. It's something to think about as you consider why you yourself love the ride (or don't, as the case may be for people I've yet to meet). If nothing else, what we can glean from Peter Pan and his Flight is that trying to define an audience's response to fantasy stories with a set of boy/girl cookie cutters simply isn't as easy as the marketing department might like it to be.

It would be parochial, though, to consider Disney's *Pan* narrowly in terms of gender. First and foremost, its story is one of escape, which is a universal and maybe gender-less fantasy. In Peter Pan's Flight, that fantasy is profound. The ride's physical sensation of flight frees us, in a way, from whatever weighs us down. "Off to Neverland!" is a call to leave the real world behind and fly to somewhere much more exciting. If *Peter Pan* is an enchanting fantasy on the screen, it's all the more spellbinding when made "real."

Isn't that what Fantasyland is all about — the magic of fantasy coming to life all around us? Disney's Imagineers locate the emotional heart of Walt's films and translate them into three dimensions, making the imaginary tangible by identifying the sentiments that made us fall in love with the story in the first place and making them manifest. Now we don't have to merely read about Neverland or see it on a TV set. We can actually *go* there. For the precious few moments we spend inside, the adults among us are children again, forever young.

I remember the first time I rode Peter Pan's Flight. With five-year-old logic, I heard the ride description and was sure I'd be sent flying through the air on some kind of wire, a very sharp hook waiting for me on the other side. Nothing could have been more terrifying. Little did I know that I should have been afraid of the ride breaking down instead. A half-hour suspended in the air gave new meaning to "never land."

The real experience isn't too far off from what I'd imagined. The ride is remarkable because it makes elaborate use of special effects — most of them more than a half-century old — to create an experience that lives up to the stories we've read and that we might imagine on our own. Those special effects are Disney's real-life pixie dust. And as the song tells us, that's all it takes to fly — faith, trust, and just a little bit of pixie dust. Disney supplies the last ingredient through the magic of Imagineering. We make up the rest with our willingness to cast off our cares and have a little fun while doing the impossible.

A lifetime ago, Walt Disney made us a promise: "you can fly." Here in Fantasyland, with one of his best rides, he makes good on the guarantee.

WATCH THIS - Finding Neverland (2004)

Disney's *Peter Pan* never really endeavors to explore the psyche of its characters. Still, what the movie lacks in depth, it mostly makes up for with an affecting spirit of adventure. Walt's film is even easier to appreciate when we bring our own outside knowledge about Peter to the table, knowledge we gain not only from the original written works but also from excellent films like Universal/Columbia's 2003 version starring Jeremy Sumpter, Spielberg's *Hook*, and the Disney-produced *Finding Neverland*.

J.M. Barrie's life story, told with cinematic finesse in *Finding Neverland*, brings invaluable context to *Peter Pan* in all its various iterations. In this creatively vivid biopic, Johnny Depp brings the conflicted dramatist to life with an air of real humanity. The movie, which was nominated for seven Oscars including Best Actor and Best Picture (it won for Best Score), keeps an eye on *Peter Pan* at all times, ensuring that the story never wanders far from the reason people are watching it — that is, to learn about the mind that created one of our most captivating fantasies. The many themes and messages found in Barrie's original *Pan* stories, Disney's movie adaptation, and the Peter Pan's Flight ride are all the easier to appreciate after having seen this outstanding film, which was distributed and co-produced by Miramax back when it was part of the Disney Studios empire (the movie is now distributed on home video by Lionsgate Home Entertainment).

It's a Small World

Type: Boat ride
Duration: 11 to 12 minutes
Height Restriction: None
Popularity/Crowds: Moderate to High
FastPass+: Yes (low priority)
Fear Factor: None (unless singing dolls give you nightmares)
Wet Factor: None
Preshow: None
Boarding Speed: Fast
Best Time to Visit without FastPass+: Anytime, but come back later if you find it very crowded.

It's a Small World[7] is kind of a tough sell: board a little boat and circle slowly around hundreds of identical child dolls as they sing the same jingle over and over again in their native tongues. Creepy, right? And yet, It's a Small World is one of the best-known and most enduringly popular theme park attractions in the world. Why? Well, gluttony for punishment is one theory, but I think there's more to it than that.

Dubbed "the happiest cruise that ever sailed," Small World takes its guests around the world, drifting from one continent to the next, a cast of children dancing modestly in each one. The wardrobe, set dressing, and language all change for each country but the children and the song stay the same. There is essentially no narrative, just an inspiring message — "a smile means friendship to everyone."

True to its word, the ride delivers on the promise of smiles and friendship before it even begins. A Disney cast member waves enthusiastically to just-boarded passengers from a control tower perch. Just around the river bend, diners inside The Pinocchio Village Haus restaurant look down at the travelers with a nod and a smile. The face on the clock tower offers an enormous grin to those waiting for their boat to arrive.[8] If they're standing there long enough, they'll see an impressive time change on every quarter-hour, but at It's a Small World, every hour is Happy Hour... just not *that* Happy Hour, of course. The only spirits in the Magic Kingdom, remember, are the happy ones at Haunted Mansion.[9]

It's a Small World lulls its passengers into a stupor all its own. Like a snake charmer's flute, the marriage of motion and music in the ride enchants everyone inside it. The attraction's methodology is not unlike the hypnotist's. The steady rhythm of the beat and the boat as it gently rocks on the water relaxes you. The colors on the stage are fluorescent and bright but everything else is pitch black, directing your focus toward the dolls and their mesmerizingly cadenced dance. The plaque at the entryway, calling this the happiest cruise that ever sailed, suggests that you should be receptive to the good vibes that will soon be wafting your way. Before long, you've entered a Small World state of mind. Hypnosis relies on the same things: relaxation, fixation, and suggestion. It's the art of using sensory persuasion to suggest an idea.

Sure enough, as Small World lulls us into its ever-so-slightly altered state of consciousness, its message starts to sink in. The serenity can make us more meditative than we might have been out in the hustle and bustle of Fantasyland. The lyrics and the visuals begin working together to impress upon us a moral.

"It's a Small World" is, according to some, including The Sherman Brothers (who wrote it), the most-performed and most-translated song in history. It's undoubtedly among the best known. A veritable earworm, the composition is wildly addictive, made all the more indelible in our minds by the fact that it plays ad infinitum in five locations around the world. The lyrics are quite simple, but in their simplicity, they're also quite meaningful. "There's so much that we share that it's time we're aware it's a small world, after all." Those words are a reflection of the historical moment in which they were written.

It's a Small World is another of the attractions that Walt Disney debuted at the 1964 New York World's Fair. Originally called Children of the World, the ride opened in the Fair's Pepsi pavilion, a notable entry in Disney's history with Coca-Cola and Pepsi, a subject worthy of a discussion all its own.[10] The original plans called for multiple national anthems to play all at once but as it turned out, a musical clash was counterproductive to the whole "global *harmony*" idea. Walt called on The Sherman Brothers to write something more pleasing to the ear. They came back with the lyrics we all know now, only they were set to a beautifully wistful ballad. Realizing he'd need a cheerier sound, Walt asked them to write something a bit more upbeat, and boy, did they deliver!

Listening to the song now, one can almost hear them saying, "You want cheery? We'll show you cheery." In a radical transformation that puts Cinderella's rags-to-riches to shame, the once-wistful "Small World" became the happiest, most buoyant song ever composed, and the music and the ride together became an instant hit. After closing at the World's Fair, the attraction opened in Disneyland on May 28, 1966, and in the Magic Kingdom on its opening day in 1971. Tokyo, Paris, and Hong Kong have their own versions, too. Fantasyland is the attraction's home in all five of those theme parks, an interesting fact when one considers that an international troupe of dancing children is not, strictly speaking, a thing of fantasy.

The right could just as easily belong to Adventureland, by virtue of its voyage 'round the world theme, or to Tomorrowland, given its message of hope for the future. So why Fantasyland? Well, besides the fact that Epcot's World Showcase didn't open until 1982, long stretches of the song have a distinctly European sound, linking it nicely to Fantasyland's Euro milieu. A large part of the score even has a Swiss quality about it, what with the yodeling and all, which connects it geographically with the Matterhorn mountain in California's Fantasyland. But beyond the music, the Small World ride represents a different notion of "fantasy" than the fanciful enchantment we typically associate with that term.

The attraction opened in the World's Fair at the peak of the civil rights movement, mere months before the Civil Rights Act of 1964 became law. The nation was facing a new future of integration in spite of lingering prejudice and racial divide. Meanwhile, international tensions were high as the Vietnam War escalated. Whether Walt and The Sherman Brothers intended it as a commentary on the changing sociopolitical climate or not, the ride and its song grew out of that especially tumultuous period in time. The fantasy in the attraction is one that imagines a more loving and cohesive world than existed in the 1960s. While strife stemming from racial and national barriers dominated the headlines of the day, the attraction contemplates humanity's potential to overcome those barriers.

The Small World fantasy, then, is not a fictive realm of magic and dragons, but a dream — the same kind of dream that Dr. Martin Luther King, Jr. famously described the year before, a dream in which little children are not judged by the color of their skin.

Small World's bold, post-racial optimism is underscored by the decision to use only children in its presentation. Their appearance together in the ride calls to mind the unforgettable lyrics in Rodgers and Hammerstein's *South Pacific*.

> *You've got to be taught before it's too late*
> *Before you are six or seven or eight*
> *To hate all the people your relatives hate*
> *You've got to be carefully taught*

The ride's design is tailored to communicating that same idea. The children look alike for a reason, to emphasize the underlying sameness that makes us all human. They sing the same song in various languages to demonstrate that our different tongues can express the same ideas. They're happy, and happiness is a thing of love.

Like "You've Got to Be Carefully Taught" in *South Pacific*, "It's a Small World" espouses a hope that the next generation of children will grow up full of love and free of prejudice and hate. They just need to be taught that it really is a small world, after all.

WATCH THIS - The Boys: The Sherman Brothers' Story (2009)

The Sherman Brothers are Disney's most famous and accomplished songwriters (Alan Menken is close behind them), but while everyone knows their music, few knew their story... that is, until their sons got together to direct this documentary, co-produced and distributed by Walt Disney Pictures and executive produced by none other than funnyman Ben Stiller. We find out that the brothers didn't really get along while working together and were barely speaking by 2009, each then in his eighties. Sadly, the elder brother, Robert B. Sherman, passed away on March 5, 2012, at the age of 86, not even three years after the documentary's debut, a fact that only underscores the tragedy of their estrangement.

In the course of investigating the rocky relationship, the film does a marvelous job of chronicling their career, including parts of it that ventured outside of Disney's walls. Special attention is paid to what are arguably the Brothers' most well-known productions: *Mary Poppins* and It's a Small World. Celebrities and insiders are on hand to share their perspectives on the attraction and its unforgettable soundtrack, making this a superb tribute to the brothers and their work.

Prince Charming Regal Carrousel

Type: Carousel
Duration: 2 to 3 minutes
Height Restriction: None
Popularity/Crowds: Moderate
FastPass+: No
Fear Factor: None
Wet Factor: None
Preshow: None
Boarding Speed: Slow
Best Time to Visit: Morning or late night (afternoons occasionally see short waits too)

You wouldn't know by looking at it, but Prince Charming Regal Carrousel[11] represents the very spark of life for the Disney theme parks around the world. Walt was first inspired to build Disneyland when taking his daughters to Griffith Park[12] in Los Angeles during the 1930s and early '40s. Every Sunday, he'd wait on the sidelines while his two little girls enjoyed the carousel there. He decided an amusement park should offer more for parents and children to enjoy together, a line of thought that would culminate in the world's most-visited vacation destinations. I suppose it's curious that his parks would end up with a carousel sitting smack in the middle of Fantasyland when that very type of ride left him unsatisfied in the first place, but Walt didn't overlook shortcomings so much as improve upon them.

Walt's original merry-go-round, the King Arthur Carrousel, opened along with the rest of Disneyland in 1955. The ride there hasn't changed much since then, though it's adopted more of a *Sleeping Beauty* aesthetic over the years. Magic Kingdom's version opened as Cinderella's Golden Carrousel in 1971, gorgeous and befitting a princess, but it doesn't belong to Cinderella anymore. In 2010, with relatively little fanfare, Magic Kingdom retitled the attraction Prince Charming Regal Carrousel. (For the record, Disneyland's version officially remains the property of King Arthur, even if he is a rather absent owner, never showing his face anywhere in the park).

Charming's taste doesn't differ much from his bride's. The eighty-six horses here look the same as ever, bobbing beautifully to the sound of Disney songs on an organ. This is still the same hand-crafted 1917 carousel that Disney acquired in 1967 and trimmed in 23-karat gold. The original, artisan-molded maidens still rotate around the top, with murals inspired by *Cinderella* between them. Those same big popcorn bulbs still cast the same romantic reflection on the castle grounds after it rains. It's still worth pulling a muscle as you try to mount your steed. Nothing really seems to have changed. But there's a different backstory now,[13] and it adds a new layer of lore to Fantasyland.

Prince Charming, better known as Cinderella's main squeeze, is a bit of a jouster as it turns out. Who knew? Apparently, after returning from his honeymoon (where do Cinderella and Prince Charming go for a honeymoon, anyway?), Charming fashioned a training machine utilizing carved horses, upon which he could practice ring-spearing, a noble game that later became known as "carrousel." His contraption was all the rage in the kingdom, so much so that the villagers, apparently oblivious to their station in life, demanded the prince give them a turn. Benevolent ruler that he is, Charming commissioned a second carousel for the commoners to enjoy, this one to be more conveniently located in the Castle Courtyard and spruced up as befits its royal locale. That's how the Prince Charming Regal Carrousel came to be — a shining example of grassroots activism in the monarchy. Now we, the commoners, can live the life of a prince for just a few minutes at a time.

Walt always envisioned Fantasyland as a real-life residence for his characters. This new carousel story aligns with that idea by telling us a little bit about their life there. True, no one spells out the backstory before the ride begins, and it is undoubtedly lost on many a guest, but those who care to investigate it will find there's more to appreciate in the attraction once they do, and that's enough to set this apart from any ordinary spin on a merry-go-round.

Vocal groups of Disney fans savaged the new name and narrative as arbitrary and unnecessary when they were first announced, but while the change did at first seem like a solution in want of a problem, there's a lot to like about it. For starters, Prince Charming — long overlooked in his own kingdom — is finally getting some recognition beyond being just Cinderella's obligatory armrest in any given parade. Through the new narrative, we now know something about the "real" Charming. Much more than just a prince (and a pushover), he's also an athlete, an equestrian, and an engineer. With all those skills, he's clearly a Renaissance man in more ways than one! And let's face it, the Cinderella we know never rode a horse. Charming's jockeying in preparation for a jousting tournament is a more credible premise, even if we aren't given lances when we climb aboard. Actually, there is a sword sitting right beside the carousel, but it's stuck in a stone.

The impression that there are villagers in Fantasyland, with a prince and princess ruling over them, lends credence to the idea that this is a kingdom we're visiting. And the suggestion that there's a sprawling countryside somewhere out there beyond the berm, with Charming's original wooden carousel in it, fits into the whole notion of the Enchanted Forest, which has a more lush and natural-feeling landscape. Prince Charming Regal Carrousel was essentially the first completed step in the "New Fantasyland" transformation.

Walt was probably put off by the carousel he visited with his daughters because there's nothing inherently enthralling to the grown mind about slowly trotting along in a circle. With a few minor touches of detail, though, he was able to tie the simple ride into the world of fantasy he'd been creating in his feature films. A carousel means more when it's King Arthur's Carrousel... or Sleeping Beauty's, or Cinderella's, or her husband's. The connection to the movies, however meager it may be, is enough to make the experience valuable. Anyone can enjoy the simple pleasure of these horses in their gold-plated shelter, but those who learn of its prince and his story will find it to be that much more… charming.

WATCH THIS – A Knight in Camelot (1998)

Following *Unidentified Flying Oddball* (1979) and *A Kid in King Arthur's Court* (1995), this Wonderful World of Disney TV movie is the studio's third (and most recent) feature-length adaptation of Mark Twain's *A Connecticut Yankee in King Arthur's Court*. The incomparable Whoopi Goldberg plays Dr. Vivien Morgan, a scientist who mistakenly transports herself to Camelot, where she impresses King Arthur (Michael York) and locks horns with Merlin (Ian Richardson). In a premise similar to the one Disney had used in *A Kid* just three years prior, Vivien employs modern technology to save herself and the royal court.

With their third take on Twain's enduring novel, Disney casts Goldberg in a role previously played by men. Gender swap in a Disney fantasy? Where else have we seen this? Oh yeah, Prince Charming Regal Carrousel! The movie seems even more at home here, given that Camelot feels a lot like the royal countryside Prince Charming would probably joust in. And let's not forget that a King Arthur story is somewhat native to this attraction in the first place — it began as King Arthur Carrousel in Disneyland, and was once also home to the Magic Kingdom's daily Sword in the Stone ceremony, in which Merlin selected one lucky child to unsheathe Excalibur and become the new king of Camelot. (The show was discontinued in 2006 but the sword still sits in the stone for brawny guests to tug on.) This funny, distinctly 1990s comedy is sure to entertain and makes a nice companion to Disney's latest redressing of the venerable carousel ride.

Mickey's PhilharMagic

Type: 3-D theater show
Duration: 12 minutes
Height Restriction: None
Popularity/Crowds: Moderate
FastPass+: Yes; low priority
Fear Factor: 1 out of 5 (3-D images; brief darkness; surprise in-theater effects)
Wet Factor: 0.5 out of 5 (in-theater misting effects)
Preshow: None
Best Time to Visit without FastPass+: Anytime
Special Comments: Giant theater usually means long lines aren't an issue.

Mickey's PhilharMagic is a symphony of synergy. Disparate characters and corporate divisions come together in a 3-D musical adventure that mines the best of Fantasyland's past, serving as a case study of the oft-cited "Disney difference."

Ostensibly a performance by Mickey's "PhilharMagic Orchestra," the show is set inside what appears to be an opera house. As stage manager, Goofy urges guests toward their seats while Minnie announces from backstage that preparations have gone awry. Naturally, Donald Duck is to blame. Guests don their three-dimensional "opera glasses" just in time to see Mickey absent-mindedly leaving his famous, mystically empowered sorcerer's hat behind while he tends to the backstage mishaps. Ever the instigator, Donald sneaks in to try the cap on for size and, before long, he's emptied out a muddled mess of magic from inside it. That's when the *real* show begins.

Cast into the darkness by his own shenanigans, Donald suddenly finds himself in a bittersweet kind of nightmare. His headpiece having gone rogue, it flings him from one Disney universe to the next. He wakes up in eighteenth century France, where *Beauty and the Beast*'s enchanted dinnerware invite him to be their guest. Then he battles the broomsticks of *Fantasia* before taking on Iago of *Aladdin* during a flight from *Peter Pan*'s London. He even winds up in the African desert, where he feels the brute force of young Simba's ambition. Decades of Disney animation come together like memories flowing from Mickey's subconscious, symbolized by his iconic cap. Audiences revisit their favorite characters and join in their favorite songs, experiencing them in new dimensions — literally.

PhilharMagic is comprised entirely of computer-generated, three-dimensional re-creations of characters originally produced using traditional animation.[14] CGI was still relatively young when production began on PhilharMagic, and the attraction would be the first attempt to wholly digitize these primarily hand-drawn characters, whose earliest appearances ranged from 1928 to 1994. That's dicey territory for computer animators, especially with characters as fiercely protected as Disney's. Naturally, the Imagineering team wanted guidance from the moviemakers to ensure that each character was faithfully rendered in the new CGI environment. That's where we find our first glimpse of synergism here. As the largest multimedia conglomerate in the world, Disney is a corporate jack of many trades. Probably its two best-known subsidiaries are Walt Disney Pictures (movies) and Walt Disney Imagineering (creative development and design for the parks and resorts). From a consumer perspective, the two go hand in hand, but they seldom work together in a production capacity. PhilharMagic represents one of the few exceptions to that rule, and arguably the most extensive.

In the end result, the show's background and character design aren't quite Pixarian, but they're better than most had hoped, at least by 2003 standards. We're forced to take a second look at familiar characters who've now been doubly transfigured — first from hand drawings to CGI and then again from 2-D to 3-D. At the same time, their stories are made immersive with an array of sensory effects, including wind, water, smell-o-vision, and even an Animatronic. We truly experience them as never before, and that is one of PhilharMagic's strong suits — it makes old ground feel new again.

Speaking of old ground, this theater was once home to a rather similar show, the Mickey Mouse Revue. An opening day attraction, the Revue looked back at Mickey's earliest short films, where audiences first came to know him as a musician. He'd assumed that role in *Fantasia* and in a number of his black-and-white cartoons during the '20s and '30s, including *The Band Concert* and the namesake *Mickey's Revue*, the latter marking Goofy's screen debut (he was called Dippy Dawg back then). A host of Disney characters came together in a "star-studded" Animatronic medley of popular songs that included "Who's Afraid of the Big Bad Wolf," "Zip-a-Dee-Doo-Dah," and "Bibbidi-Bobbidi-Boo." Tuxedo-clad and with baton in hand, Mickey took to the podium in one of his most treasured roles, that of the maestro mouse, his cinematic brethren looking on for direction.

PhilharMagic is essentially the Revue revived. Mickey returns to the theater as the esteemed concert conductor and his setlist again consists of popular Disney tunes, but the details are different. This time he's on a screen. The neat thing about PhilharMagic is that in updating the theater's original attraction, it also borrows from a few of the other shows that have called this same space home. For example, Donald's starring role here harkens back to *Working for Peanuts*[15], a 3-D flick of his that played in the theater from 1987 to 1993. Later, when Simba sings "I Just Can't Wait to be King," it's a flashback to Legend of the Lion King, an elaborate puppet show that occupied the same room until 2002.

Today, Maestro Mickey, 3-D Donald, and singing Simba collectively create a kind of mosaic of the building's history — an incidental tribute to their longstanding tenure in this location. It's an archival sort of symmetry that will go unnoticed by most, but it makes for interesting trivia and a sense of legacy.

There is more going on in PhilharMagic, though, than digital wizardry and a nod to history. There's real sentiment and emotion too, not unlike the warm feelings we get from Disney's fireworks and parades. We might explain that response by turning to a third and altogether more important kind of Disney synergy, one we alluded to earlier: the gathering of unrelated characters from different properties under one very large umbrella.

Disney is unique among movie studios in that it markets its characters as a family. Sure, Warner Brothers' Looney Tunes have that kind of kinship, for example, but you don't readily associate them with *Gremlins*, the *Harry Potter* characters, *National Lampoon's* Griswold gang, or other popular Warner properties. Disney is different in that almost every film bearing its label immediately claims a branch on the studio's sprawling family tree. That is, to a large extent, intentional... and it has been undeniably successful.

Peter Pan and Aladdin ought to be strangers. They come from different countries and eras, and from two stories that aren't remotely related. And yet finding them in this shared space makes perfect sense. Disney's pervasiveness in pop culture is sufficient for us to understand them as complements. That connection isn't limited to animated musicals. Live-action films like *Mary Poppins* and non-musicals like *The Love Bug* are similarly pulled into the Disney fold. Those characters get invited to many of these "Disney family reunions" too, celebrations invariably held inside the Disney parks.

Walt spoke of Disneyland as a place where his characters actually lived. To him, this was a solution to a problem that plagued him. With movies, there was no going back. Once in the can, a film is what it is forever. As we saw during our discussion of Pirates of the Caribbean in *Chapter One*, that was a source of creative frustration for Walt "Keep Moving Forward" Disney. His parks provided an outlet. There, the characters could live on in new adventures, telling new stories. Trips to the park were to be like visits to their homestead. Walt always treated the park that way and we, his public, have come to share in that conceit, whether in Disney World or Disneyland.

That's why Tinker Bell can fly out of Cinderella Castle every night without raising an onlooker's eyebrow about 20th century London (*Peter Pan*) suddenly colliding with 17th century France (*Cinderella*). Characters from a dozen Disney properties can dance side by side around the castle in a daily parade without the slightest inkling of narrative confusion. Each Disney character, each movie, each grouping of heroes, princesses, or villains contributes not only to its respective story world but also to the broader family of Disney characters at the same time. The interweaving of these otherwise unrelated figures strengthens the Disney identity and our sense of belonging to it. The characters aren't the only members of the family. When we're patrons in the theme parks, we are invited to feel like a part of the family, too. Disneyland's well-received Parade of Dreams laid that out in its chorus, borrowed from 2003's *Brother Bear* — "Welcome to our family!" It's a compelling invitation that keeps millions of people coming back to these parks every year.

For the most part, we know these characters. We understand their relationships with one another, and we value the connection we've had with them all our lives. Kind of like a real family.

This emotional enfranchising works better in a Disney park than in any other themed-entertainment setting because none of the other entertainment titans have cultivated their own culture to the same extent. Nor has any film studio inspired anything remotely like the passionate loyalty that Disney has long enjoyed from billions of fans. We'll take a closer look at this achievement in the context of fireworks and parades in *Chapter Six*, the Disney Festival of Fantasy Parade in particular.

Maybe, after decades of culture-by-Disney, we're all somehow born into "The Mickey Mouse Club." We might even think of PhilharMagic as a chapter meeting. Donald is there like always, still trying to steal the show. But as card-carrying members by birthright, we know how this goes... Mickey's the leader of the club. So "come along, sing our song, and join our family... M-I-C... K-E-Y... S-Y-N-ERGY."

WATCH THIS - Mickey's Christmas Carol (1983)

This twist on Charles Dickens' incalculably famous Christmas novella is among the most beloved adaptations of the story and for good reason. With Mickey as Bob Cratchit; Goofy as Jacob Marley; and Jiminy Cricket, Willie the Giant, and Peg-Leg Pete as the Ghosts of Christmas Past, Present, and Future respectively, the short film calls on something like 50 characters from Disney films to act out the indelible story of charity and change.

In the pivotal role of Ebenezer is none other than Scrooge McDuck, Donald's uncle, and so the latter stars as nephew Fred. Some rare characters turn up too, from uncelebrated properties like *The Adventures of Ichabod and Mr. Toad*, *Bedknobs and Broomsticks*, *The Band Concert*, and beyond. There aren't many nods to the characters' existence outside of the Dickens tale, but the audience is plenty aware of those on their own. Therein lies the charm of this truly great and rather faithful retelling — everybody loves a Disney family gathering, and it's even more special come Christmastime.

Enchanted Tales with Belle

Type: Interactive character performance
Duration: Varies (usually 15 to 20 minutes)
Height Restriction: None
Popularity/Crowds: Moderate to High
FastPass+: Yes; high priority
Fear Factor: None
Wet Factor: None
Preshow: None
Best Time to Visit without FastPass+: On a crowded day, catch it in the last hour or two. During slower times of the year, the attraction will only operate late at night if enough guests show up for a given show.
Special Comments: Everyone sees Belle up close, but only those who participate in the playacting will get to meet her. Guest actors are given a special bookmark to commemorate the occasion.

Chip doesn't make a lot of sense. You remember him as the adorably fractured young teacup in *Beauty and the Beast*. But how did he get there? We're told that the curse on Beast's castle, which turned the personnel into anthropomorphic housewares, has been in effect for ten years at the time we meet Chip, and he's the only child around. Meanwhile, his mother, Mrs. Potts, is a senior citizen. So how old was she when she had him? And how old was Chip at the time of the curse? Was he born a teacup? ...How?

Enchanted Tales with Belle is a lot like Chip. It's new and a little crack-headed, but loveable nonetheless. In fact, I'd argue it offers some of the Kingdom's bigger wows, even if it is intended primarily for the park's smallest guests. If we try really hard, we just might make some sense out of its story too.

Belle hails from a little town full of little people, and one of its littlest (or shortest, at least) is Maurice, her plump old dad. Enchanted Tales with Belle invites us into his countryside cottage following the events of the film. It moves us through four different rooms, beginning with his den, where we learn more about Belle than the film ever let on. There's a portrait of her mother, a beautiful young woman who must have had a thing for older men. There's also a growth chart on the wall, marking Belle's height over the years. We find plenty of books too. *Sleeping Beauty* is on prominent display, a reminder that Belle is an outsider — she lives in the Enchanted Forest beyond the berm of Cinderella's courtyard and revels in reading about her royal sistren. Later, we'll make our way into Belle's present-day dwellings. Rare is the attraction that explores a character's multiple homes so intimately, revealing little nuggets of their extra-literary past along the way. Here in her homestead, children get a chance to relate to Belle as she was at their age, and we all learn a little more about her.

The next room is Maurice's workshop. "Crazy old Maurice," Gaston calls him, and we see clearly that he's kooky to say the least. The line between genius and insanity is thinner than Maurice, but he manages to maintain balance. His workshop is filled with clever contraptions and diagrams for inventions, like the giant music box we find inside Be Our Guest Restaurant next door. Nods to da Vinci abound.[16] The centerpiece here is a magic mirror, a gift from Beast that empowers Maurice to visit Belle in the castle anytime he wants, even though the castle is literally next door. We're prompted to recite an incantation to activate the reflective portal: "Take us back to the day Belle and Beast fell in love."

The room darkens, the mirror radiates an eerie green, and there in that small and unassuming room, one of Walt Disney World's most impressive special effects unfolds unexpectedly. As the mirror grows larger, our reflection gives way to animation. We find ourselves rushing through the surrounding forest and approaching a large set of castle doors, which then open. They literally open. Somehow, before our eyes, this small and ordinary-looking mirror became a fully functioning doorway, which we're then invited to walk through. As Mrs. Potts would say, there's something there that wasn't there before.

Technically complex, the feat is an engineering marvel and has the full-fledged appearance of actual magic. It is as convincing as any special effect employed in Hollywood filmmaking, and while Enchanted Tales with Belle is certainly no Haunted Mansion, this lone sequence holds its own with any stunt that Disney has pulled off in a park. The entire premise of Magic Kingdom is reinforced whenever we experience something that defies explanation. Grown-ups who skip Enchanted Tales because it's "just for kids" are missing out on a masterpiece of Imagineering.[17]

In the fantasy genre, weird things happen to people who walk through mirrors.[18] Guests of Maurice's workshop are no exception. The stellar mirror effect is but the quarter-way point of the show, and what follows is a different kind of curious.

Upon walking through the mirror, we find ourselves inside Beast's castle, having traveled through time to the day Belle and Beast fell in love. Specifically, we enter their story just before they have dinner in the iconic ballroom sequence. Madame Wardrobe, brought to life as an enormous Audio-Animatronic in an otherwise frill-less room, greets us and says that everyone in the castle is hoping tonight'll be the night that the two finally fall for each other. (We already know that they will, but since we've gone back in time, Wardrobe doesn't know that yet.) "To help move things along," she says, "you're all going to surprise Belle and act out the story of how they met!" Um, ok.

Wardrobe assigns simple playacting parts to a few volunteers in the crowd, most of them kids. They're given props and a simple gesture to mimic, and then we all move into Beast's library, where an astonishingly fluid and limber Lumière (also an Animatronic, one of the park's best) is directing the show. Everyone not assigned a part takes a seat, while castle staff help the kids make ready for Belle. The idea is to stage a big surprise for the princess-to-be, who will then help us reenact her story up to that point.[19]

This is very strange. Belle, fresh out of the shackles of Beast's confinement and newly smitten with her captor, is going to walk into the library and find a room full of strangers eager to rehash the whole traumatizing affair. "SURPRISE! We're here to relive your kidnapping!"

When she does enter, Belle is rather unfazed and even curiously delighted by this unpredictable turn of events. She seems almost ecstatic at the prospect of acting in a play about herself. Bloggers and comics have said Belle suffers from Stockholm syndrome, but her behavior here hints that it might be Narcissistic Personality Disorder instead.[20] Has she really had sufficient time to process the difficult psychological experience of her last few months? Not having shared that romantic evening with him in the ballroom yet, is she really this comfortable with the Beast? Maybe there is something to that Stockholm theory.

Naturally, none of this is meant to be taken seriously. For all its mind-blowing technical wizardry and intriguing interweaving with a beloved story world, the principal showcase here is really just a chance for kids to see a character they love and engage in diversionary pantomime.[21] But to the adult mind, the chance to revisit — and revise — a well-known story is absolutely fascinating. Could it be that things were not as we thought? As adults, might we understand stories differently now? Is there room for more than one perspective on the same event — for more than one version of the truth? This is a very postmodern inquiry, indeed. As we will see, all three of New Fantasyland's new attractions engage in some sort of narrative revision, not unlike the recent trend that began with films like *Maleficent* and Tim Burton's *Alice in Wonderland*. Is "once upon a time" no longer sufficient for the postmodern audience — do we need "twice upon a time," at least?

Lumière ends Enchanted Tales by telling us that "as time went on, Belle realized that the Beast was not mean or cruel, but in his heart was sweet and kind, and Belle and the Beast became the very best of friends." Then Belle rushes off to meet Beast in the ballroom, where they'll soon become much more than just friends. Are we to suppose, the next time we watch *Beauty and the Beast*, that Belle famously descends that staircase in golden garb after having just spent a few moments with us in the library? Or does our tale-as-old-as-time-travel apply only on the other side of the mirror?

Hey, maybe Chip time-traveled there, too.

WATCH THIS - Cinderella III: A Twist in Time (2007)

I know what you're thinking, but A Twist in Time really is in the upper echelon of direct-to-video sequels... for whatever that's worth. The production values leave something to be desired and Cinderella herself is hard to take seriously, but it's evil Step-Lady Tremaine who steals the show.

Unable to subject herself to her stepdaughter's crown, Tremaine casts a time-turning spell and opens an alternate universe in which the glass slipper fits Anastasia instead. It's interesting, revisionist-fairy-tale fiction. Here again, traveling back in time to a fairy tale's midpoint reminds us that sometimes sci-fi can leak into Fantasyland.

Under the Sea ~ Journey of The Little Mermaid
Type: Dark ride
Duration: Approximately 6 minutes
Height Restriction: None
Popularity/Crowds: Moderate
FastPass+: Yes; low priority
Fear Factor: 0.5 out of 5 (occasional darkness and a close encounter with Ursula)
Wet Factor: None
Preshow: None, though the queue features a diversionary digital scavenger hunt.
Postshow: None, but Ariel is available for meet-and-greets in her grotto just next door. (FastPass+ available separately for the meet-and-greet; medium priority.)
Best Time to Visit without FastPass+: A relatively efficient loader, Under the Sea usually offers reasonable wait times throughout the day. But like any moderately popular attraction, your best bet is during early or evening hours, especially on a crowded day.
Special Comments: A newly "plussed" version of the ride debuted in early 2015, sporting darker black lighting and additional show elements.

1989's *The Little Mermaid* represented a return to form for Disney but also a step into the future. For the first time in decades, the studio was serving up its old bread and butter — the fairy-tale musical. But Mermaid was stamped with a distinctly modern sensibility and a distinctly Broadway-ensemble sound, relatively uncharted territory in the Walt Vault. As such, it heralded an unprecedented renaissance for the company, one that continues to pay dividends to this day. One such dividend is Under the Sea ~ Journey of The Little Mermaid, a new dark ride in Fantasyland's Enchanted Forest. Like *Mermaid* the movie, the ride is simultaneously a revival of form and a mutation — a traditional dark ride oriented toward a new goal. And it all comes down to Scuttle the warbling seagull.

Fantasyland dark rides from the past, whether in Disneyland or Walt Disney World, more or less adhere to a simple strategy: retell a Disney movie in short order, recreating key sequences from the film along the way. Each puts its own unique twist on that idea, and most home in on a particular emotion of thematic significance to the film — fear in Snow White's Scary Adventures, bewilderment in Alice in Wonderland, and lawless obsession in Mr. Toad's Wild Ride. But while all of them benefit from familiarity with the source material, they at least endeavor to achieve coherency as straightforward, stand-alone recitals of the films.

Under the Sea differs from these, making for an alternative, arguably postmodern kind of experience in which coherent narrative no longer matters as much.

In the queue, ceiling paintings recount myths about sirens, leviathans, and the sea witch Ursula, not unlike those hinted at in the movie's opening number, "Fathoms Below." But the eponymous journey truly begins when we board our "Clamobiles" and meet Scuttle the seagull, who in the film acts as a sort of ambassador between merfolk and mankind. He reprises that duty here, introducing himself as the ride's narrator, which is itself interesting. None of Fantasyland's other dark rides employ a narrator. (Alice addresses guests in her Disneyland ride, but that's more of an incidental greeting.) Scuttle, meanwhile, makes it clear that the story we're about to see is one that he's telling us — and, fascinatingly, one he can't quite remember. It is interesting that an attraction so willing to dispense with storytelling would go out of its way to feature a narrator. Then again, Scuttle isn't there to tell the story so much as to tell us that he's not really up to the task.

"Let me start at the middle," Scuttle says. "Wait, no, what am I thinking? That's a terrible place to start a story. I'll just tell you how it ends. Oh, wait, I got an idea. I'll start at the beginning!"

He never quite finds the starting point, though, reaching back to his own birth then skipping ahead to Ariel's contract with Ursula. Intriguingly, he asserts that Ariel was hoodwinked and never understood the terms to which she was agreeing — a questionable bit of lawyering for anyone who's seen the film.[22]

The story as presented is at least linear, and the uninitiated can walk away with this much: a mermaid wants to be a human but also likes the ocean, then an octo-witch gives her legs and she meets a dude with a mullet. Seconds later, they wed. The end.[23] But in this Scuttle-spun version of *The Little Mermaid*, Ursula meets a different demise, writhing alone on the water with bright flashes and zapping sounds all around her (with no evidence of her harpooning) while Ariel and Eric make out in a tower above. That is not how it happens in the movie. Is Scuttle a revisionist historian, then, or just an oaf? That's open to interpretation in light of New Fantasyland's postmodern willingness to play fast and loose with story.

The Little Mermaid is a film rich in subtext. It is, after all, the tale of a woman who loses her voice (and metaphorically, we might argue, her agency — or, stated differently, her social power) at the hands of a drag-queen-*femme-fatale*.[24] A tired argument against it is that Ariel sacrifices her own identity in order to win over a man, but those critics likely haven't seen the film in a few years. Ariel is enraptured with humanity and the idea of becoming human long before setting her sights on Eric.[25] It is, as much as anything, a story about teen angst and the immutable rebelliousness of youth. One of the most fascinating things about *Mermaid* is that it privileges rather than corrects its young protagonist's rather risky defiance of her father. One could argue that its takeaway is that disobedience is for the best. But you won't find any of that in this ride. There's a reason for that.[26]

Peter Pan's Flight conveys wonder and adventure by lifting us into the sky. Snow White's Scary Adventures conveys abandonment and horror by thrusting us into the woods at night where a witch stalks us and trees come to life on the attack. But it isn't so easy to translate teenage angst to the physical sensations and sets of a theme park dark ride. I suppose pop-up parents could surprise us at every turn with captions reading "You're always wrong!" and "No one understands!" But Ariel's dad, King Triton, plays only a small role in the ride. No, Under the Sea takes a different approach. Whereas The Many Adventures of Winnie the Pooh is very clever in the way it illuminates and comments on its source material, Under the Sea has very little to say about *The Little Mermaid*.

The ride is essentially a jukebox. With the exception of its bookends, every single sequence is a musical number. Riding it is like watching the Blu-ray and skipping chapters until you reach the next song.

In the world of musicals, that isn't unheard of. The "jukebox musical" is a staple of theater and film, usually putting music first and story second. Disney even had its own Off-Broadway jukebox revue, *On the Record*, in the mid-2000s. But Under the Sea is probably more akin to a concert musical, in which a well-known show like *The Wizard of Oz* or *Les Misérables* is performed on stage in song only, skipping the in-between altogether.

Given Imagineering's usual emphasis on "story" in most (though not all) of its guest experiences, this focus on song to the exclusion of narrative begs the question of whether storytelling is really still Imagineering's aim in an era where hyper-emotional "immersive experiences" are the new imperative.

Under the Sea is hardly our only new-age, hodgepodge theme park experience. See, for example, Star Tours — The Adventures Continue at Disney's Hollywood Studios and Forbidden Journey at Universal's Wizarding World of Harry Potter, which both value an emotional experience over a linear narrative. Why bother riding a ride if it doesn't make sense on its own, detractors ask. But then we might query just the opposite in return: why bother with a condensed re-telling if it's a story we all already know?

In approaching Under the Sea, I arrive at what might seem like a tension in this book's approach to Disney attractions. How can something like Under the Sea be worthy of serious thought and reflection if it doesn't even make sense? Well, if museums have taught us anything, it's that "making sense" is no prerequisite for art. And if Pirates of the Caribbean has taught us anything, it's that a well-told story is not necessarily the benchmark for excellence in Imagineering.

To my mind, a theme park attraction that moves its audience toward new insight — or, in this case, forges a bridge between the guest and the story in some meaningful way — is doing its job. Some artworks soar on the strength of their narratives, others on their beauty or perspective. A well-told story will always satisfy, but is it not possible for a ride to fall short in the story department and yet still offer something rewarding in some other capacity? Should we throw out that reward simply because we can't check "logical" on a list of ideal attraction elements?

Under the Sea doesn't focus on the film itself because it's more interested in us instead — that is, our emotional connection to the film, one that was forged primarily through song during the nearly 25 years that passed between the movie and its ride. Our experience of *The Little Mermaid* in this ride is informed almost entirely by songwriters Alan Menken and Howard Ashman, whose compositions are likely how people most commonly relive the film. Rather than allocating its lone few minutes of duration to narrative rehash, the ride chooses to immerse us in a three-dimensional sing-along instead.[27]

In the end, I'm not sure that Under the Sea is as dramatically effective as Snow White's Scary Adventures or Peter Pan's Flight — fear and flight are more indelible than crustacean calypso, perhaps. But it works very well as a means of bringing the Menken-Ashman songbook to new and enveloping life, and that's worth something, isn't it? Who doesn't get a thrill upon queuing up grade-A tunes like "Poor Unfortunate Souls" or "Kiss the Girl"? And how much more emotionally resonant are they when you can find yourself thrust into the middle of their original performances, recreated around you? Bringing stories to three-dimensional "life" has always been a paramount goal of the Fantasyland dark ride, and for those rare films for which Imagineers can reasonably assume universal familiarity with the underlying plot, maybe it's possible to fulfill that goal without synopsis.

Undoubtedly, there is still a place for traditional-form storytelling in the contemporary theme park experience, but Under the Sea and its New Fantasyland ilk demonstrate that there's also a place for other kinds of art. Some rides masterfully explicate their characters' adventures, but experience-oriented attractions like Under the Sea work differently by helping us to feel like a part of their world.

WATCH THIS - "Glee" (2009)

Scuttle would have a really hard time recounting "Glee" — the story didn't make much sense to begin with. But the hit Fox series, which ran for six seasons and showcased one of the most talented casts in the history of television, always saw music as an emotional experience first and a narrative device second. In spite of admittedly ridiculous storylines and countless plot holes, "Glee" succeeded as enjoyable and effective, even as it threw coherency to the wind. Its shortcomings are harder to excuse than Under the Sea's because, unlike Mermaid, we didn't know the "Glee" story beforehand. But the series proved itself affecting anyway. Incidentally, star Darren Criss auditioned for the "Glee" pilot with Mermaid's "Part of Your World." It never made it to production, but a handful of other Disney covers were among the more than 700 songs in the show's final catalog. Among them: "Bella Notte," "Breakaway," "Let It Go," "The Climb," and (depending on how liberally you define "Disney song") "No One Is Alone," "Rainbow Connection," and "Bein' Green." The soundtracks are available from Sony's Columbia Records and the episodes are available from Fox (now owned by Disney).

Seven Dwarfs Mine Train

Type: Roller coaster
Duration: Approximately 3 minutes
Height Restriction: 38 inches or taller (adult riders can switch off)
Popularity/Crowds: High
FastPass+: Yes; a top priority
Fear Factor: 2.5 out of 5 in the front-most rows; 3.5 out of 5 in the rear-most rows (sharp turns and drops)
Wet Factor: None
Preshow: None, though the queue features several diversionary games.
Postshow: None, but the dwarfs' cottage provides a nice photo-op on the way out.
Best Time to Visit without FastPass+: Early morning or late night

The mirror. The apple. True love's kiss. These are the things that come to mind when we remember *Snow White and the Seven Dwarfs*, Walt Disney's first animated feature film... the one that started it all. It's a story about vanity, jealousy, temptation, and sin.[28] But it also has plenty of musical comedy, and Magic Kingdom seems more interested in the seven silly dwarfs than in the Evil Queen's preoccupations with prettiness and poison. Once upon a time, the Kingdom had a grimmer take on the tale, but even today's jaunty joyride — the freshly minted Seven Dwarfs Mine Train — can't quite take the black out of White.

Mine Train opened May 28, 2014, the final piece in the years-long New Fantasyland expansion project, and the fourth summit in Magic Kingdom's mountain range. Practically big enough to qualify as a land all its own, the sprawling countryside hilltop is bright, colorful, and cartoonish, an embodiment of the dwarfs' personalities and a visual contrast to the cold, jagged, gray castle just behind it, symbolic of pre-Belle Beast. As pleasant and lovely as anything else in Walt Disney World, the mountain lends Fantasyland an earthy realism we might not have previously expected there. In keeping with "Once Upon a Time," "Grimm," and other contemporary productions that endeavor to tie fairy tale lore into reality, the hillside's organic landscape situates the surrealism of fantasy in a context of naturalism. But it does so with just enough aesthetic fancifulness to stay true to the area's charter.

Disney's marketing team calls it the company's first "story coaster," presumably a reference to the Mine Train's hybrid nature — part dark ride, part roller coaster. In truth, it's hardly the first "story coaster" in the plain sense of that term.[29] Nearly all of Disney's roller coasters have a backstory and many even have show scenes. But it is fair to say that Mine Train probably goes further than any other in balancing theme parks' two most iconic genres of ride.

The first few moments are reminiscent of Big Thunder or Splash. Mine carts zoom, zip, and dip as buzzards eye their occupants from above. But then the vehicles slow down and descend into a slow-moving "show scene" recreating the film's legendary "Heigh-Ho" sequence. We don't stay there long, quickly rising back up out of the cave and roller coastering again until the very end, where a second and final "show scene" finds the witch arriving at Snow's cottage with poisoned pomme in hand.

Viscerally, the most interesting thing about Mine Train's mechanics is that its carts can swing. The sensation is pronounced at key pauses or pivots in the ride sequence while essentially undetectable at others, but the daffy rhythm in those moments smartly calls to mind the dwarfs' nonsensical "The Silly Song," which we hear in the distance as the ride comes to a close.

But it's "Heigh-Ho" that steals the show. The dwarfs begin to sing just as their shift ends for the day. It's a song that rejoices in leaving work, and that's a cause for celebration that vacationers understand all too well. A happy and bouncy escape, "Heigh-Ho" find us in emotional alignment with the dwarfs as we embrace the carefree quality of life in the Disney bubble, far away from the responsibilities of the world. The ride's second lift hill is carefully timed to begin just as Doc bellows his big "Heigh-hooooo," launching us up and out of the mine as the dwarfs march by our side, the lot of us cottage-bound. The interplay between the lift in the track and the swell in the song in that moment is brief but powerfully effective, particularly for those seated toward the front of the train.

The Audio-Animatronics are something else. Today's theme park designers take it on the chin for their excessive reliance on screen technology, but Mine Train's dwarfs are showcases for tasteful employment of projection effects.

The problem with over-screen-ification in the parks is that screens are nothing special. Unlike Animatronics, screens are part of our everyday lives. We carry them in our pockets. There's neither novelty in their appearance nor mystery in their apparatus. Audio-Animatronics in physical sets built just for them, though? That's something you don't see every day. The dwarfs here are full-bodied Animatronics, life-like and fluid. They aren't breathing, but they *are* standing right there in front us. The digital projections on their faces are integrated subtly and almost seamlessly, enhancing the presentation without calling attention to the effect, making this a corporeal confrontation that projections could never manage on their own.

Outside the mine, there's just as much to marvel at. The mountain itself is magnificently crafted and its sightlines are a treasure. As Dumbo the Flying Elephant did when it once stood behind the castle, Mine Train offers an exquisite view of Fantasyland. Those lucky enough to catch a ride during the park's evening fireworks will find it especially enthralling (bursts abound in every direction).

But after the whistling and whooping are all over, the ride pulls into its final destination, where we find the wicked witch knocking at the cottage door, Snow and the dwarfs cavorting just inside. Clearly, this story is far from over. Danger has come a calling, and Snow White's about to help herself to some fatal fruit. That's a curiously morose note on which to end such a jolly outing — but then maybe not so curious if we look at Magic Kingdom's previous Snow show and the film itself.

Snow White's Adventures opened with the park in 1971, inspired by a similar attraction running in Disneyland since its own debut in 1955. It was a conventional dark ride but an especially terrifying one. The dwarfs made only a fleeting appearance and the eponymous princess was nowhere to be found — the idea being that guests would "play" the part of Snow White instead. Without her, the ride was all witch, witch, and more witch. As she stalked the guests, they also had to deal with careening mine carts, mobile skulls, and other eerie objects that lurched toward them from the ceiling, the walls, and the floor. There was no music inside, only a piercingly loud cacophony of howling wind, shattering jewels, and cackling screams. Even without the alarming visuals, the sound experience alone was enough to horrify guests of any age. The witch leapt out at every opportunity, creating the feeling of hot pursuit and narrow escape. At the end, she dislodged a giant jewel, which she hurled down atop Snow White (that is to say, the guests). The crash appeared to be a fatal one. The last sight guests would see before the ride came to an abrupt end was the explosive flashing of shattering diamond all around them — a most unsettling finale.

That all changed in 1994, when the ride reopened in the Magic Kingdom as Snow White's Scary Adventures. But while its name finally owned up to the fear factor, the new edition was actually less intense. There was happy music now, less harshness, more of Snow White herself and her dwarfs, and an extended happy ending that bid a much more cheerful farewell to guests than their apparent death did previously. Where people once complained that the ride was much more frightening than they would have expected, some now found it surprisingly light, the "Scary" title having led them to expect something more menacing.[30]

Alas, in the wake of this decade's New Fantasyland expansion, Snow White's Scary Adventures, one of the park's all-time greatest attractions and arguably the best Snow White ride anywhere to date, closed for good on May 31, 2012. It's now Princess Fairytale Hall, a meet-and-greet in which you can sometimes talk to Snow herself atop the ruins of her original ride.[31] (Fortunately, a different version of the dark ride still operates in Disneyland.)

Snow White's Scary Adventures reflected not only the inherent darkness in the Snow White story but also Walt Disney's unflinching willingness to get deep. Though edifying in their morality and usually uplifting by the end, Walt's first five features were astonishingly dark in content and tone. Despite the fact that these movies have been around for seventy years, that seems to be a continual surprise to the world. Perhaps adults forget how frightening the films were when they saw them as children, or assume that youthful impressionability is to blame for their reaction at the time. When they get around to revisiting the movies as grown-ups, however, they're often surprised to find them incredibly stark for viewers of any age. That's true for Fantasyland's supposedly childlike dark rides too. The debate about how scary a ride like Snow White's ought to be arises out of audiences' long-standing ambivalence toward children's entertainment as a whole, and it shines a light on just how bold an artist Walt Disney was.

Walt never made movies for children. He was quite adamant about that. "You can't live on things made for children," he said, "or for critics.

I've never made films for either of them. Disneyland is not just for children. I don't play down."

Indeed, he did not. Walt never saw fit to reduce his content to the lowest common denominator. What's often confused for "kid's stuff" is actually "family stuff" — universal entertainment designed to connect with a wide audience of all ages. There is surely a difference between a story written primarily for children and one that has no age group in mind but just happens to be appropriate for children as well as adults. Walt was always interested in the latter, but he had an enormous respect for the young mind. He believed that murder, witchcraft, and sinfulness were not at all unsuitable subject matter for a family film. In fact, those were recurring elements in much of his work.

"I didn't treat my youngsters like frail flowers," he once said, "and I think no parent should." He went on to add, "Children are people, and they should have to reach to learn about things, to understand things, just as adults have to reach if they want to grow in mental stature. Life is composed of lights and shadows, and we would be untruthful, insincere, and saccharine if we tried to pretend there were no shadows. Most things are good, and they are the strongest things, but there are evil things, too, and you could do a child no favor by trying to shield it from reality. The important thing is to teach a child that good can always triumph over evil, and that is what our pictures do."

Walt's creations are replete with misfortune in addition to joy. He was fond of bleak murder plots by villains who turn toward evil to achieve their selfish desires. Early Disney animation is no stranger to violence, weaponry, or death. Weighty issues touching on life and loss are common too, as is religious contemplation of the eternal and the divine. So many animated features are hesitant these days to go anywhere near a topic potentially divisive or disturbing, but Walt is the one who built the genre by hand, and he did it with deeply mature themes and an abundance of dark imagery.

In *Dumbo*, poor Mrs. Jumbo is locked away in a cage and subjected to terrible cruelty while also having to endure as witness to her son's humiliation. Dumbo gets drunk, too. Pinocchio does the same and smokes cigars to boot, after which he is rather violently transformed into a donkey. Cruella de Vil has puppies slaughtered for profit. Alice breaks down in tears of abject loneliness and despair because Wonderland is so heartless. Bambi's mother is killed in one of the most depressing scenes ever committed to film. In *Sleeping Beauty*, Maleficent summons "all the powers of Hell" as she turns into a dragon. In *Fantasia*, an actual demon raises wicked spirits from the dead to frolic in the moonlight until subdued by the prayerful procession of Christians. And then there is *Snow White*.

While *Dumbo* is probably thematically darker than any other Walt Disney film, *Snow White and the Seven Dwarfs* is his most classically frightening. The protagonist is as innocent and as naive as they come, making her victimization all the more abhorrent. Having already lost her mom, Snow has to flee from her own home while her stepmother plots her murder. Using venom, sorcery, and deceit, the Queen hunts the young princess and makes multiple attempts on her life.

Legendary director Steven Spielberg has many times publicly reflected on the horror in *Snow White*, and he singles out this moment in the movie: "One of the most frightening sequences in film history is not the shower scene in *Psycho*," he said, "but the huntsman coming to get Snow White and her retreat into the woods, which come alive and try to kill her... Disney wasn't afraid of scaring children in those days..."[32]

Disney is still scaring kids today, sometimes still using Snow White to do it, but their commitment to the film's fearful side has wavered over the years. Edgy material like *Snow White* puts Disney in a tough spot, having to balance the artistic freedom to explore mature themes against the demands of a paying public that seems uncomfortable with darkness in the family setting, but then that tension is hardly unique to Disney. The field of children's entertainment — and children's literature in particular — is filled with dark works that were rebuked in their time as too mature for young readers but which finally found an audience with them nonetheless. From *Alice's Adventures in Wonderland* and *The Wonderful Wizard of Oz* to *Adventures of Huckleberry Finn* and *Charlie and the Chocolate Factory*, right on up to the *Harry Potter* series today, nearly every major work of children's literature has faced substantial condemnation and weathered enduring firestorms.

The criticism follows into the film, television, and theme park adaptations. Despite their typically mixed reception, the most durable works of "children's entertainment" (that is, works commonly consumed by children, whether or not they were made for children or are also consumed by adults) relentlessly engage with darkness and have since the day of the fairy tale. If anything, Disney's variations tend to be lighter than their source texts. Had Snow White's Scary Adventures been as grim as the Grimms, we'd have seen the witch feasting on Snow White's cooked heart, strangling her with lace, and ultimately dancing to her death in red-hot iron shoes. Even the 1971 ride seems tame by comparison!

Ms. White's whole history in this park encapsulates the history of children's literature itself. The age-old debate over how much darkness is appropriate for a younger audience is alive and well here in Magic Kingdom, where Snow has been known to both sing and scream at one time or another.[33]

Seven Dwarfs Mine Train is unquestionably a turn toward mildness, but its final moments are interesting and unexpected. Recall that the ride finds the witch waiting outside the door while Snow and the dwarfs dance and sing. That is not what happens in the film. As in Under the Sea ~ Journey of The Little Mermaid, the Imagineers have concocted a new ending here. In the movie, Snow is home alone when the witch visits, long after "The Silly Song" ends. But in the ride, the scenes are combined. The implication in this newest ending seems to be that even in our merriest moments — even when life is riding high — evil lurks for us outside, just a door knock and an apple bite away.

I'd like to think that's how Walt might want it.

Creating the first animated feature film was bold enough. Choosing for that project a story as scary as *Snow White* was even more daring. That was Walt Disney, though: a visionary innovator and a daring pioneer. With *Snow White*, he saw to it that so-called "children's films" would enjoy the same legacy of complexity and maturity that has defined "children's literature" for centuries. And Magic Kingdom ensures that that legacy carries on in "children's rides" too. Mine Train may be neither the chiller nor the treasure that Scary Adventures was, but its back-row thrills and subversive conclusion go to show that Snow White and her adventures — whether in prose, park, or film — are never quite as peaceful or pure as her name would imply.

WATCH THIS –
Something Wicked This Way Comes (1983)

Noted author Ray Bradbury adapted his own novel for this eerie fantasy film, set during an ominous autumn in the 1930s. A carnival is coming to town but right from the start, something seems not quite right. A tall and mysterious man named Mr. Dark (Jonathan Pryce) runs the show and he's promising to fulfill the townspeople's deepest desires. He can deliver, but always for an unpleasant price. Our protagonists, two young boys named Will Halloway and Jim Nightshade, sense that there's something sinister lurking within the carnival's closed tents. So does Will's father, local librarian Charles Halloway (Jason Robards). A little research reveals that this isn't the first time the carnival has come around, and things didn't go so well last time.

Released during Disney's most experimental phase of moviemaking (the 1980s), *Something Wicked This Way Comes* is an incredibly atmospheric, unsettling, bizarre, and downright dark movie. The PG rating means that it's technically family friendly, but there's a serious edge that is sure to give audiences of all ages the creeps. Like *Snow White*, *Something Wicked* was a brave endeavor for the studio. It's a great illustration of the darker side of family entertainment, and its circus-like setting jells with Mine Train's view of Storybook Circus across the way.

The Many Adventures of Winnie the Pooh

Type: Dark ride
Duration: 4 to 5 minutes
Height Restriction: None
Popularity/Crowds: High
FastPass+: Yes; medium priority
Fear Factor: None
Wet Factor: None
Preshow: None
Boarding Speed: Slow to Moderate
Best Time to Visit without FastPass+: Morning or night

Winnie the Pooh first ran for President in 1968. If you don't remember his name on your ballot, you probably didn't vote in Disneyland. In a brilliant effort to promote their newly acquired character, the Disney Company tapped into electoral tension that year and launched the first of several Pooh for President campaigns. While the United States shifted from blue states to red, the theme park went all yellow.

Unfortunately, even with support from Mickey Mouse and an expected endorsement by the Seven Dwarfs, the pudgy bear failed to win a single state. He's been a perennial candidate since then, but the country still hasn't put its first fluff-stuffed President in office. Well, I suppose that's up for debate. But while some blame his simple-minded reputation and few can forget his frequent "Oh, bother" reply when pressed on the issues, one might pin his more recent defeats on his surprisingly divisive presence in the Disney theme parks. It all began with the opening of his signature attraction, The Many Adventures of Winnie the Pooh.

Author A. A. Milne first published *Winnie-the-Pooh* in 1926, a collection of short stories inspired by his real-life son, Christopher Robin, and the stuffed animals in his nursery. A second anthology soon followed, *The House at Pooh Corner*, published in 1928. The stories delve into young Christopher's imagination, where animals come to life and talk him through life's simple lessons. All the while, he moves closer to adulthood, the point at which he knows he'll have to leave his imagination behind.

Among the toys in Christopher Robin's room were a bear, a tiny pig, a donkey, a tiger, and a kangaroo. As you might have guessed, that's how Pooh, Piglet, Eeyore, Tigger, Kanga, and Roo were born (Milne thought up Rabbit and Owl on his own). The characters' roots in reality were manifested in Milne's stories, which always presented them as material objects — toys. One needn't look any further than Eeyore, his tail forever falling off, for evidence of the animals' artifice. The original illustrations are consistent with that idea, too. Only Rabbit and Owl look like actual creatures in the drawings.

The characters' existence as anthropomorphic toys contributes to a marked self-awareness in Milne's prose, in which the author addresses the reader directly as he frequently acknowledges that he's telling fictive stories about the imaginary lives of inanimate toys. That idea would later become important at the cinema and in the Magic Kingdom, but the author's unique writing style also found him an early English audience.

The *Pooh* tales were an instant success in Europe, much to the chagrin of real-life Christopher Robin, who grew up harboring deep resentment toward his father, believing that he had exploited his childhood and doomed him to certain hardships as an adult. Milne wasn't thrilled with the success either, feeling stifled by a public that now expected him to concentrate on children's literature despite his desire to move on.

The characters never caught on in the same way for Americans — at least not until Disney came along. Walt licensed Milne's characters in 1961 but waited a few years to begin adapting the stories, realizing that audiences would need to acquire a taste for Pooh before they'd be ready for a whole load of it — er, him.[34] *Winnie the Pooh and the Honey Tree* introduced Pooh Bear to the American cinema in 1966, the first of three short films that would together comprise the seminal Pooh film oeuvre. Disney's Pooh was similar in many ways to Milne's, but initially put less emphasis on some of the major themes, such as Christopher Robin's emerging manhood and readers' awareness of the characters being mere toys. Walt also reached out to stateside moviegoers by introducing a new, decidedly American personality in the Hundred Acre Wood — Gopher, a hardworking and wisecracking miner. Walt's efforts were a success. At long last, Pooh had a lot of fans in the United States, too.

Walt died just when the characters were getting off the ground. Creatively frozen in the wake of his sudden passing, the company did very little with the franchise for years. That changed in 1977, when the ailing studio desperately needed to make a quick buck. To do that, they blew the dust off the Pooh projects and revisited the three short films, putting them back in theaters as a single, full-length feature. *The Many Adventures of Winnie the Pooh* added new animated sequences and live-action bookends to interweave the stories beautifully while also situating them in their original literary context. The movie finds the characters playfully interacting with the literal letters printed on the pages of a *Pooh* novel, and it ends with Christopher Robin reflecting poignantly on what it means to grow up. Through meaningful touches like those, the movie moves Disney's *Pooh* much closer to Milne's approach. The film has arguably become the most recognizable entry in the Hundred Acre Wood canon and has helped create tremendous worldwide affection for its characters.

Almost right off the bat, Milne had aggressively marketed and merchandised his characters, and Disney followed suit, particularly in the 1980s, when a new fervor for the lovably aloof bear swept the United

States. Pooh quickly became one of the company's most reliably profitable franchises. Milne had been a relentless marketer himself, licensing the characters to so many people that Disney has wound up in a number of legal battles with competing rights holders in the years since.

Pooh's popularity waned slightly during the early 1990s, a new golden age of animation having claimed his spotlight. By the late '90s, though, the bear's star was again on the rise, thanks in part to the success of a new direct-to-video movie, *Pooh's Grand Adventure: The Search for Christopher Robin*, in 1997. Following that release, Disney unleashed a tidal wave of new Pooh products that would continue over the course of the next decade.[35] The time was right at last for Walt Disney World to develop a theme park attraction based on the Hundred Acre Wood, something Disneyland had considered but abandoned several times before.

The Many Adventures of Winnie the Pooh opened in Magic Kingdom in June of 1999, based on the film of the same name. Given that the Bear of Very Little Brain was enjoying a resurgence in popularity at the time, Disney fans would be thrilled about a large-scale dark ride built in his honor, right? Actually, they protested instead. The objection was nothing personal, mind you, but as much as Disney fans like a bumbling bear, they love amphibious aristocrats even more. You see, the trees in the Hundred Acre Wood were planted atop the ruins of Toad Hall, once home to the highly acclaimed Mr. Toad's Wild Ride. When Disney announced plans to demolish that beloved attraction in preparation for The Many Adventures of Winnie the Pooh, fans mounted rallies and petitions with such zeal that even major media outlets picked up on the fuss. Nevertheless, without an invite, Christopher Robin's imaginary gang crashed the party.

Four years later, the same thing happened in Disneyland, where The Many Adventures of Winnie the Pooh steamrolled The Country Bear Jamboree. (Unlike Magic Kingdom's crowds, Disneyland loyalists love the Country Bears and always will.) The dust settled with time in Florida, but in California, it never really has. Disneyland fans insist the ride's a big "pile of Pooh" and they're still waiting for someone to clean it up. Hell hath no fury like a Disney dork scorned.

Back in Magic Kingdom, the attraction is actually pretty popular today, in spite of its divisive beginnings. There's good reason for that.

The ride begins in the thick of the woods on a particularly blustery day. Those just happen to be the same atmospheric conditions found in the middle and most iconic segment of the film, so the gusty breeze instantly ushers us into a familiar place. Later, Tigger bounds into view, and our ride vehicle starts to hop around with him for some bouncy, trouncy, flouncy, pouncy fun, fun, fun, fun, fun! It's one of the more memorable surprises in Fantasyland.

But the most interesting thing about the ride comes before it even begins. Giant paper pages decorate the queue, appearing to have been freshly ripped out of a book, their text adapted directly from Milne's stories. They lead the way to the loading platform, made to look like a giant-sized bookshelf with gargantuan tomes stacked in the corner. *Pooh* pages are scattered everywhere.

We climb into an oversized honey jar as it inches toward one of those books, already opened to Chapter II, "In Which We Join Pooh and His Friends in a Very Blustery Day," which sounds quite a bit like a Milne chapter but actually isn't one. The jar turns us toward a giant hole in the middle of the right-hand page and we pass through a portal into the book. At once, the characters spring to colorful life, just as they do in Christopher Robin's imagination.

The many giant books serve as reminders that these characters are the stuff of fiction. The oversized pages pave the way toward the entrance and away from the exit, but they also continue throughout the ride itself, framing each show scene inside. In this way, the attraction is every bit as self-aware as Milne's books. It's one thing for guests to know that Eeyore isn't a living donkey, but it's another altogether for the storyteller (in this case, Disney) to subtly point that out for them. The torn-out pages do that. Most fiction asks us to suspend disbelief and buy into the fantasy until the final page turns. When authors choose to "break the fourth wall" and address their readers directly, they're opting to make a point by *sustaining* disbelief instead. The Many Adventures of Winnie the Pooh wants us to sustain disbelief.

Pooh is nothing if not an interrogation of the imagination. The ride inspires reflection about the ways our imagination can help us work through dilemmas. That's really all a first-time reader takes away from Milne's books, too, which don't exactly lend themselves to easy interpretation or definitive conclusions about a deeper meaning. What is clear in those texts is that Christopher's imaginary playmates are helping him come of age and his interactions with them all play out inside his mind. This ride takes guests inside those dreamed-up adventures for a firsthand look at his imagination in motion. To even begin to appreciate that, though, guests must first know that they're inside an imagined world, and that's where all of those torn-out book pages come in.

The characters' in-ride design echoes that same self-awareness. Here they are largely inanimate constructions that budge only when moved by a lever or some other device controlling them from afar. In other words, these aren't the same kind of full-fledged, elaborately animated Audio-Animatronics one finds in The Hall of Presidents or Pirates of the Caribbean. While the three-dimensional cutouts certainly do look like the cartoon characters we all know and love, they also look fairly fake — as they should. Remember that Milne always emphasized the materiality of Christopher Robin's toys. In both description and illustration, they never looked lifelike and were never meant to. Not until Disney came along did the characters take on a more organic design, and even then they didn't entirely lose their doll-like configurations. Now, in Magic Kingdom, the Disney characters are more toy-like than ever. By putting guests face-to-face with physical, tangible recreations of these characters, The Many Adventures of Winnie the Pooh asserts their materiality in a way that the film adaptations never have. The moving figures have the same effect as all of those book pages — they remind the audience that the characters are only make-believe.

Pooh and his pals take the next step into the material world when the ride ends and we exit directly into a store. While Disney rides exiting into gift shops is anything but uncommon, the transition is refreshingly sensible here. For many years, the store was called Pooh's Thotful Spot, a right proper name given all the thinking to be done in Many Adventures. Now it's Hundred Acre Goods, where we sometimes find honey for sale, a useful part of our post-ride thought process. As Winnie himself will tell you, honey makes very good food for thought, indeed. He didn't become a savant on an empty stomach, you know.

More importantly, the shop offers a selection of Pooh dolls, available in a variety of costumes, colors, and sizes. There, on those innumerable, plush-stocked store shelves, Winnie the Pooh comes full circle at last. The toy-turned-playmate-turned-cartoon star becomes a toy again, ready to be taken home to enjoy new exploits inside another child's imagination — or maybe even in an adult's. That's what Milne's Hundred Acre Wood is all about, and in bringing it home that way, the Magic Kingdom's Pooh experience is every bit as full and well rounded as the tubby bear's little tummy.

WATCH THIS - Pooh's Grand Adventure: The Search for Christopher Robin (1997)

Pooh's first direct-to-video feature breathed new life into the franchise. Without it, there might never have been a Pooh ride in Fantasyland. A direct sequel to the 1977 theatrical film, this venture into the Hundred Acre Wood doesn't quite measure up to the original but nicely captures its tone and engages the same overarching themes. When Christopher Robin leaves for his first day of school, Pooh and his pals misunderstand a note he left behind, concluding that he's trapped inside a giant skull and must be rescued.

Pooh's Grand Adventure does away with the meta-story elements that define both the first film and the theme park ride, but that's because it isn't based on any of Milne's works. The original screenplay does, however, retain the author's interest in Christopher Robin's imagination. Despite its slow pace, the movie is a charming exploration of how a child might reckon with the major change that the first day of school represents.

Mad Tea Party

Type: Spinning teacups
Duration: 2 minutes
Height Restriction: None
Popularity/Crowds: Moderate
FastPass+: Yes; low priority
Fear Factor: 2.5 out of 5 (fast spinning; some guests experience motion sickness)
Wet Factor: None
Preshow: None
Boarding Speed: Slow
Best Time to Visit without FastPass+: Morning, early afternoon, or night

Walt Disney was a man ahead of his time. He filmed his TV shows in color when there were no color TVs. He made a major investment in a theme park when the market for one didn't really exist. He produced the first animated feature film when conventional wisdom had it that audiences would never sit still for a long cartoon. In nearly all of his endeavors, he was ahead of the curve. He even got a jump on the 1960s drug culture with the release of *Alice in Wonderland* in 1951, though something tells me that wasn't his intention.

Alice was a relative flop when it hit theaters in '51. Critics tore it apart for taking substantial liberties with author Lewis Carroll's source texts and audiences didn't connect with it either. The tepid reception and underwhelming box office led even Walt Disney himself to later lament that the film had no heart. That's not really how audiences view the movie today. While *Alice* doesn't enjoy the popularity of, say, *Lady and the Tramp* (at least not when measured by home video sales), it's now widely revered as a classic and continues to perform well on home video. So what changed? The times.

With the rise of the counterculture movement in the 1960s and its affinity for recreational drug use came a phenomenon slangily referred to as "head films," movies that hippies liked to watch while high. By the late 1960s, Disney's *Alice* had become one, as had *Fantasia*. Strange, isn't it, that *Alice* would emerge as a head film when so much of its dialogue concerns the removal of heads? Then again, stoned college kids probably weren't using their heads at all. They were too mesmerized by the movie's mushroom eating and flower singing, all of which seemed to resonate so profoundly with their favorite extracurricular activities. Also enchanting the psychedelic set were all the film's bright colors, Alice's constantly altering body size, the Mad Hatter's tea-induced inebriation, the hookah-smoking caterpillar... okay, maybe they were onto something. But even if the flower children missed the whole point of the movie, they did serve a very important function — they brought *Alice* and *Fantasia* back from the dead. The psychedelic era largely faded away but those movies' renewed renown never did. Both unsuccessful in their initial runs, they're widely embraced and celebrated as family standards today.

Fortunately, when Disneyland opened in 1955 there weren't that many Disney movies to choose from. That meant that even the less successful ones were on the table as possible inspirations for new attractions, *Alice* included. The most famous *Wonderland* attraction is Mad Tea Party, which was running on opening day at both Disneyland and the Magic Kingdom. The spinning teacups are easy enough to describe — climb into an oversized teacup and spin yourself around until the music stops. While you twirl in one direction, the giant platform below you moves in the other. The surrounding cups whirl both ways at the same time. Basically, there's a lot of spinning going on, like a hip hop DJ with a giant turntable — and everybody in the cup's gettin' dizzy. Mad Heave Party is more like it.

Disorientation is its signature sensation. Taking their first steps out of the teacups, off-balance guests stagger toward the exit with all the grace and precision of a zombie freshly back from the dead. (Incidentally, this is one of Magic Kingdom's top spots for people watching.) Like a sudden bout of vertigo, a ride on the teacups can make the whole park spin before your eyes. Fortunately, the effects are temporary and their incidence varying. In my many whirls 'round the teapot, I've been plenty dizzy, but I've never been sick. But you don't have to get on the ride to consider all the ways it takes us down the rabbit hole and into Wonderland.

The feeling of dysequilibrium approximates for us Alice's profound sense of bewilderment, one of the major themes in both Carroll's books and Disney's film. The very idea of Wonderland is inherently horrifying — a realm where nothing is as it seems, no one can be trusted, and nonsense pervades. In the first *Wonderland* book, the Cheshire Cat confesses to Alice, "We're all mad here." How utterly nightmarish! The Mad Tea Party echoes that madness while in motion. As the Fantasyland vista becomes a streaking blur, what once was clear becomes cloudy and indecipherable. Before long, we struggle to stay sure of the direction we're moving in. The temporary discombobulation is uncomfortable, just as Wonderland is for Alice.

In the moments after the ride ends, the theme of confusion sets in with even greater depth. Producing in us actual, momentary malaise, the teacups make real for us the sickening sense of being lost and muddled that moves Alice to tears in Disney's film. Few attractions can so physically unite us with a character's feelings. If you were wondering whether Wonderland is a place you'd want to visit, Fantasyland has an answer, which makes it a kind of Wonderland all its own.

WATCH THIS – Alice in Wonderland (2010)

Disney's big-budget, Tim Burton-directed sequel to Lewis Carroll's *Alice in Wonderland* novels made major bucks at the box office but didn't quite get its due with critics.[36] The philosophically robust premise finds Alice all grown up and barely able to recall her first visit to Wonderland. So distant is the memory that when she sees a rabbit running through the garden in a waistcoat, she doesn't think twice about chasing after it. We viewers know where she's heading, or so we think. She falls down the rabbit hole again, but when she gets to the other side, it isn't Wonderland. This time, she's in a place called Underland.

Tim Burton masterfully takes us through the original *Alice* story all over again, seen not through the eyes of an easily befuddled and overwhelmed child, but from a young woman's perspective. Wonderland is not what Alice thought it was the first time she went there. As we realize that so much of what she misconstrued as nonsense is in actuality sinister and real, we're challenged to reconsider the observations we've taken for granted from our own childhoods.

Dumbo the Flying Elephant

Type: Flying, steerable elephants
Duration: Ninety seconds
Height Restriction: None
Popularity/Crowds: Moderate
FastPass+: Yes; low priority
Fear Factor: 0.5 out of 5 (moderate heights)
Wet Factor: None
Preshow: On busy days, families can wait in an air-conditioned, circus-themed play area (fun for kids, uncomfortable for adults). Restaurant-style pagers may be given to those waiting without FastPass+.
Boarding Speed: Slow
Best Time to Visit without FastPass+: Anytime, but come back later if you find it crowded. Storybook Circus is reliably empty at night.

Dumbo the Flying Elephant is one of Disney's simpler rides — charming, yes, but no Splash Mountain. 32 gray elephants revolve around a central axis, each of them bearing the lovable likeness of the eponymous, big-eared hero. Riders use a joystick to raise themselves approximately 17 feet into the air, and then — ninety seconds later — they're back on the ground. That can mean a long wait for a very short ride, and yet it's one of the most beloved and iconic attractions on Disney property.

Adults are allowed to ride Dumbo alone or bring a small child or two aboard with them. Technically, two adults can ride together, but that's best avoided, lest we draw depressing comparisons between our collective size and that of the elephant (he's a young elephant — let's not be so hard on ourselves). Age seems to have very little effect on one's affection for the ride, though… adults are as eager as kids. Why?

We used to explain that with location. For more than 40 years, Dumbo the Flying Elephant stood directly behind Cinderella Castle, just beyond the carousel. As we sailed through the sky, a gentle breeze brushing our face, the full majesty of Fantasyland was laid out for us like a hand-drawn map. The castle seemed even more beautiful from up in the air, and The Flying Elephant afforded a chance to savor its extravagant architecture. After the Skyway to Tomorrowland closed,[37] this was the only ride offering an elephant's-eye view of this part of the park. Taking it all in, even for a short time, allowed us to forge an emotional bond with Fantasyland that you couldn't quite make anywhere else.

But then Dumbo closed on January 9, 2012 and moved to the whimsical carnival town of Storybook Circus, an area once known as Mickey's Toontown Fair and later annexed as part of Fantasyland.[38] The relocated ride offers twice as many elephants as before, with two hubs spinning in opposite directions for a sort of "Dueling Dumbos" effect.

Now the ride is situated in a whole new context. Storybook Circus is essentially "Dumboland," a grand foyer for an old favorite. Right in the middle sits Casey Jr. Splash 'N' Soak Station, a simple little train-theme playground where mechanical animals squirt copious amounts of water at any guest walking by, showing neither mercy nor restraint.

Whether you run toward the deluge or away from it, turn a careful eye down toward the ground near Casey. A single train track runs from the Splash 'N' Soak Station all the way back to the Walt Disney World Railroad, which encircles the whole perimeter of Magic Kingdom. The suggestion is that Casey himself exited off the WDW Railroad track to make Fantasyland his next circus stop. As you might recall, Casey is the very train on which Dumbo's circus travels in the movie. It stands to reason that his many animal friends might have followed him in. Sure enough, the ground is stamped with elephant footprints, horseshoe-shaped indentions, and peanut shells — clear signs of a circus invasion. At some point, Casey must have negotiated relocation terms with Mickey Mouse, who moved his own meet-and-greet to Main Street and allowed his Toontown Fair to become the Storybook Circus instead. It only makes sense that if Casey has set up shop in the back of Fantasyland, Dumbo should join him there.

But the nakedness of the mechanics, beautifully designed as they are, means that Dumbo doesn't create the same illusion of flight found in the *Peter Pan* ride over yonder. With an unmasked apparatus lifting other guests into the air right in front of us, there's no mystery to Dumbo's takeoff. Without dark lighting, show scenes, or the use of forced perspective,[39] the flight here isn't quite as thrilling and imaginative as our voyage over Neverland. And the fact that we can see 31 other Dumbos next to us must surely make the opportunity to ride inside one of them less special, no? And yet this is one of the most enduring and quintessential Disney attractions, as likely to turn up in a Walt Disney World TV commercial as any E-ticket or brand-new offering. So what gives?

In today's themed entertainment industry, "immersion" is the end-all, be-all buzzword in ride design. Cast members at the new Star Wars: Galaxy's Edge in Disneyland and Disney's Hollywood Studios won't acknowledge life outside their fictional universe, and certainly not the fact that they're in a theme park. Pandora — The World of Avatar at Disney's Animal Kingdom is said to be a distant planet in the future, and once you cross the bridge to get there, there's to be no mention of anything foreign to that place and time. A great deal of attention is given to blocking your view of things you aren't supposed to be able to see from within the story setting, and all of this is an extension of the way Walt Disney wanted things, or so we've come to believe. Is it, though?

Walt Disney cared about theme integrity, that's for sure. But he wasn't so obsessed with it that guests needed a signpost to tell them why they weren't wearing jackets on the Matterhorn. No one needed blinders on Snow White's Scary Adventures to keep them from realizing that, though they were playing the part of the princess, they weren't the *only* "fairest one of all." Frontierland wasn't special because guests believed they had actually traveled back to the Gold Rush, nor because anyone working there stubbornly swore it were so. On the contrary, Frontierland was and is special *because* it's make-believe — the most elaborate and fun-spirited make-believe you've ever seen, but make-believe nonetheless. All the attention to detail makes it easier to suspend disbelief, but you still must suspend. Today's hyper-immersive environments are fun and incredibly impressive, engaging our imaginations in a different way, and I'm glad we have them. But are they *inherently* better than a Wild, Wild West with a plain-view castle in its skyline? In the industry's mad dash for more "immersion," have the company's creative teams lost sight of Disneyland's simple hub-and-spoke appeal?

To Walt, I think, theme integrity meant committing to a theme but not denying that there was one. Disneyland didn't exactly break the fourth wall in the way that The Many Adventures of Winnie the Pooh does today (e.g. sustaining disbelief), but it didn't build a wall around its audience either, the way we might say today's new theme park designs endeavor to do (e.g. denying disbelief). In that sense, his Disneyland was a postmodern experience ahead of its time, unafraid to weave one world into the other, thus breaking away from the confines of conventional narrative. That's why it's perfectly natural, within the laws of Disneyland or Magic Kingdom, to climb aboard one Dumbo while looking at your friend in another without feeling that the whole experience is a lie. On the contrary, it's a luxury — someone else has given you permission to pretend and a platform for doing so, and the pretending feels less forced because you're allowed to acknowledge that it's happening.

On Dumbo the Flying Elephant, as on the Jungle Cruise, the artifice is laid bare before us. Yet even with all the logistics exposed, it affords us the chance to connect with a character we've loved all our lives but have never been able to engage with outside of a screen. In a sense, we fly with him in his moment of triumph here, following all the sorrowful darkness that preceded his ultimate flight in the film.[40] Still, I don't pet Dumbo or feed him peanuts. I don't ask the ride attendant about the circus workers' labor union or whether Timothy Q. Mouse has been lapping up the champagne again. If I inquire about a FastPass, I'm not confused or thrown out of the story if the cast member knows what that is. I don't need to believe that there's not another Dumbo vehicle beside me. While the attention to consistency and immersion in today's new theme park lands is admirable, somehow the fantasy rings true on this little flat ride here in Storybook Circus too. Maybe the simplicity of the pretense is what makes it so accessible. Suspending disbelief invigorates the imagination.

Undoubtedly, the ride wouldn't mean much of anything to anyone if it were Ed the Elephant. But it's not. It's Dumbo, and that theme — simple as it is — makes all the difference. The ride operates as an extension of the movie's ending, a celebration of the character's liberation from judgment and injustice. It's the emotional closure the movie never *quite* gave us, the budget constraints of 1942 having forced Walt to bring it to an abrupt end.

In his movie, Dumbo is a conquering underdog. In the Magic Kingdom, his victory lives on in perpetuity, forever inviting us to share in it with him. Undoubtedly, audience's expectations escalate over time. The "hedonic treadmill" of human psychology ensures that we constantly adjust our standards to the "new norm." A world with Galaxy's Edge is probably one where building a new Dumbo will never do. But the little guy's been going for some sixty years now, and this is his legacy: the elephant ride is one we never forget.

WATCH THIS - Disneyland, U.S.A. (1956)

During the 1950s, the Walt Disney Studios produced a series of feature-length travel documentaries entitled *People and Places*. The sixth entry in the series focused on Disneyland itself, just one year after it opened.

The way narrator Winston Hibler talks about the park speaks volumes as to how Walt & Co. understood the Disneyland experience in those early years. "Rainbow Ridge is a frontier traffic center," Hibler tells us when we get to Frontierland. "Here, stage coaches and conestoga wagons arrive and depart just as they did in the days gone by." In that quote alone, we see both the pretending — "Rainbow Ridge" *is* a frontier traffic center — and the acknowledgment of the pretense — "just as they did in the days gone by." Again, just a few minutes later: "To visit Frontierland and travel along its high roads and byroads is to relive in this modern day all the high adventure of the American pioneer." We even see a cactus giving a thumbs-up on the Nature's Wonderland ride route, something Hibler tells us "could only happen in Disneyland." (Compare that to the "Whaddya mean 'modern times'?" and "What's Disneyland?" responses we might hear from cast members playing their parts today, or the three-page treatise we'd expect on the cactus's origin story.) On the flip side, Hibler is also eager to point out that things at Disneyland are always changing and always will.

It's worth a watch for any Disneyland fan. But come for the commentary, stay for the views. Shot in stunning Technicolor widescreen, *Disneyland U.S.A.* gives us an aerial view of the entire park in detail, capturing the same kind of up-in-the-air magic we sense while riding Dumbo. The elephant himself turns up, too, with close-up footage reminding us just how exceedingly simple the Flying Elephant was when it debuted. And it comes with a reminder of what Walt said when dedicating Fantasyland about what it should be: the place where "magic and make-believe are reborn."

The Barnstormer
Type: Junior roller coaster
Duration: Under 1 minute
Height Restriction: 35 inches or taller
Popularity/Crowds: Moderate
FastPass+: Yes; low priority
Fear Factor: 1.5 out of 5 (zippy speed, modest drops and turns)
Wet Factor: None
Preshow: None
Boarding Speed: Slow
Best Time to Visit without FastPass+: Anytime, but come back later if you find it crowded. Storybook Circus is reliably empty late at night.

If Magic Kingdom is home to the young and young at heart, Storybook Circus is a place for the small and we-can-pretend-we're-small. That's the spirit of The Barnstormer featuring Goofy as the Great Goofini,[41] a revamped attraction that strains the whole idea of "Fantasyland" and makes us question whether we're really the grown-ups we thought we were.

Mickey Mouse turned 60 in 1988, and to celebrate, Magic Kingdom opened a sparsely decorated and supposedly temporary "land" just behind Fantasyland. One of the quickly-built offerings there was Grandma Duck's Barn (sometimes referred to as Grandma Duck's Petting Farm), where children could interact with live animals, including Minnie Moo, a real Holstein cow with a naturally occurring Mickey Mouse silhouette on her side.

But Mickey's Birthdayland never went away. By 1996, it had turned into Mickey's Toontown Fair, and Grandma Duck's Barn became the framework for The Barnstormer at Goofy's Wiseacre Farm,[42] a so-called "kiddie coaster." The idea was that Goofy maintained a country farm here at his Toontown vacation home, and he managed his expansive cornfields by way of crop dusting. In an obviously handmade airplane, he also have his guests 60-second "flying lessons."

Junior roller coasters like The Barnstormer are supposed to be gentle and mild. Now, I don't know about you, but I've seen some of Goofy's work over the years, and the idea of flying with him in an airplane that he built himself sounds like anything but tame to me. Sure enough, The

Barnstormer packed a surprising punch for a ride of such tiny size. Not that great a pilot after all, Goofy took us through quick dips and zips and, ultimately, right through the wall of his barn. Adults like myself ended up having at least as much fun as the younger target audience — more than we'd ever care to admit — and that made The Barnstormer the indisputable star of Toontown.

Perhaps surprisingly, 9/11 did little to quell the ride's popularity, despite its airplane-through-building storyline and the international concern about crop dusters in the weeks and months following the terrorist attacks. Eventually, though, Goofy's Wiseacre Farm did close, because Storybook Circus was steamrolling Mickey's Toontown Fair and everything in it. But then Disney announced to the relief of all children (and, secretly, many adults) that The Barnstormer would return with a brand-new title, backstory, and theme.

The Barnstormer featuring Goofy as the Great Goofini opened on March 12, 2012. Not one inch of the steel track changed, which means it's the same ride that's been delighting children and surprising adults for nearly two decades. Only the scenery is different. One small barn remains, and that's where guests squeeze into the tiny "stunt planes" (no longer crop dusters). After that, the ride offers a beautiful, heightened vantage point for surveying the immersive circus environment that makes up this back corner of Fantasyland. It may be a junior coaster of simple frills and modest thrills, but the Barnstormer is a fully realized and completely satisfying experience.

The new storyline posits that Goofy has set up shop as Storybook Circus' resident daredevil. As we approach his plane, we see posters advertising his recent performances — getting shot out of a cannon, juggling tigers, dodging swords, and riding a rocket, among others. The Barnstormer is his latest feat and the circus's newest signature attraction, in which Goofy takes to the sky for a stunt show of aerial acrobatics. And we get to tag along for the ride. To quote the press announcement, it's "plane crazy."

"Barnstormers" once referred to pilots who would travel around the country, selling short airplane rides. They usually took off from — or flew over — farmland, essentially what Goofy was doing in Toontown. (The fact that his plane also "stormed," i.e. crashed through, an actual barn added a fun layer of wordplay to the name.) The 1920s then saw the advent of "barnstorming shows," aerial performances at county fairs and the like in which stunt pilots would show off flying tricks and daring maneuvers in small aircraft. That, of course, is the type of barnstorming Goofy's engaged in now. That the Imagineers were able to keep the title despite completely reworking the ride's theme is pretty serendipitous. (Fun fact: when multiple planes barnstormed together, it was colloquially referred to as a "flying circus," and since there are two planes on The Barnstormer track at any given time, this ride becomes a circus act in more ways than one!)

But in talking about all of this story's virtues, one thing we are not talking about is magic. Goofy is not a wizard. He can't fly on his own, he doesn't cast spells, and he is not the ruler of a kingdom. Sure, he's a dog who walks and talks, but the Disney universe has never really treated "the fab five" (Mickey, Minnie, Pluto, Donald, and Goofy) as enchanted animals. Rather, they've usually been presented as Hollywood stars in their own right, bona fide celebrities who just happen to be anthropomorphic animals.[43]

As Goofy's Wiseacre Farm, Barnstormer contributed to the Mickey's Toontown Fair theme in a way that made sense. If the land was a country vacation home for the characters, why shouldn't Goofy maintain a farm there? And how better to explain a short flight over farm crops than with a crop dusting storyline? Even in a ride primarily intended to give youngsters their first taste of roller coastering, the attention to detail matters.

But how does Goofy fit in Fantasyland? That's the question many were asking when The Barnstormer featuring Goofy as the Great Goofini was announced for Storybook Circus. Remember that unlike Mickey's Toontown Fair, Storybook Circus is not its own land inside Magic Kingdom. Rather, it is a subset of Fantasyland. Dumbo qualifies as fantasy because he's an elephant who flies and hangs out with a mouse who talks. No one questioned Dumbo the Flying Elephant as part of Fantasyland back when it was located right behind the castle, and no one questions it now. Goofy's different, though.

The Great Goofini might sound like a magician's name, but that's not the story here. He's a professional daredevil, Fantasyland's answer to Evel Knievel. In the Great Goofini meet-and-greet, guests pose with

Goofy next to a steel motorcycle cage, his bike upside down and fuming. Those are the kinds of wonders he performs. You need any number of things to stage those types of shows, but a spell book isn't one of them.

There is more of cartoon than of fantasy here. Whereas Dumbo's flight and Casey Jr.'s railway journey require a bit of imagination to embrace, The Barnstormer's story about a hijinksy plane could easily unfold in real life. Indeed, in the 1920s, such stories often did. The extent to which Goofy's flight goes awry (crashing through a billboard and whatnot) *is* a bit outlandish, borrowing from the spirit of Walt Disney's short-subject cartoon films, but that's what we'd expect to find in the old Toontown, not necessarily New Fantasyland.

The fact that The Barnstormer can't be adequately defended as a work of "fantasy" might give us pause if we were to consider the attraction by itself. But I prefer to look at it in the context of its next-door neighbor — Dumbo the Flying Elephant.

Dumbo hit theaters in October 1941, a time when feature-length films were frequently accompanied in theaters by one or more short-subject cartoons. The cartoon short enjoyed a golden age between the 1930s and 1960s,[44] when toons would play before the feature as an appetizer and added value for the price of admission.

We might think of the Great Goofini in the same way. It's the roller coaster equivalent of a cartoon short, playing for Storybook Circus audiences as an adjunct to Dumbo next door. Given that nearly everything else in Storybook Circus is *Dumbo*-themed, it stands to reason that Goofy is there as a sort of add-on, a role that he and his "fab five" brethren have filled well for nearly a century.

Cartoons bring out the kid in all of us, and The Barnstormer does that too. It's probably the ride's best quality. Kids love it because the thrills are tailor-made for them, and we adults love it precisely because the thrills *aren't* made for us. Disney lets us experience them anyway, and there's something about how our adult bodies fling around those tiny, sharp curves that exhilarates us.

Perhaps there is a little bit of fantasy in the Great Goofini, after all, then. It lets grown-ups pretend that they're young again, with body sizes and recreational sensibilities to match. If we're to be entirely honest with ourselves, it's a teeny bit ridiculous that we're riding it (and I'm sure there are some readers who wouldn't go near it and think I'm crazy for doing so), but the ridiculousness is half the fun, isn't it? That's what being goofy is all about, and in Storybook Circus we learn how to get goofy from the best.

WATCH THIS – The Big Wash (1948)

Goofy plays a circus worker in this animated short film, which ran in theaters during 1948, just seven years after *Dumbo*. He tries his best to bathe a circus elephant named Dolores, but she's having none of it. This was the second of Dolores the Elephant's three appearances in Disney's cartoon canon. She's also seen in *Tiger Trouble* (1945) and *Working for Peanuts* (1953).

At just over seven minutes, *The Big Wash* provides plenty of the character humor and sight gags that made Disney cartoons reliable box office diversions. We experience the same kind of fun in our short jaunt aboard The Barnstormer. Seeing Goofy in circus garb makes this one feel like a natural opening act for Storybook Circus.

The Big Wash even gets a little nut-sized nod in the attraction. A rocket by the entryway bears the name Dolores on its side. The same can be seen in one of the posters on display there. It's Imagineering's subtle nod to Disney's second-most-preeminent pachyderm.

Cinderella Castle

Type: Walk-through environment
Duration: Unlimited
Height Restriction: None
Popularity/Crowds: Moderate to High
FastPass+: No
Fear Factor: 0.5 out of 5. Pyrotechnic effects during the "Mickey's Royal Friendship Faire" castle stage show cause loud noises.
Wet Factor: None
Preshow: None
Best Time to Visit: Anytime
Special Comments: There is very little to tour in the castle itself, unless you're visiting Bibbidi Bobbidi Boutique (makeovers for kids) or Cinderella's Royal Table (character dining). Reservations are imperative for both. But you should definitely walk through it if you can. Note that the castle is closed off just before, during, and after stage performances and fireworks. See the daily Times Guide for scheduled performances of "Mickey's Royal Friendship Faire" and the "Move It! Shake It! MousekeDance It!" street party (more on that in *Chapter Six*).

For those who haven't been to Walt Disney World before, there might not be anything higher on the bucket list than merely laying their eyes on the castle. Cinderella Castle has emerged as an icon for not only the Magic Kingdom but also for the culture at large. Visiting it in person is something of a rite of passage. As the park's colossal centerpiece, rising high above the rest of the Kingdom, it is visible from the other side of Seven Seas Lagoon, which guests must cross just to get there. Like a skyscraper or a star on the horizon, it beckons travelers from afar. It is the ultimate visual beguiler and also the thing that makes the rest of the park's narrative click. If the basic premise of the Magic Kingdom is an escape into fantasy, then the castle, just by being there — a full-sized storybook palace in the real world — makes that escape credible. It transforms fantasy into reality.

Even in Europe, where castles are common, they don't look quite like this. Cinderella's home is surreally opulent, sparkling and massive, sporting all the elegance of royal luxury but few of the practical features that would have been mandated by the need for defense in times of war. This is the kind of estate that only a make-believe monarchy could call home, and yet the castle *is* part of a kingdom. That's the story anyway, and when we venture inside its mysterious corridors and along its perimeter walls, we discover the extent to which the building really does reinforce that idea.

Walt has already built a castle for Aurora of *Sleeping Beauty* in Disneyland, so it only made sense to switch things up and build Cinderella's digs in Florida instead. The blueprints, borrowed from a long list of famous castles,[45] most of them in France, also drew inspiration from the art of *Cinderella* (1950). The end result is that Magic Kingdom's castle is substantially larger (and much less pink) than Disneyland's, but each boasts its own, unique charm.

That most of the source castles are French is significant. The "Cinderella" fairy tale that inspired Walt's movie is French too, or at least the most famous version of it is, written by Charles Perrault[46] in 1697. The main floor of the castle interior is open to the public and inside it, the walls are intricately decorated with colorful glass mosaics that illustrate the "Cinderella" story as told by Perrault, with just a few touches of Disney's version. Opting for less cartoony, more old-world character designs makes the passage more effective in establishing Fantasyland as the realm of olden fairy tales.

Once upon a time, we found one of the resort's most intriguing gift shops inside the castle itself. The King's Gallery dealt not in plush dolls and collectible pins, but in shields and swords, and was also well stocked with impressive porcelain and glass. This knightly retailer recognized both the obligations of battle and the spoils of war that were all part of royal life.

In 2007, The King's Gallery shipped some of its merchandise over to Main Street and closed for conversion to Bibbidi Bobbidi Boutique, a fanciful salon in which little girls can be given a makeover as a princess of their choosing and boys can be dubbed knights. Whereas Prince Charming Regal Carrousel shifted attention away from Cinderella and toward the oft-overlooked men of the kingdom, the opening of Bibbidi Bobbidi Boutique erased a rare nod to *Cinderella's* king (who, as the movie shows, really has no business with a sword).[47] But while the loss of The King's Gallery was sad, the new boutique is just as good at engaging with the fairy tale.

The story goes that the Fairy Godmother, who we all know to be proficient in rags-to-riches makeovers, is teaching her apprentices the art of transformation, and Magic Kingdom's littlest guests get to be their guinea pigs — for a price. Fortunately, the godmothers in training do a decent job. With a curtsy, they bid beaming tykes adieu with fancy new face paint and hairdos. A "Knight Package" (previously known as the "Cool Dudes" package) is available as well.

Across the hall from Bibbidi Bobbidi Boutique is the entrance to Cinderella's Royal Table, long the most coveted dining experience in Walt Disney World (though Be Our Guest has recently given it a run for its money). The Royal Table, located on an upper level within the castle, serves three meals a day and all of them require reservations, usually months in advance.[48] While the royal chef warms up the kitchen, the castle staff seats us at our table, which might be beneath a canopy of imperial flags or in front of beautiful windows overlooking Fantasyland. Cinderella is on hand to greet all the diners, and so are a handful of her princess friends.

Cinderella's Royal Table was known as King Stefan's Banquet Hall until 1997. That's odd because King Stefan is Sleeping Beauty's father. Cinderella was very gracious to allow another king to randomly host his banquets in her castle for all those years, but we can see why the name needed to change — the real mystery is why it took until 1997 for that to happen. With the deed transfer complete, the Royal Table stands as a unique storybook experience hidden inside one of the world's most famous castles — even if the consensus is that there's better food elsewhere at Walt Disney World. Knowing that the giant building is more than just a hallway and a façade makes it more credible as an actual castle. The fact that it's so hard to snag a reservation means you really do feel like royalty when you get in.

If the Royal Table is exceptional because it's on the second floor of the palace and hard to get into, the Cinderella Castle Suite is once-in-a-lifetime extraordinary. Originally intended as an apartment for Walt and his family, this room perched high up in one of the castle towers used to be just some storage space and an office, until Disney converted it into the single most luxurious hotel room in all of Walt Disney World. During the "Year of a Million Dreams," which ran from the fall of 2006 through early 2009 (more than a year, I know), one lucky family visiting the park each day was selected at random by Disney's elusive Dream Team to stay in the suite overnight for free. When the promotion ended, so did the chance to sleep in the castle, and until something new is announced, there's no way to reserve it for even one night.[49] Still, as with the Royal Table, just knowing the suite is there makes the whole castle that much more exciting.

The castle narrative extends beyond *Cinderella*, though, all the way to the outskits of Fantasyland. The building itself is used to tell a broader story about the entire park, supporting the idea that the Magic Kingdom is a *kingdom*. Fortress walls extend out from the palace itself in two directions, as if the castle walls are protecting the medieval village[50] of Fantasyland from outsiders. Behind every attraction façade in the courtyard, we can see the castle's familiar blue-gray brick and stately turrets.

The next time you're in the great open plaza that greets you after you have walked through Cinderella Castle, just take a moment to stop in the middle and turn around in a circle. You'll see that you're standing in a *proper* castle courtyard, protected by the impenetrable walls of the royal estate.[51] Ancient kingdoms had barrier walls; so does this one. Here again, we see the attention to detail that has made Disney's theme parks famous.

Earlier, we observed that Cinderella Castle isn't saddled by the defensive mechanisms that real castles would use to fend off attack, but we might think of the barrier walls as an exception to that. They suggest that Fantasyland does need protection, and that begs the question — from what? For many years, there was a castle show with an answer. "Dream Along with Mickey" was built around the idea that Fantasyland is under attack by Disney's own evil villains. The Sorcerers of the Magic Kingdom game, which we will cover in *Chapter Six* explores that same idea.

There's a new show in town today: "Mickey's Royal Friendship Faire." It's less interested in the castle's defenses than in the idea of daily life here, suggesting that some of the company's characters (Sir Mickey and Lady Minnie, apparently royalty now) live in Fantasyland while others (Anna, Elsa, Rapunzel, Tiana, and so on) visit from far-off realms. Minnie has never seemed more like a real person than when she straight-up fangirls over "Let It Go." The idea that she has heard of the royal family of Arendelle but hasn't met them yet speaks to this broader notion of the kingdom as a real community.

But as I was preparing to update this chapter to include "Mickey's Royal Friendship Faire," Disney fan columnist Blake Taylor[52] posted his own reflections on the show, and they caused me to consider this silly little stage play in a light I hadn't before. A very different, much more meaningful light. "Mickey's Royal Friendship Faire" premiered in the summer of 2016 on the heels of tremendous tragedy in Orlando.[53] Debuting mere days after multiple incidents of violence and misfortune had impacted the Central Florida community in the span of a week, its songs about inclusivity, being stronger together, and making the most of the day you have in front of you took on new meaning. Grieving masses held candlelight vigils in front of the castle that same week, the castle an obvious gathering point and a meaningful place of memorial in a city known for its magic but rocked to its core. I remember feeling that same sense of comfort but hadn't since considered it as part of the show's legacy. Now, as persistent rumors suggest "Mickey's Royal Friendship Faire" may close sometime before the end of 2021, I suspect that may be its legacy after all.

The castle has come to mean so many things to so many people — a place of refuge, an escape, a source of comfort, a symbol of aspiration, a marker of memories, a home away from home. It is more than the gateway to a land of carnival rides. It is a powerful cultural artifact with symbolic significance that goes well beyond any castle party or parade.

Cynics could (and do) scoff at the idea of anyone finding any real meaning in something as silly as a theme park fairy tale façade. But is Cinderella Castle anything less than a landmark?

We travel from afar to visit national monuments like the Statue of Liberty or the Eiffel Tower, contemplating their symbolism and admiring their every detail. Just as they are monuments of history, Cinderella Castle and Disney's other theme park icons have become monuments of culture, and for those who've come to associate them with something of substance in their life, they are as important as any other.

WATCH THIS - Enchanted (2007)

Princess Giselle (Amy Adams) spends most of her days whistling and playing dress-up with the woodland animals in her entirely hand-drawn, hyper-cartoony world. That changes when the nefarious Queen Narissa (Susan Sarandon) banishes her to the live-action real world of New York City circa 2007. There, she meets a disillusioned attorney (Patrick Dempsey) and spices up his life with the kind of cheery housecleaning and random musical outbursts that only a true Disney princess could provide.

Part tribute, part parody, *Enchanted* is a hilarious, brilliant, and loving satire of Disney feature filmmaking. It's a delicious Disney-on-Disney spoof. The confusion Princess Giselle feels when she's maliciously expelled from her animated kingdom and hurled into New York is not unlike Alice's experience when she falls into Wonderland. Be that as it may, in this winning musical, the perplexity is played for laughs. Here as in Fantasyland, the intersection of the fairy tale with modern-day reality remains eternally appealing.

Chapter 5

Tomorrowland

> *"A vista into a world of wondrous ideas, signifying man's achievements... a step into the future, with predictions of constructive things to come. Tomorrow offers new frontiers in science, adventure, and ideals: the Atomic Age, the challenge of outer space, and the hope for a peaceful and unified world."*[1]
>
> Walt Disney, "Dateline: Disneyland," July 17, 1955

Walt mentioned a "challenge" here, but I wonder if he realized then just how challenging the concept of Tomorrowland would become.

Tomorrow is always just two days away from being yesterday. Sadly, theme parks don't change as quickly as the times. Tomorrowland's name is in tension with its limitations. That makes the attractions here harder to read as parts of a whole. The whole is in a perpetual identity crisis, with one foot in the future, one in the past, and one in a sci-fi fantasy. (Three legs because Tomorrowland *loves* itself an alien.)

We'll keep this challenge in mind as we walk through the seven major attractions here — the Tomorrowland Transit Authority PeopleMover; Buzz Lightyear's Space Ranger Spin; Tomorrowland Speedway; Astro Orbiter; Monsters, Inc. Laugh Floor; Space Mountain; and Walt Disney's Carousel of Progress.

So much of the future is found in the past, and any good exercise in time travel takes us through that crossroads. What's a sci-fi adventure without a few wrinkles in time?

Tomorrowland Transit Authority PeopleMover

Type: Tram ride
Duration: 10 to 12 minutes
Height Restriction: None
Popularity/Crowds: Moderate
FastPass+: No
Fear Factor: None
Wet Factor: None
Preshow: None
Boarding Speed: Very fast
Best Time to Visit: Anytime

I can't urge you enough to make the PeopleMover your first stop in Tomorrowland. Not just because the line is never long or because there's a cream cheese pretzel stand on the first floor, but because it lends essential context to a Tomorrowland that wouldn't make much sense otherwise.

Its unwieldy title — three words plus a portmanteau — tells the story of its evolution over time. Here we have yet another attraction with roots in the 1964 New York World's Fair, where Disney first created the Ford Magic Skyway. Sponsored by the motor vehicle giant, the ride took guests on a slow-moving tour of prehistoric dinosaur dioramas and then through vignettes of human innovation and a futuristic cityscape, all from the comfort of the latest Ford model cars.[2]

After the World's Fair closed, the Magic Skyway moved to Disneyland where, on July 2, 1967, it opened with a new sponsor (Goodyear) and a new name — the PeopleMover.[3] Sleek new train cars stood in for Ford's convertibles. Moving along an elevated track, they gave guests an up-in-the-air view of the recently redesigned Tomorrowland, while onboard narration provided a rundown of the attractions below.

The name remained unchanged until 1982, when part of the ride (an enclosed sequence called the SuperSpeed Tunnel) took on a *Tron* overlay in support of the cutting-edge sci-fi flick's theatrical premiere. PeopleMover Thru the World of Tron, they called it, and it stayed that way until Disneyland shuttered the ride for good in 1995. Imagineers decided to put a thrill ride in its place, but 1998's Rocket Rods was a rocket fraud, thrilling precisely no one and closing just three years later. The track still stands in Disneyland, empty and unused, taunting nostalgic Disneyland fans who long for the PeopleMover of the past.

Fortunately, Magic Kingdom had opened its own version on July 1, 1975, and no one in Florida had ever tried to strap a rocket pack on its back. Walt Disney World's version did sport some enhanced tech, though, and a new name: the WEDWay PeopleMover. "WEDWay" referred to the track itself, inspired by Walter Elias Disney's initials. "PeopleMover" referred to the long, roofless train gliding along a highly stylized, partially enclosed, tunnel-like highway in the sky (as opposed to Disneyland's individually covered cars running along an open-air track). Magic Kingdom's on-ride audio was similar to Disneyland's until a "Commuter Computer" took over as narrator in 1985, spieling guests well into the next decade.

Then came 1994, the year that Magic Kingdom decided to do something big about its Tomorrowland problem. The massive, land-wide renovation came with two chief goals. First, work around the challenge inherent in a land themed around the future — the fact that society's vision for tomorrow is forever changing. Second, enhance the overall urban vibe.

Heeding the directive, Imagineers dreamed up a new approach to Tomorrowland that could kill both birds with the same stone. Billed "the future that never was," the new Tomorrowland posed as a fictional city of the distant future, but not one that anyone expected might come to pass. No, this was the type of city one would have found in early twentieth century comic strips like *Flash Gordon* and *Buck Rogers*, with maybe just a hint of H.G. Wells and "The Jetsons."[3] In this new narrative, the city of Tomorrowland is Earth's ambassadorial center for the intergalactic League of Planets. The new metropolis has all the makings of a living, breathing city, including a major metro system — the WEDway People-Mover — only it wasn't called that anymore.

With the new theme came yet another new name, the Tomorrowland Transit Authority, more commonly referred to as "the TTA." The renovated ride, now outfitted in a showy metallic finish, reflected

Tomorrowland's new direction more than any other attraction. Riding it became the best way to understand "New Tomorrowland"'s backstory. New narration flesh out the storyline in some detail, telling guests they had boarded the "Tomorrowland Metroliners," part of a mass-transit system that would take them from the city's central spaceport to a variety of stops along the route (none of which actually existed). The booming, almost otherworldly voice lent new personality to the ride and referred to the TTA with a number of nicknames — the "Blue Line," the "Super-Skyway," the "Grand Circle Tour," etc. — all of them now a part of the Disney fandom's vernacular.

The 1994 version of the ride lasted longer than any other to date, now an indelible part of Tomorrowland memories for many millions of visitors. But by 2009, the script was starting to show some age again, Tomorrowland slowly starting to look less and less like the city of the future it described. When it came time to spruce up Space Mountain with a soundtrack and a fresh coat of paint, Disney decided to do the same for the TTA. All-new narration debuted in September 2009, marking something of a return to the personality of Disneyland's original PeopleMover ride, with a more friendly-sounding narrator acting as a sightseeing guide.

The next year, in August 2010, Disney went and renamed the ride once again, now the Tomorrowland Transit Authority PeopleMover, a tribute to the pre-1994 nomenclature. It's a nice nod but a long name. I like to call it the T-TAP. Lots of other people like to call it lots of other things, too, so you practically need a PeopleMover lexicon to communicate coherently about the thing.[4]

This newest iteration is arguably less effective than the one that ran from 1994 to 2009. Before, the spiel served as a dramatized municipal orientation of sorts. Welcoming guests who'd traveled through time to a fictional city of tomorrow, it told them how the Metroliner worked and where it could take them. Now, the narrator is positioned more as an instructional guide for visitors in the *present* age. His spiel advertises attractions as attractions, rather than as important hubs for galactic travel. Guests still get an overview of the land below, but the storytelling element is seriously diminished. Without it, the inviting premise of Tomorrowland-as-metropolis is harder to discern. Unaware that they're visiting a futuristic fantasy rooted in an earlier era and not a contemporary designer's prophecy for tomorrow, fans and casual guests alike might wonder why so much of Tomorrowland feels decidedly passé. Even when state-of-the-art isn't their goal, the attractions can't help but feel dated with the rapid passage of time.

As the land's lifeblood, the T-TAP is always changing in an attempt to adapt at minimal expense. It doesn't always succeed, but hey, accommodating transformation on a budget is something real cities grapple with all the time. So maybe Tomorrowland is more realistic a municipality than it seems.

In its present form, the ride still works to suggest city life. For starters, the idea of a metro isn't absent altogether. We do still hear references to this being a mass-transit system. The new script encourages people-watching too, always a favorite urban pastime. The Imagineers have even preserved a loudspeaker page for a "Mr. Tom Morrow," a creative touch that lends credibility to the cityscape. That particular announcement was so popular during the 1990s and 2000s that when it briefly disappeared in 2009, outraged fans successfully demanded its return the next year (well, almost successfully — the current recording is slightly different than before[5]). Still, unfortunately, what you *hear* on the ride now makes less of an overall impact than what you see and feel.

Even if only as a visual statement, the T-TAP defines Tomorrowland in a snapshot. Encasing the perimeter, wrapping around the curvature of each attraction, winding across the walkways, and curling up around the Astro Orbiter in the center, the PeopleMover makes quite the impression upon a single glance. The ride never stops running, its perpetual motion making Tomorrowland look positively kinetic. The PeopleMover's motion contrasts nicely with the divergent movements of the Astro Orbiter's spinning jets, the Speedway's racecars, the Carousel of Progress's rotating show building, and the Walt Disney World Railroad's train. Everything's moving, a veritable Tomorrowland motionscape, and the T-TAP pulls it all together.

The sights seen from the tram are pretty out of this world too — quite literally, if we buy into the story. The T-TAP travels inside two Tomorrowland attractions, passing by a scale model of Walt's original dream for EPCOT along the way (more on that at the end of this chapter). One of those is Buzz Lightyear's Space Ranger Spin, which ostensibly takes us out of Tomorrowland and into the evil Zurg's outer space empire (more on that a bit later too). The other is Space Mountain, the Magic Kingdom's star attraction (no pun intended). As its name implies, Space Mountain is set in the cosmos and looks the part. As our T-TAP pulls into those rides, the Tomorrowland storyline takes us from a thriving city center into outer space in the blink of an eye — a very futuristic idea. That optimistic prediction for transportation might be one of the most intrepid ideas in Tomorrowland, even if the Imagineers never call our attention to it.

From a storytelling perspective, the journey into Space Mountain is terrifically effective as a foreshadowing device. Though T-TAP's thrills are modest, Space Mountain's looming galaxy of the unknown is a real source of apprehension for many guests. The suspense starts to build with the first step into Tomorrowland, when the mountain's intimidating spires first appear on the city skyline. The T-TAP knows that and is a total tease about it, showing just enough scream-filled blackness inside the ride to really psych us out.

Among the many phrases Walt Disney is famous for are these three words: "Keep moving forward."[6] The Tomorrowland Transit Authority PeopleMover does just that. In one sense, it contemplates the future, looking forward to a day when the subways will be sky-borne. In another, it literally never stops. Barring a breakdown, the tram keeps moving, but eventually, you have to get off. When you do, you'll have a better sense of how to fully appreciate the rest of what Tomorrowland has to offer.

WATCH THIS - Meet the Robinsons (2007)

"Keep Moving Forward" is a key phrase in Disney's 47th official Animated Classic,[7] which follows a genius orphan boy named Lewis and another young man, Wilbur Robinson, who whisks him off to the future in a time machine. Together, they travel to the year 2037, where Lewis meets the idiosyncratic Robinson family, a clan so eclectic that he fits right in. Wilbur needs Lewis's help in repairing an older time machine, but his motives seem less than straightforward. Meanwhile, he and Wilbur must always stay one step ahead of the evil Bowler Hat Guy, a great among comedic villains.

Bob Iger became CEO of the Walt Disney Company just a month

before *Chicken Little* was released to theaters in November 2005, so *Meet the Robinsons* is generally considered to be the first Disney Animated Classic of the Iger era. Following years of a nasty and very public battle[8] between previous CEO Michael Eisner and Roy E. Disney (Walt's nephew and a big player in the company at the time), Iger was intent on sending a message — things will be different now. To that end, *Meet the Robinsons* is dedicated to Walt and his legacy, and it is built around several Walt-ish themes, including innovation. The movie's imagination for the future is vivid and creative, right down to transportation by floating bubble. In one memorable scene, Lewis and Wilbur pass over Tomorrowland itself, only 17 years from now (that was 30 years into the future when the movie was released), winkingly presented as "Todayland."

Buzz Lightyear's Space Ranger Spin

Type: Dark ride with interactive laser guns
Duration: 5 minutes
Height Restriction: None
Popularity/Crowds: Moderate to High
FastPass+: Yes; medium priority
Fear Factor: None
Wet Factor: None
Preshow: None
Boarding Speed: Fast
Best Time to Visit without FastPass+: Early morning or later in the evening

Buzz Lightyear's Space Ranger Spin is a world within a world within a world. Two of those worlds are set in the future, one is not, and it's the middle layer that creates a big problem for Tomorrowland's premise. Yet somehow, the video game-inspired ride gets away with playing fast and loose with the whole future theme. Video games are *virtual* experiences, after all, and "virtual" is just another way of saying "close enough." That's Buzz Lightyear's Space Ranger Spin for you: close enough... and a fair amount of fun.

The ride opened in the Magic Kingdom on November 3, 1998, in a building that had been occupied by an airplane-themed ride (in various incarnations) since the park's opening day. While it kept the same basic layout, Space Ranger Spin did away with the airways idea altogether and introduced a more ambitious kind of ride.

Thanks to a few optical illusions — passable if not wowing — guests walk out of Tomorrowland and into Star Command, where they instantly shrink to the size of a toy.[9] A towering and life-like Buzz Lightyear awaits them inside, ready to induct all newcomers as instant space cadets. The new recruits are ordered into the cosmos where they'll do battle with the galaxy's most notorious buzzkill, the evil Emperor Zurg. Space vessels arrive in no time, and cadets are paired off and given one laser gun each. The ride vehicles follow a typical dark ride track, steadily inclining to simulate entry into outer space, where the cadets come under attack right away. It's never spelled out explicitly, but they've entered what is supposed to be — and certainly looks like — a Buzz Lightyear video game.

Zurg's army of toy aliens and accessories are outfitted with infrared targets bearing a giant "Z." Some are easy to tag; many are not. Each successful shot earns the responsible marksman a given number of points. The values are determined in large part by the difficulty of the target. Fortunately, the cadets have an advantage over some of their alien adversaries because the space vessels are equipped with a joystick that can rotate the vehicle a full 360 degrees for optimal aim. Immensely interactive, the ride keeps its gamers on their toes.

That means most riders will spend their time thinking about the innermost level of the ride — the Buzz Lightyear video game in which the ride's primary narrative unfolds. Walking into Buzz's virtual world from Tomorrowland outside, one might easily overlook the storyline that gets us from the Magic Kingdom to Buzz's Star Command — the world of *Toy Story*.

Tomorrowland takes place in the future and Buzz Lightyear's video game seems to as well. *Toy Story*, on the other hand, is set in the late 20th century. Conceptually, then, we must first travel back in time before continuing on in the future. The theme park asks its guests to leave the imaginary land of Tomorrow and return to a present-day mindset, where a contemporary video game provides the characters and future-oriented storyline used in Space Ranger Spin. I doubt many guests pause to reflect on the narrative time warp but I do think many come away thinking that the ride doesn't *feel* particularly futuristic. That's because the whole thing is about playing a video game, which isn't at all on the cutting edge of recreation. Video games are nearly as old as the Magic Kingdom itself, and the point-and-shoot style of Space Ranger Spin is a better fit for Yesterland (or your local mall).

As established during its major 1994 reboot, Tomorrowland is intended to be a future fantasy inspired by early twentieth century visionaries. Space Ranger Spin's galactic battle is a future fantasy, but it was created by late, not early, twentieth century imaginations. The attraction breaks away from New Tomorrowland's founding narrative and requires a momentary departure from the otherwise-immersive illusion that guests have traveled into the future.

But perhaps the ride is due some leeway, given that video games are all about approximation. Space Ranger Spin is ultimately a life-sized video game and a very unusual one at that. How many electronic games manage to physically transport guests inside their world and make them part of the action? Okay, there was Nickelodeon's 1992 game show "Nick Arcade," but unless you were a lucky young teen at the time, you never got to take part in that. For most of us, laser tag dark rides like Buzz,[10] Duel: The Haunted House Strikes Back! at England's Alton Towers, and Men in Black: Alien Attack at Universal Orlando are the closest we can get to total immersion inside the video game universe, and Tomorrowland's Space Ranger Spin is the most fully realized of its generation.[11]

Feature-length animation hasn't been the same since *Toy Story*'s release in 1995. Pixar revolutionized the movie industry by delivering the first major CGI success at the box office. More importantly, their team told a good story with a cast of endearing characters. That's true of the *Toy Story* sequels, too (not to mention most other Pixar films). *Toy Story* captivated audiences with a supremely intriguing premise — when the child's away, the toys will play. The Pooh stories had charted similar territory decades prior, but Pixar brought a delicious air of mystery to the idea. Whereas Christopher Robin knows that his toys are alive (albeit only in his imagination), Andy doesn't have a clue what's going on when he's not home. And *his* toys are adventuring in the real world, to boot.

To some extent, Buzz Lightyear's Space Ranger Spin does for the video game what its inspiration, *Toy Story*, does for the toy. In the ride, a video game is brought to life and made immensely appealing, just as toys are in the films. The parallel isn't perfect. I doubt you'll feel the same compassion for a game cartridge that you'd have for a pull-string cowboy. No one supposes that a video game — a thing of bits and bytes — would have a personality of its own or get up and roam the entertainment center at night, so Space Ranger Spin wisely doesn't pursue that line of conjecture. What the ride does do, however, is three-dimensionalize the video game experience, making it exciting in a whole new way. Like a multi-player game, riders ward off attackers and compete for points against the person beside them. Only here, the environment isn't generated on a screen by a computer — it's real!

That experiential relationship with the video game format might not matter much in another ride, but Space Ranger Spin's *Toy Story* lineage shouldn't be ignored. Guests already saw Buzz Lightyear come to life in the movies. Now they get to see his video game world come to life, too.[12]

The ride also provides the perfect case study for an ongoing debate among those who study video games as a cultural medium. Are the games first and foremost about storytelling, the way that books and movies are? Or are they primarily about gaming, where objectives and instructions and rules are the underlying purpose and draw? Buzz Lightyear's Space Ranger Spin might lend support to either view. As to the former, the queue and boarding area set forth a straightforward narrative, and the ride also ties into the *Toy Story* saga, including the "Buzz Lightyear of Star Command" TV series, which itself spawned an actual video game release. At the same time, the game is defined by an objective (defeat Zurg) and numerous opportunities to make progress toward that objective (hit as many targets as possible in each level), all in accordance with the game's physical layout and rules (cars can spin in a full circle except during set times when the rotation device is automatically locked, for example).

Would the game be played any differently if the backstory was completely changed but everything else stayed the same? Would the story be worth telling without the element of gameplay? Clearly, both narrative and gaming are at work in the attraction, having fused two different theme park genres — the dark ride and the shooting gallery.[13] And yet the marriage of gameplay and storytelling isn't unique to theme parks. (Space Ranger Spin mirrors many narrative-heavy video games in that regard.) Because the level of player interaction is so high in the ride, video game theorists might do well to spend some time away from their TV sets and in the Magic Kingdom instead!

Perhaps the most game-like of Space Ranger Spin's qualities is its repeatability. Even on the fiftieth ride, the attraction remains engaging, if only because you have the chance to come away with a better score. Even with only one of Buzz's giant plastic feet planted in the future, then, the ride is still more forward-looking than most (and arguably more than Tomorrowland's original airplane rides ever were). It's just a shame the aesthetics and the fundamental novelty are all trapped in the past. Still, even as its technology fades into irrelevancy, the ride's appeal to competitive instincts gives it a longer shelf life. While much might change in the near future, our desire to best a friend in a game of laser tag likely never will. Buzz may not quite be a light year ahead of his time, but he's at least worth some playtime until something better comes along.

WATCH THIS - Tron: Legacy (2010)

Tron isn't exactly a video game, but the action surrounding it plays out a lot like one. In point of fact, Tron is a *program*, one of many that interact inside The Grid, a labyrinthine virtual world that exists inside a computer. The mechanics get kind of complicated, and yet the core idea of an electronic universe is pretty simple (and arguably flimsy). Suffice it to say that humans can enter The Grid too, but some of the programs lurking there are hostile and getting back out isn't easy.

Legacy is the unexpected sequel to a movie that came nearly 30 years before it, 1982's *Tron*. Both movies have their fair share of problems, but each contains flashes of brilliance. Following them to a T isn't the easiest task, nor the most appealing to the technologically disinclined. Still, there's a lot of story to chew on, and the audience is invited to take up some intellectual exercise. All blockbusters should be so substantive.

Legacy is more mainstream, more traditionally action-oriented, and more human than its predecessor. It imagines what it might be like for mortals to travel inside a computer system or video game. (The portal to The Grid is found inside an abandoned 1980s arcade). It has that curiosity in common with Buzz Lightyear's Space Ranger Spin. While the movie isn't set in the future, The Grid is as sleek and bold in design as anything I've seen presented for the days ahead. As both a Buzz Lightyear counterpart and a companion piece to Tomorrowland, *Tron: Legacy* works.

> Need another reason to watch? How's this? Magic Kingdom is building a major, massive, E-ticket roller coaster inspired by *Tron: Legacy*, currently under construction next to Space Mountain and behind the Tomorrowland Speedway. Modeled after Shanghai's popular Tron Lightcycle Power Run ride, it's sure to be the toast of Tomorrowland when it opens around the time of Walt Disney World's fiftieth anniversary in 2021.

Tomorrowland Speedway

Type: Slot car ride
Duration: 4 to 5 minutes
Height Restriction: 54 inches or taller to ride alone
Popularity/Crowds: Moderate
FastPass+: Yes; low to medium priority
Fear Factor: None
Wet Factor: None
Preshow: None
Boarding Speed: Slow to Moderate
Best Time to Visit without FastPass+: Morning or evening

The Tomorrowland Speedway might be a decent ride if it were at least remotely tethered to either tomorrow or speed. On the contrary, it's rather antiquated and tortoise-like. Far from the car race of the future it purports to be, the ride forbids lane changing, bumping, and all but the most meager acceleration. A more appropriate title might be something like The Slow and the Spurious (which we'd probably all still prefer over Universal Orlando's new Fast & Furious ride, but that's neither here nor there). Dull as the "Speed"-way may be, there is at least some peripheral justification for its continued existence.

After what is usually a lengthy boarding process, the Tomorrowland Speedway kicks off with a... I would say "bang," but if you hear one, it's probably just the noisy old racecar behind you backfiring. When given the green light, drivers put the pedal to the metal and zoom from zero to seven in under a minute. Along the way, they're thrilled by the sights passing by — understated shrubbery, cautionary signage, and heavyset tourists handily outpacing them on foot.

The yellow warning signs urge drivers to keep at least one car's length in between each vehicle, but at seven miles per hour, the only way anyone can catch up with anyone else is if the first car comes to a sudden halt. As it so happens, cars do frequently halt on the Tomorrowland Speedway because they're hard to drive. Petrified by the prospect of low-speed collision, Disney has shackled each vehicle to an ill-fitting rail that takes the driving out of an attraction that's supposed to be all about driving.

In its present form, the Tomorrowland Speedway offers little reason to ride, despite occupying more real estate than most other attractions in Walt Disney World. That hasn't always been the case, though, especially in Disneyland, where the ride first opened in July of 1955 under the name Autopia, quite modern for its time. Believe it or not, there were no U.S. Interstates in 1955,[14] but the prospect of limited-access expressways running across the country had spawned a lot of excitement and chatter in the early 1950s. Wisely foreseeing the future potential of these new roadways — President Dwight D. Eisenhower commissioned the first interstate highway a year later, in 1956 — Walt wanted an attraction built in their honor.

When Autopia debuted, it was utterly chic — adults got a taste of this new mode of transportation and unlicensed children got an early start on their driver's ed. That was important to Walt, who very much wanted Disneyland to promote learning and responsible citizenship among both children and adults. Like most things in Disneyland, Autopia was in high demand and stayed that way for many years, popular enough to warrant multiple spin-off attractions over the years (only the original survives today).[15]

When Magic Kingdom was in development, Autopia was still a big attraction in Disneyland; so naturally, the company wanted to bring a similar experience to Florida. The only problem was that while Eisenhower's Interstate project was still far from finished, it was hardly the source of excitement it had been fifteen years prior. So the Magic Kingdom version was themed as an international raceway instead — not a very futuristic idea, but there's at least something optimistic about international sportsmanship. Called the Grand Prix Raceway, the ride was one of Tomorrowland's opening day attractions on October 1, 1971.

The first big change came in 1988, with a slight shortening and shifting of the track to make way for what was then Mickey's Birthdayland[16] (hard to believe, given that the current track runs for an astounding 2,260 feet as it is). In 1996, on the heels of the "New Tomorrowland," the ride's name changed to Tomorrowland Speedway. It kept that name until December of 1999, when the Indianapolis Motor Speedway stepped in as a new sponsor, asking for a few cosmetic changes to make the Speedways match. In January 2000, the name officially changed to the Tomorrowland Indy Speedway. That partnership lasted just eight years. In the spring of 2008, Disney formally dropped "Indy" from the name, reverting to the former title. In 2019, Disney shortened the track ever so slightly to accommodate the upcoming Tron roller coaster and repainted the Speedway at the same time. Otherwise, not much has changed.

Neither driving nor the Interstate is in any way revolutionary to our present state of mind. There's no real discernible international theme anymore either. There's not even a good view of Tomorrowland from the track, unlike in Disneyland, where the raceway's integration with Tomorrowland is Autopia's saving grace. Children are more likely to learn about driving from a local go-kart park than from this restrictive plod-along. For the very young who are seeing a motor track for the first time, there might be an enticing newness in the experience, and for others, there's nostalgia. But you've probably driven faster in parking lots, over speed bumps, and through thick layers of mud or snow than you ever will on the Tomorrowland Speedway.

So why ride? Well, on a tight time budget, maybe you shouldn't. On a more relaxed schedule, though, the racetrack *can* lead to some insight. By taking us back to the past, the ride unwittingly leads us to think about the future. The Speedway is the product of a time when cars and state-to-state roadways could stir tremendous national excitement. The fact that they're a basic part of travel just sixty years later inspires optimism about how much further transportation might progress over the next half-century or so. Most of the people visiting Magic Kingdom on a given day probably got there on an Interstate. The Speedway's marginal value isn't in the replication of that experience, but in the way it implicitly challenges it. Maybe some of the more cutting-edge transportation in Tomorrowland, like rocket ships or highways in the sky, will be equally commonplace in another fifty years. That's an idea worth pondering on a lethargic putter through the park.

WATCH THIS – Freewayphobia (1965)

The educational short film starring Goofy is a Driver's Ed classroom classic, sometimes called *Freewayphobia No. 1* (or by its official subtitle, *The Art of Driving the Super Highway*). In it, Goofy plays several different kinds of dangerous drivers, each of them inevitably causing a multi-car pileup on the freeway. The Disney Studios created *Freewayphobia* to introduce Americans to the Interstate back when that idea was new, opening with an animated map that charts the growing Eisenhower system.

The film is still relevant as an instructional tool today, but its focus on the newness of Interstate driving reflects Walt Disney's desire to excite and prepare the public as he did with Autopia.

For more great moments with Goofy behind the wheel, check out the sequel to this cartoon, *Goofy's Freeway Troubles* (1965, sometimes called *Freewayphobia No. 2*), and 1950's *Motor Mania*, in which road rage triggers a Jekyll-and-Hyde transformation in the dippy driver. Oh, and while you're at it, don't forget the wonderful "On the Open Road" sequence in 1995's *A Goofy Movie* either!

Sadly, Disney Educational Productions has retired its trusty old *Driver Safety* DVD with this and other short films on it, but until it gets a new release, there's always YouTube... and the hope that *Freewayphobia* turns up on Disney+.

Astro Orbiter

Type: Flying, steerable rockets
Duration: Under 2 minutes
Height Restriction: None
Popularity/Crowds: Moderate to High
FastPass+: No
Fear Factor: 2.5 out of 5 (tall heights)
Wet Factor: None
Preshow: None
Boarding Speed: Very slow
Best Time to Visit: Morning or night

Astro Orbiter immediately calls to mind two other iconic Magic Kingdom attractions: Space Mountain and Dumbo the Flying Elephant. Space Mountain because they both involve a rocket ride through space, Dumbo because they're both simple hub-and-spoke rides.

Unlike Space Mountain, though, Astro Orbiter towers in the open air. When guests take off inside Astro's rockets, they're gazing up toward the heavens, hefty clouds billowing across the beautifully blue, sun-stamped Florida sky. The ascent begins with an elevator lift to a third-story platform atop the PeopleMover, where the rockets are ready for launch. Once the guests have boarded and strapped themselves in, the space jets lift off for the skies, swooshing in a steady revolution.

Like a look at Earth from outer space, the view from Astro Orbiter extends well beyond the park, offering a vantage point that even Dumbo can't match. To the extent that heights are thrilling, the Astro Orbiter holds its own as a thrill ride too (albeit a mild one). At the peak, guests find themselves much farther off the ground than they expected, and at what feels like a faster speed. Enormous, planet-like spheres spin around them (or are supposed to, at least — they rarely work these days[17]), creating an illusion of acceleration.

Positioned quite literally in the center of the land, Astro Orbiter underscores the centrality of space travel in Tomorrowland's twentieth century-inspired vision of the future. Its colorful swarm of planets creates an eye-catching "weenie" for Tomorrowland, drawing crowds closer to Space Mountain and the PeopleMover — a sky-high monument to intergalactic voyaging.

The ride's lineage traces back to 1956, when Disneyland first opened Astro Jets (renamed Tomorrowland Jets in 1964). That ride was basically the same as today's Astro Orbiter, only it loaded from the ground, like Dumbo. When Disneyland premiered its brand-new Tomorrowland in 1967, the Tomorrowland Jets became the Rocket Jets, newly perched high atop the original PeopleMover. That's the version Magic Kingdom recreated as Star Jets in 1974, built around the giant white NASA rocket that used to be at the center of Florida's Tomorrowland. When Walt Disney World unveiled a new Tomorrowland of its own in 1994, the Star Jets became the Astro Orbiter, complete with all the planets around it, and that's what we have today.[18]

Tomorrowland wouldn't feel quite right if it didn't afford its visitors some air time. Astro Orbiter makes sure that happens, aptly fashioned as a blast-off to the cosmos. Who knew Cinderella Castle was visible from outer space, though? Or that it's still so darn humid up there? Or that it takes only two minutes to go in and out of orbit? Well Tomorrowland *is* a future fantasy. With Astro Orbiter, that fantasy takes flight.

WATCH THIS - Moon Pilot (1962)

This little-known sci-fi comedy is both a spy movie and a romcom, the story of Captain Richmond Talbot's (Tom Tryon) reluctant voyage to the moon.

Government forces try to compel Capt. Talbot to make man's first mission to the moon on behalf of the United States, but there's a catch: he has to keep the whole mission top-secret. Talbot begrudgingly agrees, but on one condition: he gets to go home and visit his family first. Against their better judgment, the officials acquiesce. When Talbot gets home, though, no one shows much interest in him, except a pretty lady with a foreign accent that eludes identification. Talbot has no idea who she is, but she clearly knows entirely too much about him. Afraid that she's a Soviet spy, he plans to escape back to NASA and shake her off his trail on the way.

Opening with a still-cool rocket launch sequence, *Moon Pilot* memorializes Walt Disney's fascination with the national space program. Remember that this was released to theaters in 1962, seven years before Neil Armstrong landed on the moon (and five years before Don Knotts made another great movie along the same lines, *The Reluctant Astronaut*). Here, as in most things, Walt was way ahead of the curve. His early and eager attention to space travel manifested itself in Tomorrowland and the Astro Jets.

Disney has never given the movie a wide release on DVD, but subscribers to the Disney Movie Club can purchase it as a members-only exclusive. Fortunately for everyone else, those members often resell their purchases, so plenty of copies turn up on the second-hand market (as does the 1997 VHS release). *Moon Pilot* is also available digitally for rental and purchase.

Monsters, Inc. Laugh Floor

Type: Theater show
Duration: 15 minutes
Height Restriction: None
Popularity/Crowds: Moderate
FastPass+: Yes; low priority
Fear Factor: None, but some guests are randomly put on the spot for interaction (very scary for me).
Wet Factor: None
Preshow: Funny introductory video in a standing-room-only preshow
Best Time to Visit without FastPass+: Anytime
Special Comments: The front doors open at regular intervals. After watching the preshow video (which cannot be skipped) guests move into the main theater. Shows run continuously throughout the day.

As the old saying goes, laughter is the best medicine. For the monsters living in Monstropolis, it's the best fuel too. That's the lesson learned in the hit 2001 movie, *Monsters, Inc.,* a fantastic film that too often gets lost in the Pixar shuffle. Picking up where the movie left off, Walt Disney World opened its highly interactive stand-up comedy show in April 2007, focusing on the eponymous monsters' energy needs. Noting that comedy clubs are alive and well today, Disney fans on the net widely lambasted the attraction as a Tomorrowland misfit. They've got a point, but maybe there's more here than meets Mike Wazowski's one giant eye.

Our entrance to Monstropolis is said to be a special portal put in place just for the human residents of Tomorrowland. While waiting, we humans can text jokes of our own to a special phone number provided in the queue. If the punchline's good enough, the monsters just might use it in that very show. When the doors open, we're ushered into a dimly lit comedy club, complete with tables and lamps. At the front of the room are several giant screens and a big, empty, yellow canister. Roz, the movie's hilariously annoying administrative type, appears on one of the screens to set up the premise — the monsters need to harvest human laughter to energize their world. If we humans want the exit doors to ever open again, we better laugh up enough energy to power them.

Then the real fun begins. Roz introduces Mike Wazowski, the diminutive, Billy Crystal-voiced green monster who serves as the movie's star and the attraction's "Monster of Ceremonies." He brings onto the stage a cavalcade of monster comedians who, through the impressive technology of digital puppetry, interact with the human guests in real time. Theater attendants bring a microphone over to randomly selected audience members, who have the chance to converse with on-screen monsters, voiced by backstage actors. The effect is quite remarkable, creating the illusion that the characters are real, living, thinking beings. They're pretty darn funny too, routinely delivering fresh jokes that vary from one show to the next. Naturally, the laugh tank fills up in no time at all.

Right off the bat, the Monsters, Inc. Laugh Floor suffers from the same temporal dilemma as its next-door neighbor, Buzz Lightyear's Space Ranger Spin. *Monsters, Inc.* is set in either the late 1990s or early 2000s. The transition to Monstropolis, where not much time seems to have passed, spoils the retro "city of tomorrow" illusion that Tomorrowland supposedly strives for (unless we are to believe our portal also takes us back in time, in which case the monsters are working way too hard for a laugh). I doubt the early twentieth century visionaries saw wisecracking monsters as part of the future. They might have been impressed with the show's digital puppetry, though. To its credit, while the production may not take place in anyone's version of the future, it is at least a showcase of cutting-edge technology . . . for now, anyway. Remember that the whole point of Tomorrowland's 1994 relaunch was to adopt a vintage vision of the future instead of trying to keep technological pace with the one we're actually creating today. The Laugh Floor is nevertheless more in keeping with the latter. The show probably won't feel fresh for long, but for the time being, it gets by.

The attraction keeps in touch with tomorrow in another, more rhetorical way, too. The monsters on the laugh floor are harvesting laughter to power their world, a goal not unlike humanity's quest for alternative energy in planning our own future. The monsters found a way to become less fear-dependent in the movie and now they're tapping into a new kind of energy (Mike's very green, you see). Perhaps our own future will include alternative power sources. We probably won't find ours in canned laughter, but the Laugh Floor nevertheless resonates with one of the major forward-looking issues of our time.

However tangentially futuristic the attraction may be, the truth is that it's ultimately less interested in preserving the Tomorrowland theme than in simply showing guests a good time (and maybe promoting Pixar a little bit along the way). To that end, admittedly, the show succeeds.

The monsters specialize in the same brand of tongue-in-cheek, pun-laced, occasionally (and knowingly) cheesy humor that spreads throughout the whole resort. Partly scripted but highly improvisational, the show ensures variety from one performance to the next and gives the talented voice actors the freedom to work in their element. The material is nearly always funny, but while the laughs in the show are plentiful, the biggest joke of all just might be the attraction's name — or at least its acronym.[18]

Having originally entitled it the Monsters, Inc. Laugh Floor Comedy Club, Disney quickly dropped "Comedy Club" from the name about a month after opening. Maybe they were concerned that the name was too long (but then how do you explain the Tomorrowland Transit Authority PeopleMover?) or that people would expect a live comedy show. It may be that the term "Comedy Club" reminded guests of raunchy stand-up routines and had parents keeping their distance. Worry not; the humor here is wholesome, and there's just enough to crack at least one smile from everyone in the room. That's just what the monsters need.

Here in the human world, laughter isn't going to turn on our lights or cool down our houses anytime soon, but it does play an important part in giving us the energy we need to get through a busy and exhausting day at the Magic Kingdom. In the midst of thrill rides, sit-down shows, and a lot of potentially stressful time spent standing on foot, the Monsters, Inc. Laugh Floor is one of a few Magic Kingdom attractions chiefly designed to provide some much-needed comic relief... in the cool, in the dark, and on a seat. The show may not be a perfect fit for tomorrow (far from it), but it does give us a bit of the good-humored sustenance we'll need to make it there.

WATCH THIS - The Emperor's New Groove (2000)

Another underappreciated Animated Classic, *The Emperor's New Groove* is Disney's 40th in the official canon. The movie had originally been developed as a serious musical drama entitled *Kingdom of the Sun*, with Sting set to pen the original songs. For the better part of a decade, the project underwent numerous revisions as corporate turmoil began to brew. The movie was way behind schedule, the filmmakers couldn't agree on a stylistic approach, and a firm release date had already been set. By the time it saw the light of day, the project had a different director, a new title, and a lot less Sting. The pop/rock star's wife, Trudie Styler, produced a documentary about the whole ordeal, *The Sweatbox*, which was screened at the Toronto Film Festival in 2002 but has never been released to home video (perhaps because Disney owns those distribution rights — don't look for it on Disney+).

While the final product is less epic and grand than Disney had planned, it's still an abundantly entertaining comedy. With a voice cast that includes David Spade; *Monsters, Inc.* star John Goodman; and Patrick Warburton, it became the first outright comedy in the Animated Classics canon.

Space Mountain

Type: Roller coaster
Duration: 3 minutes
Height Restriction: 44 inches or taller (adult riders can switch off)
Popularity/Crowds: E-ticket
FastPass+: Yes; a top priority
Fear Factor: 4.25 out of 5 (near-total darkness; sharp turns and drops at moderately high speed; heights)
Wet Factor: None
Preshow: None
Boarding Speed: Moderate to Fast
Best Time to Visit without FastPass+: Very first thing in the morning or very end of the night
Special Comments: An absolute must, despite the long waits

Space Mountain is Walt Disney World's pride and joy, the crown jewel of the whole Resort. No other attraction inspires anxiety, commands crowds, or brings people back for more like Space Mountain, the great big granddaddy of WDW rides. The roller coaster just happens to be a Magic Kingdom original, granting the park bragging rights for what has become one of the most popular rides in the world. There's a lot to brag about too. Though a little scant on story, this psychologically intimidating behemoth of a ride is a mountain in more ways than one.

To Disney, a "mountain" is a member of an elite class of top-of-the-line Disney thrill rides: Splash and Big Thunder in Frontierland, Everest in Disney's Animal Kingdom, and Grizzly Peak over at Disney California Adventure, among others. The first such mountain was the Matterhorn Bobsleds attraction at Disneyland, a project Walt thought up himself but also initially had doubts about. Were he to open the Matterhorn, which his team had designed as a zippy steel roller coaster through the mystical Swiss Alps, he'd be introducing Disneyland's first real thrill ride, something he wasn't sure it needed. He'd always envisioned his parks as a place where story mattered more than speed, and kids would and could ride the same things their parents did. But as design work on the attraction progressed, Walt began to see it as a ride with universal family appeal, its modest thrills notwithstanding. Ultimately, he warmed to the idea, and it opened to the public in the summer of 1959.

Following the Matterhorn's wildly popular reception, Walt and his team started thinking that another family-friendly thrill ride might be in order, so Walt dreamt one up — Space Voyage, a lights-out coaster through the stars. Disneyland's creative team was already at work on a major Tomorrowland revamp, set to debut in 1967, and Space Voyage seemed an ideal headliner for the project. Walt lived just long enough to see his idea put on paper and given its current name, Space Mountain, before he died in December 1966. After his passing, the company's attention turned almost entirely to Walt Disney World (still a few years away from opening), and Space Mountain was put on hold.

Disney kept its focus on Florida for several years after the Magic Kingdom's big premiere in the fall of 1971. The park opened its gates without any thrill rides behind them, but when the new resort became an even bigger success than anyone had imagined it could be, Disney scrambled to change that. Rather than replicating the Matterhorn, which Fantasyland didn't have room for anyway, the Imagineers pulled out Walt's Space Mountain idea and went right to work. Space Mountain officially opened in Walt Disney World's Tomorrowland on January 15, 1975,[19] the second crest in the Disney mountain range and the first of its summits to rise in Florida. (A Disneyland version opened in 1977.)

We really can't go any further without acknowledging that, unlike Splash, Big Thunder, Everest, Grizzly Peak, and the Matterhorn, Space Mountain is not a mountain, at least not in the usual sense of the word. Mountains are geological formations. Space Mountain is just a building — a very cool building, but just a building nonetheless. Granted, Splash and those other mountains are technically just buildings too, but they at least look like mountains. The Space Mountain structure, meanwhile, is something altogether unique, resembling a futuristic space station of some sort, and it's incontrovertibly manmade. So what's with the name?

We've already said that the word "mountain" has a different meaning in the Disney dictionary than it has in Webster's. By bestowing the "mountain" banner upon a ride, Disney signifies that the attraction is one of its premium offerings, the Kingdom's crème de la crème. But whether the word had the same import in the mid-1960s, when Space Mountain got its name, is questionable. Only one Disney mountain existed then and the word wasn't even part of the proper title in Matterhorn Bobsleds'. The Imagineers probably had something else in mind when they came up with the name Space Mountain.

Early designs for the exterior reveal an earthier appearance than the smooth concrete and sleek steel we see today. Regardless of its final countenance, the whole concept for the ride makes it a mountain in the figurative sense of the word. Mountains don't refer merely to geological features; they can be personal challenges too. For a newcomer to thrill rides, Space Mountain is a fiercely intimidating prospect. Even for the roller coaster aficionado, the totally enclosed, pitch-black nature of the experience makes it a harrowing experience. The ride's sheer unpredictability arouses uneasy apprehension in all who approach its colossal edifice for the first time. It has proven itself capable of psyching out guests more than any other attraction in the Magic Kingdom, so those who summon the nerve to "climb the mountain," so to speak, emerge as conquerors.

Despite the fact that much of it is cloaked in darkness, Space Mountain is as attentive to detail as any other E-ticket Disney attraction. Here, each of the details is aimed at making the space setting both realistic and nerve-racking. The effect begins in the queue, ominous and entirely enclosed. Walkways that tilt ever upward and seem to grow increasingly narrow create a sense of claustrophobia. Low lighting and eerily soothing, rippling music create a mood of intrigue. Faux windows are placed throughout the skinny corridors. Through them, strangely warped panoramas of the cosmos are just barely visible. Whether you're supposedly in space at this point or not isn't clear. For that matter, nothing about this strange and mysterious experience is clear at all. Space Mountain is extraordinarily skimpy on narrative and always has been, especially in the Magic Kingdom. Almost paradoxically, the non-specificity of the story contributes brilliantly to the experience Disney wants to create. Disorientation is one of Space Mountain's key ingredients and everything about the ride is tailored to that aim.

Most of the attraction's story elements play before or after the ride itself. Space Mountain is not about being *in* space; it is about traveling *to* space from Earth — more specifically, from the thriving future metropolis that is Tomorrowland. In 2009, Disney substantially revised the queue to make that important point clearer than ever. This updated edition of the ride welcomes guests to "Starport Seven-Five," a new name that appears in a beautiful, recurring logo incorporating the mountain's exterior design. The boarding guests are greeted as "space travelers." Maps charting the galaxies and their various travel routes adorn the narrow hallways. These enhancements tell guests they've entered a spaceport. In that concept we find the visionary premise and promise of Space Mountain, an idea that Walt and the Imagineers had all along but which has often eluded guests.

The ride imagines a future in which a quick ride through space is as commonplace and easy as a flight across the country is today — or even easier, given the total absence of the TSA in Starport Seven-Five. (Keep your belt and shoes on, please.)

The ride itself is almost incidental to the experience as a whole, and yet the steel coaster shooting through the dark is immeasurably fun. Two tracks run parallel inside the building, occasionally coming close for a near-miss with the other. The 2009 upgrades label the two tracks Alpha and Omega and each has its small distinguishing idiosyncrasies. Though their close encounters are minimal and the other track can barely be seen, the divergent nature of the paths ensures that one ride can differ from the next and even adds something of a dueling component to the ride, giving a whole new meaning to the term "space race."

Careening through the blackness, sharp turns and surprisingly steep drops come without warning. In terms of speed, the ride is relatively tame by today's standards, but the wind blowing in the darkness and the giant projections on the ceiling make it a kind of hyper-speed planetarium. As stars and asteroids whiz by, passengers feel that they're flying much faster than they really are. In 2010, Disney added new music and sound effects to further enhance the intensity of the sensation. The world's fastest outdoor roller coaster couldn't pull off the kind of sensory illusions that make Space Mountain so mesmerizingly unique.

Remarkably, the ride even works under both the original concept of Tomorrowland (a future city seen through contemporary eyes) and the 1994-present premise of a future imagined by those who lived more than a hundred years ago. Its spaceport story could only unfold inside a city of the future, where citizens could embark on travels that simply aren't within our reach today and likely won't be anytime soon. Recreational space travel has long been an enduring dream for tomorrow, and the ride is every bit as timeless as that aspiration. Standing back and surveying the whole breadth of Tomorrowland, with Space Mountain towering majestically over its horizon, we can see that the ride really is in many ways a mountain. It's both peak Tomorrowland and Tomorrowland's peak.

WATCH THIS - The Black Hole (1979)

The Black Hole was a highly experimental movie for Disney, their first foray into serious science fiction. The movie borrows elements from both "Star Trek" and *Star Wars* but ends up less memorable or epic than either of them. Nevertheless, *The Black Hole* is an engaging and suspenseful movie that tells an interesting story with great acting and incredibly impressive visuals for 1979.

The big-name cast includes Ernest Borgnine, Anthony Perkins, Maximilian Schell, and the voices of Roddy McDowall and Slim Pickens as friendly robots. They play members of two different space crews who meet in the vicinity of a black hole, where they encounter the mysterious Dr. Hans Reinhardt (Schell).

Unfolding entirely aboard stations and ships in outer space, the movie has the immediate look and feel of Space Mountain. Disney could re-theme the ride as a *Black Hole* attraction and the story would fit right into place. (They shouldn't, but they could.)

Disney fans often talk about *The Black Hole* and *Tron,* the studio's two big sci-fi efforts in the pre-Eisner era, in the same breath. When *Tron: Legacy* hit theaters in 2010, one of its opening scenes featured a *Black Hole* poster. Later, in 2015, Disney's park-inspired *Tomorrowland* epic went to theaters with yet another *Black Hole* poster visible in a background shot. The *Tron: Legacy* team has long expressed interest in a major *Black Hole* remake, but it's been to slow to progress. Fans speculate that those poster shots might just be the studio's subtle reassurance that we ought not give up hope. Alas, at the time of this writing, the Mouse House has yet to give the project an official go-ahead. The fact that *Tron 3* has been in limbo for ten years does not inspire confidence. But maybe if we wish on one of Space Mountain's stars...

Walt Disney's Carousel of Progress

Type: Theater show
Duration: 18 minutes
Height Restriction: None
Popularity/Crowds: Low to Moderate
FastPass+: No
Fear Factor: None
Wet Factor: None
Preshow: A brief documentary on the attraction, featuring archival footage from its early days and development, plays while guests queue up outside.
Best Time to Visit: Anytime

Carousel of Progress is the longest ride in Magic Kingdom, but it might be the one I've ridden most. The infectious music, the easy-going temperament, the air conditioning, the guarantee you won't wait in a line. What's not to love? It's a four-act play where the actors are Audio-Animatronics, each act gets its own stage, and the seated audience rotates around them — a real "theatre in the round"!

To love the Carousel is to embrace its... shall we say... eccentricities? It is the story of a family not *quite* like any family I know. And their journey through time is not *quite* like the passage of time as I've experienced it myself. To work through all that and get to the bottom of what makes Carousel of Progress so great, we're going to dive a little deeper than we have with some of our other attractions.

Maybe the best way to understand the ride here in 2020 is to ride through it with someone seeing it for the first time. I wonder what it must be like to board this attraction, first conceived in the 1950s and last updated in 1994, as a newcomer with no context and a skeptical eye. Let's imagine.

Like a Virgin:
Carouseling for the Very First Time

The theater doors open and we take our seats in front of a sign that says this ride is "Walt Disney s" with no apostrophe but the empty space for one. George Orwell was right: English gets easier in the future. There are curtains here. I wonder what's behind them. The apostrophe, maybe? No, wait. We're moving. The curtain was a lie.

It's Act I. We meet a middle-aged man named John and his extended family, a gangly Cleaver clan and the apparent victims of a hereditary movement disorder that grows worse as hydraulic fluids run dry. The year is 1900-something, it is Valentine's Day, and Thomas Edison is the Elon Musk *du jour*. John introduces us to his daughter, despite the fact that she's dressed in the 1900s version of lingerie, and to his son, who is using the 1900s version of an iPhone to watch the 1900s version of porn. There's also a grandmother who sits dangerously close to the horn of her gramophone; a second daughter who will become a missing person by the 1920s; two pets (a parrot and a Bearded Collie, both of them sassy); and John's wife, Sarah. She irons. Here at the turn of the century, people have telephones, they can travel coast to coast in a week's time, and someone finally invented a box you can put ice in. Could life *be* any better? Probably not, but let's sing a song anyway: There's a great big beautiful tomorrow, and tomorrow is just… right now, I guess, because we're already in another room.

Act II. It's 1920-something on the Fourth of July: the hottest one in years. John's arms have been growing for two decades now, but the rest of him is still the same age. He's learning how to hold a fan and almost has the hang of it. There's time for stuff like that now that Mr. Edison has revolutionized the American kitchen. Things are so great, in fact, that his youngest daughter's disappearance doesn't faze John in the least. A face on the milk carton is a small price to pay for milk cartons that keep for more than a week. Still, there's a limit on progress: John blows a fuse (blowin' the whole neighborhood, he calls it). He flips it back on in time to show us his Uncle Orville taking a bath. Orville's a houseguest for the holiday, just like Grandfather Progress, who likes to sit inside and feel the thrill of an unlit firecracker in his wrinkled rubber hands. Even the littlest Progresses are getting into the spirit: Patty puts on a Statue of Liberty costume and Jimmy dresses like a Revolutionary guard. It's a regular ole Carousel of Cosplay. And Sarah's there too! She sews.

Act III. The 1940s. Rover is immortal but Thomas Edison is dead. By now, John stays behind a table to hide his arms altogether. Patty has inherited her father's blind belief in technology: she thinks she'll lose *a few inches* off her waistline in time for *tonight's* Halloween party. Meanwhile, Jimmy has inherited his dad's penchant for chauvinism: he calls

Patty an ugly wolf and howls. Rover, impervious to death and unafraid of consequence, wholeheartedly agrees. TV's a thing now, and the world is caught up in a "do-it-yourself" craze. John never does anything himself, though, except blowin' the neighborhood. That's why Sarah's in the next room, thinking she knows how to put up wallpaper. She does not.

Act IV. We have transcended time and ventured into the multi-verse, a version of the mid-1990s where HDTVs have already been invented and ovens respond to voice commands. Or maybe it's a version of the future where everyone still wears Bugle Boy shirts and the video games have gone vintage. I can't quite tell. Sarah's brainy now. She wears glasses. Grandmother looks younger somehow, but Jimmy is way, *way* older. Patty hasn't aged a day, though, so I guess that exercise machine *did* work, *Dad!* Speaking of Dad, if you had told John in 1900 that someday he would not only stand up inside his own kitchen but also *cook* something, he'd have blown the whole neighborhood. But here he is, burning the Christmas turkey. I guess man's biological ineptitude in the kitchen is one problem technology just can't solve. Group laugh. The end.

Easy, Rover. We're just having some fun with John Progress and his time machine.[20] Putting a finger on exactly how time passes in this play isn't easy. And yet the Carousel of Progress is widely, and rightly, considered a classic. Maybe its weirder elements and wonky timeline make it more endearing. Maybe its less progressive elements, particularly where gender is concerned, invite us to pause and reflect on what's really happening here — and how we got here.

Tomorrow's Yesterday: A Brief History of the Carousel of Progress

The Carousel of Progress made its grand debut at the 1964 New York World's Fair, but the concept dates back to Walt's plans in the '50s for an attraction called Harnessing the Lightning, part of his proposal for Disneyland's Edison Square. It was the same basic idea, but a robot would have hosted, and guests would have walked around the theatre instead. When Edison Square fell by the wayside, Harnessing the Lightning went back on Walt's shelf of ideas. We're lucky he didn't get to build it when he wanted to.

The standards at the World's Fair were high. General Electric wanted (and was willing to pay for) a spectacle, and in 1964, Audio-Animatronics that looked and moved like humans would fit the bill. Sure enough, newspaper reports from the time indicate that for all the marvels on display at the World's Fair (including demonstrations of thermonuclear fission explosions), the biggest hit by far was Disney's Audio-Animatronic technology.[21] The ride we now know as the Carousel of Progress became the flagship attraction in GE's Progressland, a strikingly domed pavilion dedicated to "the ways in which electricity, put to use for human betterment, is changing our world and our lives."

After the Fair ended in the fall of 1965, Progressland packed up the show and shipped it to Disneyland, where it reopened in 1967 as the Carousel of Progress. GE stayed on as sponsor and the show remained largely unchanged. In its original edition, each scene looked rather different from what we see today, with a different script and different voice actors too. But the gist was the same. Audiences traveled through the era of electricity twenty years at a time, originally ending in the then-present 1960s. That's more or less the version guests rode in Disneyland for the six years it spent there. Then GE started pining for Walt Disney World's newer, bigger, and more diversified tourist population. At GE's behest, the Carousel of Progress migrated from California's Tomorrowland to Florida's, where it opened on January 15, 1975 (the same day as Space Mountain).

Magic Kingdom's first version of the show introduced a number of substantial changes, including a new cast of voice actors, an updated finale set in the 1970s, and a new song from the Sherman Brothers. The world had fallen in love with "There's a Great Big Beautiful Tomorrow," but GE wondered why guests should bother with a great big beautiful tomorrow when they could buy great big beautiful GE appliances today. Heeding the request, Disney commissioned a new soundtrack celebrating the promise of the present. And so "The Best Time of Your Life" took its place in what would become a footnote of Disney history: the brief period of time when the Carousel of Progress had that song nobody liked. Its opening lyric, "Now is the time," spoke volumes. Was it a bad song? Not really, truth be told. Can the Sherman Brothers do wrong? How dare you. But this new ditty lacked the original's forward-looking optimism and the catchy refrain. If anything, it offered a "Second-Best Time," and who wants that?

The original song would return, but not until GE got out of the way. First came the '80s, when "progress" meant big hair and electric guitars. The Carousel of Progress had to have both. So 1981 brought yet another newly updated finale, now 40 years removed from the preceding scene, with the rest of the ride unchanged.

By the time the next decade rolled around, GE had already withdrawn its sponsorship (bowing out in 1985 after 21 years with the Carousel of Progress), meaning Disney could approach the attraction on their own terms. Out with the new and in with the old: "There's a Great Big Beautiful Tomorrow" reclaimed its rightful place in the ride's loudspeakers. It was just one of the many changes that would come in 1994, including a new voice cast (the original John, Rex Allen, now played the part of Grandfather, with Jean Shepherd assuming the starring role) and — you guessed it — a new finale. Disney's fourth take on the final scene went in a new direction: rather than setting itself in the current decade, as had become tradition, this new ending was ostensibly set in the year 2000 instead, looking six years into the future with an eye toward fast-approaching developments in home theater, gaming, and kitchen appliance technology. A few tiny adjustments and a new HDTV aside, the 1994 version still runs here today.[22]

"Yes, Dear": Progress, Gender Roles, and the Passage of Time

Once upon a time, in Walt's time, the word "progress" meant the march toward an inevitably better tomorrow... and not much more than that.

Thomas Gale Moore, a Stanford University scholar who, though controversial, has written extensively on the concept of progress and its evolution over the years, poses this question: "Will our sons and daughters be better off at the dawn of the third millennium than our grandparents were at the start of the twentieth century?"

But "nobody would have posed this question in 1900," Moore writes. "The answer was too obviously yes."[23]

Moore's point is instructive in our understanding of the Carousel of Progress. Though the version we ride today dates back to 1994, it is fundamentally the same attraction that debuted in 1964, which in turn grew out of plans that trace back to the 1950s, conceived by a man born in 1901. The Disney theme parks are largely reflective of Walt Disney's personal and creative interests. He was captivated by the promise of the future but also positively in love with the past, specifically his own past, wrapped up in the early-20th century optimism that Moore describes here.

Today, our concept of "progress" is at least as sociopolitical as it is technological, part of the new political patois. It is at the root of contemporary social concepts like "progressivism": the millennial measure of woke-ness and a term one would probably *not* use when describing Walt Disney's Carousel of Progress.

...Then again, maybe one could, if one tried.

It is impossible to be in the audience today and watch, without any sense of awareness or irony, as John sits comfortably in the square center of his house and speaks patronizingly to (and about) the women of the house, who are quite literally kept on the sidelines.

Notably, it is only John — the man of the house — who is allowed to address the audience directly. In the first three scenes, at least, the other characters speak only when in conversation with John. His role as narrator is not unlike that of the nightly news anchor, who sits in a similar position of power behind the news desk. Meteorologists, field reporters, and interviewees must speak to the anchor, not to us, unless the anchor has given them permission ("Amy, tell us what's happening there on the scene"), after which the reporter must cede authority to the anchor ("Back to you, Jim."). Some scholars have criticized this dynamic as dangerous to society because it privileges news anchors (and, by proxy, the corporations that put them behind the desk) as authoritarian filters for the truth.[24] Here in the Carousel of Progress, we might say that John's kitchen table is his news desk, and Sarah's "Yes, dear" is her "Back to you, John." His center seat on that stage is, like Archie Bunker's armchair, privileged and powerful.

That's the easy, surface-level read on the Carousel of Progress: charming, optimistic, well-meaning, but also a product of its time and, at least on some level, brazenly sexist. But when we start studying how earlier iterations of the attraction dealt with gender, we can come to two realizations: it might be that the attraction is sexist by design, and the whole point of that design might have been to challenge sexism in the first place — even in (and especially in) the 1960s.

The Progressland script of 1964, for example, presented an even more unabashedly paternalizing version of John — at least in the first three acts.

From Act I (Progressland, 1964)

John: That's my wife, Sarah.
Sarah: ...With my new wash day marvel, it takes only five hours to do the wash. Imagine!
John: That's right, folks. Now Mother has time for recreations like, uh...
Sarah: Like canning, and polishing the stove?
John: Okay, Mother. You just iron the wrinkles out of my shirts.
Sarah: Yes, dear.

From Act II (Progressland, 1964)

John: ...We can run as many wires as we need, in any direction, for Mother's new electrical servants: electric sewing machine, coffee percolator, toaster, waffle iron, refrigerator... Well, the days of lugging heavy, hot irons from an old stove to an ironing board are gone forever. And with an electric iron and electric lights, Mother has something to do to fill in her evenings. Now it's no problem at all to get my collars smooth. Right, Mother?
Sarah: Yes, dear.

From Act III (Progressland, 1964)

John: ...Mother's remodeling my basement workshop into something called a rumpus room. Be careful now, Mother.
Sarah: Don't worry about me, dear.
John: Mother's pretty ingenious, like using her food mixer for stirring... paint!? Well, that's my wife Sarah. You know, I remember when...
Sarah: Oh!! Darn!

> *We hear a loud crash.*
> **John:** Is there a doctor in the house?
> **Sarah:** Never mind. I'm all right, dear.

In each of these acts, we see John adopting a loving but also dismissive tone toward his wife, whose domain is entirely domestic and who seems to labor in his service (it's *her* food mixer but it's *his* basement). Their dynamic is one of subservience. As on the evening news, Sarah speaks only when spoken to, and only to John.

But then there is a change as the Progressland audience rotates into Act IV. Gone is the familiar house with a big, central kitchen and rotating rooms on the side. The Progresses are movin' on up, and their new digs sport an open floor plan, with the kitchen off to one side and the living room in the center (not unlike the layout we find in Act IV today). John and Sarah are sitting together, co-anchors, both of them in the living room and neither engaged in any household chores. *She* speaks first. To us.

From Act IV (Progressland, 1964)

> **Sarah:** Merry Christmas!
> **John:** Merry Christmas. We were just reminiscing about Christmas in the old days—
> **Sarah:** When getting ready for the holidays meant hectic days of cleaning house and preparing extra food…
> **John:** And as I started to say—
> **Sarah:** When Christmas Day arrived, I was too exhausted to enjoy it.
> **John:** But today, our new—
> **Sarah:** Yes, today our new, all-electric home gives us lots more time to enjoy ourselves.
> **John:** In fact, it's a—
> **Sarah:** And would you believe it? I'm cooking dinner, or rather, my electric range is. I just set the time and temperature controls and relax. It even has a self-cleaning oven. And we were able to pick our appliance colors from so many beautiful combinations.
> **John:** All of the appliances are improved today. Take a refrigerator; why, I remember when—

Sarah: When the man of the house had to work twice as many hours to earn one as he does now. And today we have a better product.
John: You took the words right out of my mouth, dear.
Sarah: And I'm thrilled with my new dishwasher. And doing a big family wash is simply a breeze now. Oh, how I used to dread doing that job.
John: Now Mother has time for—
Sarah: Activities like my Garden Club, the Literary Society, Ladies Bowling League, and…
The dog growls.
John: Quiet while Mother's interrupting!
Sarah: Home entertainment for our family is centered in one area. And from here we can enjoy radio, hi-fi, and stereo music anywhere in our home….
John: …Mother—
Sarah: It has brought convenience and enjoyment we never knew before.
John: …Mother—
Sarah: Dear, you've hardly said a word. Why don't you say something?

The contrasts between this scene and those that precede it are unavoidable and undeniable. No longer servile and deferential, Sarah now commands the conversation, and when she talks to us about technology, it isn't just about kitchen gadgets but also "radio, hi-fi, and stereo music." She's tech-savvy, confident, and assertive. She has a life outside the home too: gardening, reading, and bowling.

Granted, it is less than ideal to position the female character as "an interrupter" (not far removed from the stereotypical "nag"), or still to assign Sarah with the responsibility of cooking dinner, or for Sarah to appraise a refrigerator's value in terms of a man's labor hours. But by early 1960s standards, I dare say this is bordering on progressive (a word we'll return to later), and it's making a point. What seemed like casual sexism in the first three acts is now revealed to have been sexism by design. In Act IV, it becomes clear that John's attitude toward Sarah in those earlier scenes is as outmoded and passé as the ice box, the cistern, or the wash day marvel. Here, we find Walt and his team acknowledging that the domestic gender dynamics that were so pervasive during their childhoods and early adult lives are now antiquated, and that times have changed — even if the show never comes right out and says it.

Magic Kingdom's first version of the show, though, *does* come right out and say it. Here's an excerpt from 1975 (note that daughter Patricia was known as Jane in earlier versions of the show, and the dog went by a number of names, including Queenie and Sport[25]):

From Act II (Magic Kingdom, 1975)

John: ...I'm also getting a little static from my daughter.
Jane: I don't see any harm in my looking for a job, Daddy.
John: It's a man's world out there, Jane.
Jane: Well it won't always be, Father.
The dog grumbles in support of Jane.
John: Now cut that out, Queenie. You're supposed to be *man*'s best friend.

From Act III (Magic Kingdom, 1975)

Jane: ...We still Jitterbug but I'm having some trouble with the Rumba. I can't quite get the hip action...
John: Hmm, any more hip action and she'll disconnect something.
The dog growls.
John: Quiet, Sport. You can never underestimate the power of a woman. And speaking of women doing things, Mother is caught up in the new do-it-yourself craze. She's remodeling our basement into something called a rumpus room. *(John chuckles.)* Mother's pretty ingenuous, like using her food mixer for stirring... paint!? Well, that's my wife Sarah.
Sarah: John?
John: Yes, dear.
Sarah: I was just thinking.
John: About what?
Sarah: That if you hired a man to do this, wouldn't you pay him?

John: Well of course, dear.
Sarah: Then I should get equal pay.
John: Well, um, we might negotiate something later on, dear.
Sarah: When??

The cuckoo clock strikes.
The cuckoo bird sings, "Now is the time, now is the best time."
John addresses the clock.

John: You stay out of this! Well, if it's time for anything, it's time to move on…

From Act IV (Magic Kingdom, 1975)

John: Well, it sure is nice to have the whole family home for the holidays. Right now, I'm cooking my one and only specialty…
Sarah: My, that chili sure sounds good.
Grandmother: Mmm, smells good too!
John: And it better be good, Grandma. With Mother spending all of her time on the Clean Waters Committee, I may be the only one with time left to cook.
Sarah: Now dear, you encouraged me to get involved.
John: Good grief, did I do that?
Jane: My mother the activist. I think that's kind of neat!
Sarah: I think it's kind of neat too! Did I show you the letter from the mayor, thanking us for getting the bond issue passed?
Jimmy: You've done it again, Mom.
Grandmother: In my day, women only had time for fun things, like—
Sarah: Canning and polishing the stove?
Grandfather: Now, Grandma, things haven't been all that bad. We've been a pretty good team.
Jane: But on *your* team, Grandma spent most of her time on the bench!

Group laugh.

Here we see the Carousel of Progress engaging directly with the women's liberation movement that emerged in the late 1960s and was in full swing by 1975. This version of the play reveals John to be sexist by design much earlier than Progressland did. Jane's Act II retort to her father's reminder that this is "a man's world"— "Well it won't always be, Father" — is a winking nod to the audience, which understands that Jane's answer is prescient.

Act III's discourse on equal pay for women is practically ripped from the headlines of the '70s (which, regrettably, look a lot like our headlines today). I suppose we might read the exchange as playful or flirtatious — tongue-in-cheek banter between husband and wife — and to his credit, John *does* refer to it as "*our* basement" this time. But his staunch opposition to equal pay makes him something of a good-natured cad. Here again, Archie Bunker is a useful point of comparison: a character can be charming despite espousing regressive viewpoints *if* the character's very purpose is to serve as a foil for the more enlightened characters around him, and if he is shown to have a heart. I submit that John's casual sexism — in the first three acts of *each* version of this show — serves the same essential purpose as Archie Bunker's backward blowhardedness, even if John is much friendlier and more genial than Archie on his best day.

It is interesting, though, to compare 1975's final act to the one we find now. Whereas the 1970s finale was at least as much about women's liberation as technology, the characters don't even touch on the topic today.

What are we to make of that change? Has the current version taken a step backward by wiping away all its self-awareness? I don't think so. It seems to me that the attraction is still very much aware of the shift in gender dynamics that takes place between Acts III and IV, only it's made less explicit (read: in your face). John's reply to his dog in 1974 — "You're supposed to be *man*'s best friend" — is an astoundingly transparent line, and even a little bit on the nose. Might this new version be more powerful in its restraint? When we arrive at the "future," it's one where the husband and wife are standing together to the side of the stage and neither is talking about the other's proper role in the household. Sarah isn't an environmental activist anymore, but we find her at a desk, bespectacled, and working at a laptop. There's not an ironing board in sight. She's programing the 'smart house' system, setting up the oven controls so that

John can roast the turkey. Here, as in the versions that ran in the 1970s and '80s, John is cooking dinner, but this time, he and Sarah are contributing equally to the task at hand, as partners. If anyone is sitting center stage, it's the daughter, who gets the lion's share of the dialogue this time around and sits holding a ski boot in her hands — she's athletic, and not because she wants to get in shape for a boy. And for the first time, no one addresses the audience directly. They talk to each other instead, everyone on equal footing in the same household.

Today's finale might not *expressly* call our attention to the shift in gender dynamics that has taken place throughout the play, but the shift is there nevertheless, made plain for us to see. It is my feeling that art is often more powerful when it is less overt, when the audience is trusted to make the observations and connections for itself.

Mind you, this newest version probably isn't quite a feminist ideal, and I won't go so far as to say that the attraction tries to be, or that I'd be qualified to determine whether it is (I'm certainly not). Likewise, I acknowledge that there are problems beyond gender. (As scholar Stephen M. Fjellman writes, "The final scene shows how we would live if we were white, rich, and residing in California.")[26] But Thomas Gale Moore reminds us that progress isn't the same thing as perfection; in fact, it is its opposite.[27] Perfection, were it attainable, would represent the end of progress. Does that mean the Carousel of Progress has no room for improvement where its depiction of gender roles in the household is concerned? On the contrary, it means precisely that there *is* room for improvement still. But there's more at work in this attraction than meets the eye. Upon the careful kind of study we've done here, the attraction reveals itself to be a plea for gender equality, an endorsement of *cultural* progress (beyond merely electrical progress), and even an admonishment of the past — an admonishment that Walt Disney conceived of himself and one that carries his name today. Somebody tell Meryl Streep.[28]

Improving on Progress:
How to Fix the Final Scene Today (and for Tomorrow)

The passage of time creates problems for the Carousel of Progress, as it does for most things in Tomorrowland. When the attraction first opened, only 20 years separated the last two acts. Then with the updates in each decade, the gap widened to 30, then 40, and now 60. The year-2000 finale was a thing of the future when it opened in 1994. Today, it's two whole decades into the past, meaning that audiences are already separated from the preceding 1940s scene by some 80 years — longer than the entire timeline of the original World's Fair attraction.

Speaking strictly from a Tomorrowland perspective, the finale isn't out of date. The living room gathering in the year 2000, with its self-automated kitchen and high-tech gadgetry, is probably pretty consistent with what early twentieth century visionaries might have imagined for the year 2000. So even a hundred years from now, the fourth act will always be in keeping with what the Imagineers set forth in 1994 as Tomorrowland's mission — presenting the past's future that never was. That said, the jump from 1940 in one scene to 2000 in the next is quite a jolt for audiences, and the selection of the year 2000 increasingly feels as random as would any other year drawn out of a hat. The first three acts depict a time that actually came to pass in the United States, but the 1994 version of 2000 never did. The current finale therefore feels lost in time — neither vintage, nor contemporary, nor futuristic.

This uncomfortable time warp was inevitable. There's a reason the Carousel of Progress used to update its finale every ten years or so. Today, the last scene has gone unrevised longer than ever before, likely because waning attendance in the spinning theatre has discouraged Disney from investing in an overhaul. Rumors of closure have dogged the attraction for years now, but Walt Disney World insists that the Carousel isn't going anywhere. Let's hope that's true.

But audiences already openly laugh when Grandpa and Patty marvel over LaserDiscs and car phones. Sooner or later, something's got to give. One can imagine various solutions: setting Act IV in the year 2020, or going the other direction and reverting to 1964's original ending, or maybe fast-forwarding to the year 2071 (Magic Kingdom's 100th anniversary) or a Jules Verne-ian future fantasy.[29] Another solution might be to add a fifth act.

In Disneyland and at the World's Fair, there *was* a fifth act. Guests exited the carousel and walked upstairs to view a diorama of "Progress City," a metropolis of the future as presented by GE. John and Sarah narrated, building on their dialogue in Act IV and excitedly explaining that everything in Progress City was already within reach in 1964. But Magic Kingdom never offered that second-story tour, choosing instead to display just part of the Progress City model inside the Tomorrowland Transit Authority Peoplemover.

As the ride runs now, there are two additional rooms with stages, one for entry and the other for exiting. If operational logistics would allow it, facilitating both entry and exit within a single room (and during the course of a single act) would open up the additional room for a fifth act. Alternatively, Magic Kingdom might consider doing something with that second floor.

With Mind and Heart: The Ride's Appeal

Though it first opened more than fifty years ago, the ride's central concept remains a novelty today. Whatever else you might say about the Carousel of Progress, you can't deny it this: it's the only play you'll ever ride. But I think the attraction's appeal comes down to more than just its mechanical novelty.

The winter holidays have always been a part of Carousel of Progress (today as in the 60s, the ride ends at Christmas; in the 1970s and '80s, it ended on New Year's Eve), but the other holidays didn't get in on it until 1994. Previous versions cycled through the seasons but never tied them to a particular celebration. While some have lamented this change, and I understand the desire to return to the way Walt designed it, I think the festivity does a lot to bond us with these characters. It's similar to the effect *Meet Me in St. Louis* has as we watch a single family observe various holidays throughout the year, or that Netflix's "Stranger Things" has as each season of the series ties itself to a particular holiday or time of year. We get the sense that we've lived with these characters throughout distinct times of their lives — times that they would likely count among their most special.

Speaking of Netflix, I am always struck by the tone of bemusement these characters have when talking about the up-and-coming technology of their day. The Wright Brothers are foolish, snap-on electric lights are laughable, and television is fluff. How often do we talk about the up-and-coming innovations of our day with similar sarcasm, whether it's Siri, Snapchat, selfie sticks, or new math? Hindsight is 20/20. Watching the Progress clan laugh at things that would go on to change the world can remind us that what might seem to be the silly whims of a younger, distracted generation may go on to become not only commonplace but also essential to society, the building blocks for the *next* wave of progress, and may even end up saving lives or enriching the world.[30] Maybe the tech and trends we all tend to laugh at today aren't quite so silly or worthy of exasperation as we might think, and the Carousel of Progress gently reminds us to keep an open mind. After all, if perfection is progress's opposite, closedmindedness is surely its foe.

There's also a kind of comfort that comes from realizing just how much effort the simplest things used to take, such as when Sarah tells us about the five hours she spends doing the wash. It makes us feel grateful for the modern conveniences we take for granted, and such opportunities for gratitude are always welcome. There is also the Swiss Family Treehouse effect: knowing that human beings got by in such conditions confirms for us that we too are capable, perhaps of much more than we realize. And that as busy as we are, the demands on our time could be even worse.

Watching the show, it's easy to imagine yourself up on that stage, telling the story of your life. Which decades, chapters, or seasons would you choose if you could only pick four? What would be the prevailing narrative? For the Progress family, it's the betterment of their lives by way of technology and evolving gender norms. How much has technology or cultural change impacted *yours*?

One of the best insights we can take away from the attraction is this: the past wasn't long ago, and change — both technological and cultural — comes fast, even if it seems slow while it's happening. It's what happiness guru Gretchen Rubin calls a "secret of adulthood": "The days are long but the years are short."[31] On the Carousel of Progress, the better part of a century passes in under 20 minutes. Real life can feel like that too.

Perhaps most importantly, the attraction stands as the most significant vestige of Walt's personal presence in the park. This ride — entitled Walt Disney's Carousel of Progress since '94 — has the distinction of being not only the longest-running theater show with the most performances in American history but also the oldest exhibit in all of Walt Disney World, one of only two Magic Kingdom attractions to bear Walt Disney's name in its official title,[32] *and* the only one in the whole Florida resort that he actually touched with his own hands.[33] For a Disney destination that opened after its benefactor died, that's an important connection to the man whose creative vision is the reason people come here.

Walt spoke often of his ambition for innovation and his deep sense of personal responsibility to make a difference in people's lives. He was fascinated by America's development from the late nineteenth century into the mid-twentieth. That's how we end up with a Tomorrowland attraction that takes place principally in the past.

The Sherman Brothers thought of "There's a Great Big Beautiful Tomorrow" as a personal anthem for Walt, and by all accounts, they got it right. He believed fiercely in The American Dream, having fully lived it himself, and so while the lyrics aren't so specific as to narrowly pertain to it, we might easily read them as a meditation on The American Dream in particular: "Man has a dream, and that's the start," but he must "follow his dream with mind and heart," and "when it becomes a reality, it's a dream come true for you *and* me."

That was, fundamentally, how Walt seemed to understand The American Dream: it required hard work ("hard facts… have created America," he said when dedicating Disneyland), but once realized, the benefit wouldn't be for the individual alone, but rather for the good of society. From Fantasound and Technicolor to the storyboard, the monorail, the multi-plane camera, and even the Experimental Prototype Community of Tomorrow, Walt was in love with ideas and technologies that would improve our way of life.[34] His Carousel of Progress wholly embodies those values and aspirations, almost as if he designed a living monument to his personal worldview. It's no coincidence that the original attraction opened at the turn of the 20th century and closed in the 1960s; it was literally the story of America as Walt knew it during his lifetime. No wonder the Carousel of Progress is said to have been his single favorite attraction.[35]

You know, the Carousel was in the middle of migrating to Disneyland when Walt passed away. The Progress City diorama that sat on top of it would have been the basis for his EPCOT city, but he passed away before that could be finished too. But both those projects — and the world — kept going without him. There's no stopping progress. None of us can escape it. But as long as the Carousel of Progress continues to operate here in Tomorrowland, Walt Disney will always be a part of tomorrow.

WATCH THIS - Pollyanna (1960)

Despite disappointing box office returns, *Pollyanna* was one of Disney's most critically acclaimed films up until that time. In the movie that made her a household name, young Hayley Mills plays an orphan girl whose unbounded optimism genuinely changes the town she lives in. The heartwarming story is set in 1910, which falls halfway between the ride's first and second acts. Not only does the movie look the part as an ideal accompaniment for this ride, it feels it too. *Pollyanna* isn't just about the virtue of optimism; it's about the *power* of optimism. That's a belief Walt Disney cherished and it compelled him to deliver some of his best work, including both Pollyanna and the Carousel of Progress.

Chapter 6

Main Street, U.S.A.

*"Main Street, U.S.A. is America at the turn of the century —
the crossroads of an era. The gas lamps and the electric lamp —
the horse-drawn car and auto car. Main Street is everyone's hometown —
the heart line of America."*

Walt Disney

Our final dedication is one Walt never gave, at least not at Disneyland's grand opening. He was later credited with describing Main Street this way, as everyone's hometown. It is, but more particularly, it is Walt's hometown. Main Street, U.S.A. is his love letter to the world he knew as a small boy in Marceline, Missouri. It has all the charm of any real-world, turn-of-the-century main street, but this one isn't boarded up and dry. It's alive and in its prime, probably shinier and snazzier than the real thing ever was.

Main Street, U.S.A. is a different sort of land, and we'll take a different approach. The attractions on Main Street are never *on* Main Street for long. There are the olden Main Street Vehicles, but you'va gotta catch 'em while you can; they clear out when the crowds get thick. There's the Walt Disney World Railroad station sitting atop the park's main entrance — but after the "All aboard!" it's on its way. The interactive

Sorcerers of the Magic Kingdom game starts on Main Street but soon sends us off to other parts of the park. The afternoon parade and the evening fireworks work their magic and then evaporate for the day. So before we contemplate its attractions individually, let's take a moment to consider Main Street as an attraction all its own. Here's a toast to the shopping, sugar, and shindiggery that make this razzle-dazzle boulevard an instant pick-me-up that even its own Starbucks can't beat.

Main Street, U.S.A.
Type: Themed Environment
Duration: Self-paced
Popularity/Crowds: High
Best Time to Visit: Anytime, but expect major congestion during fireworks, nighttime shows, and parades.
Special Comments: The live entertainment here is not to be missed. Check the daily show times guide for the Dapper Dans (Disney's resident barbershop quartet), the Main Street Philharmonic (the park's own brass marching band.), and the Main Street Trolley Show at the very least.

Walking down Main Street is like an orientation on day one in the "Disney bubble," that special headspace where we close off the worries of the world and find the unburdened version of ourselves that used to feel so free. On one end is Town Square, a plaza we'd expect to find in any small town of the early twentieth century. On the other is a massive castle, which we don't expect to see anywhere in America at any time. There must be something magical about this road and the destinations it can lead us to — a yellow brick road in red.

Fans have likened Magic Kingdom to a movie and Main Street to its opening credits reel. The windows at the top of each little building bear the name of someone instrumental in the resort's development. Alternatively, we might think of the park as a giant theater, with Main Street the red carpet leading to the five genre "films" showing today: the adventure epic, the western, the historical period piece, the fantasy, and the sci-fi spectacle. Street vendors sell popcorn and concessions to round out the metaphor. The Main Street Cinema, even if now just a façade, captures the excitement of motion pictures at the dawn of the twentieth century.

While Disneyland's Main Street is modeled entirely after Marceline as it was when Walt was born in 1901, Magic Kingdom's incorporates other regional influences too, most notably turn-of-the-century New England architecture. Its bigger cross-section of the country reflects Walt Disney World's status as the Disney resort more Americans call their home away from home. It's a literal Memory Lane for America, or at least its eastern half. There's the hattery, the candy shop, the bakery, some penny arcade games, Casey's Corner for corn dogs, and traffic of the under-twenty miles per hour variety. A horse-drawn trolley crosses paths with a fire engine, a horseless carriage, and a double-decker omnibus. You can catch any of them for a quick ride to the castle or devote your morning to round-trip tours on all four if they strike your fancy.

These antique vehicles putter past prancing horses while a brass band marches and a barbershop quartet sings. The archetypes of small-town politics bring character to the place. Will Helpya shakes hands as presiding City Council Chairman. Hildegard Olivia Harding and Bea Starr campaign for the woman's vote along with larger-than-life personalities like Inga DaPoint, Victoria Trumpetto, Sheila Shufflehop, and Constance Purchase. Chief Smokey Miller keeps the fire station in ship shape while Noah Lott shares the 4-1-1.

Main Street is so immersive largely because there's so much activity here. Surely it must be one of the world's busiest thoroughfares, the Shibuya of the southeast U.S. There aren't any real rides or big-banner shows, and yet there is so much to do. This is the gathering place for parades and fireworks... home to ice cream, cookies, coffee, and a gift shop the size of Missouri. If other small towns made this much money, they wouldn't stay small for long!

We walk into the Magic Kingdom expecting to find "The Most Magical Place on Earth," or to borrow Disneyland's better-known motto, "The Happiest Place on Earth."[1] Main Street tends to that from the moment we step inside; the hustle and bustle teems by design. The beaming faces of the storybook cast, the buoyant greeting from the chairman, the toe-tapping ragtime ditties, and the foot traffic from tens of thousands of park guests exuding their contagious excitement all foster a pervasive sense of joy.

Each morning kicks off with a remarkably talented cast dancing to the earwormy "Walking Right Down the Middle of Main Street," unfolding right there on the walkway like a flash mob or a movie musical brought to life. It doesn't stop there. From the piano player at Casey's Corner to the impromptu pal-arounds with Pluto and friends in Town Square, there's always something happening on Main Street. There's the daily flag retreat, the glass blowers, the hand chimes, and an effervescent street party with the catchiest theme song you've ever heard ("It's a Good Time," the anthem for Main Street's MousekeDance). At night, each building lights up with a warm white trim. Nothing glows quite like it. Nighttime is probably the best time to be there.

Main Street is both the first and last of the six lands in Magic Kingdom. It's the only way to get in or out, which means it's the one part of this park every guest is guaranteed to experience — twice. By the end of the night, you're on such a high from junk food and good times that you're dangerously susceptible to giddy delirium. The urge to buy a lollipop the size of your face and dance the Charleston is nearly irresistible. It isn't unusual to see teenagers skipping or grown men dancing a jig with their kids. Everyone is whistling or laughing or marching to the relentlessly up-tempo beat of the world's cheeriest music. There is literally a song in the air. If this isn't The Happiest Place on Earth, I don't know what is.

WATCH THIS - Meet Me in St. Louis (1944)

Everything about *Meet Me in St. Louis* feels like Main Street. The time's right, for one thing. Set in 1904, the movie takes place just three years after Walt Disney's birth and unfolds in St. Louis, Missouri, just a few hours' drive from the small town of Marceline where he grew up. This is the film that gave us "Have Yourself a Merry Little Christmas," as well as "The Trolley Song," which is sometimes performed as part of Main Street's morning trolley show.

The movie, starring Judy Garland, follows one family over the course of a year. Special attention is paid to Halloween and Christmas, which also happen to be cause for major fanfare on Main Street each year. The importance of family and home are among the movie's prevailing themes, and those sentiments are obviously integral to the Main Street atmosphere, too.

Meet Me in St. Louis was produced by MGM and is currently distributed digitally and on Blu-ray and DVD by Warner Home Video.

Walt Disney World Railroad

Type: Train ride
Duration: 20 minutes for a full circuit tour around the park
Height Restriction: None
Popularity/Crowds: Low to Moderate
FastPass+: No
Fear Factor: None
Wet Factor: None
Preshow: None
Boarding Speed: Moderate to Fast. Trains depart on a regular basis.
Best Time to Visit: Anytime, but the attraction typically closes one hour prior to the evening's first fireworks show.
Special Note: As this book goes to press, the Walt Disney World Railroad is expected to remain closed well into 2020, and possibly for the entire year, in order to accommodate construction at the TRON project in Tomorrowland. While the attraction is closed, the train is available as a backdrop for photos at the Main Street Station.

The Walt Disney World Railroad (WDWRR) is a ride without a home. This scenic train trip around the outer berm doesn't belong to any one of the park's six lands, but by the time it's made a single loop around the park's perimeter, it has chugged through all but one of them. Much is said about the railroad's train stations and the destinations they serve, but too often, the ride itself goes overlooked

It's no secret that Walt Disney loved trains, so much so that he built a scaled-down but fully functional steam engine railway in his own backyard. Walt's inaugural train ride into Disneyland even kicked off the opening day ceremony in 1955, that park's rail line having been inspired by Walt's own backyard *Carolwood Pacific*. (Televised for all to see, Disneyland's grand opening ranks as one of history's most-watched live broadcasts.) With the exception of Shanghai, each of Disney's castle parks around the world has opened with a train station as its foyer and a real railway running through the park.

The WDWRR uses four trains, each named after someone integral to the Disney legacy — Walt, his wife Lillian, his brother Roy, and Imagineer Roger E. Broggie. Lillian's, the *Lily Belle*, is doubly special because it was built in 1928, the same year Mickey Mouse was born. Its trips are usually limited to each morning's opening ceremony.

The other trains take guests around the park, making three stops along the way. The first and easiest to find is Main Street Station, the turn-of-the-century depot at the front of the park. When Magic Kingdom first opened, Main Street's was the *only* train station, meaning that if you got on, you were committing to a full 20-minute "grand circle tour" of the park. That changed when a second train station opened in Frontierland the next year. Tucked away on a second-story platform just behind Splash Mountain's entryway, Frontierland Railroad Station is charmingly rustic with a ticket booth inside, old newspapers that treat the land like a real place, and "wanted" posters for various frontier bandits.

The third and final stop is Fantasyland Station, which opened in 1988 as part of Mickey's Birthdayland, considered the park's seventh land at the time but since annexed by Fantasyland and converted to Storybook Circus (see *Chapter Four* for a more detailed history). With the circus came a whole new train station for Fantasyland, a lovely barn-like building with a covered walkway and a train-shaped weather vane rising from the roof. The face on the depot clock reads "Carolwood Park," a tribute to Walt's backyard railroad.[2]

Assuming you board at Main Street, the ride begins in early nineteenth century small town America and embarks on a most unusual journey through different eras and realms. Within moments, the train is chugging through the jungles of Africa and Asia. Steel drums and the sounds of wild animals wash over the tracks. A minute later, the train has returned to America, but it's half a century earlier than where it started. The train pulls up alongside the cars of Big Thunder Mountain Railroad as they careen through the enormous buttes of the Wild West. Then the WDWRR crosses over an antique bridge and behind Tom Sawyer Island, where a hidden part of Frontierland is visible only to railroad riders. There's a teepee outpost, but no sooner has it passed them than the train rolls out of reality altogether and into the world of cartoons and fantasy.[3] Then it's off to the future!

The train's narrator used to became audibly confused as he saw spaceships and the like. After all, one wouldn't expect a steam engine in a city of tomorrow, and yet here it is... but not for long. As quickly as it came in, the train travels back in time to the familiar environs of Main Street, U.S.A. We've just taken a voyage across continents, through centuries, and into the imagination — all in under 20 minutes.

Like the Liberty Square Riverboat, the Walt Disney World Railroad experience is a postmodern narrative that journeys across myriad settings and stories to piece together an adventure all its own. That's the Magic Kingdom in a nutshell, so the railroad is effectively a pastiche of the whole park experience. In the tradition of the *Polar Express*, the *Hogwarts Express*, and Mr. Rogers's neighborhood trolley, the Walt Disney World Railroad train is a magical and mysterious one. Disney doesn't market it that way, but that makes its surrealistic movement through the park all the more alluring, like a great and wondrous surprise. Those first boarding at Main Street haven't the slightest hint of the time warps and hidden scenery waiting ahead. More than a simple transit system or a sightseeing tour, the ride turns out to be an enchanted expedition that defies the constraints of place and time.

A magical train trip suits the Magic Kingdom, where an ordinary perimeter tour just wouldn't do. But to appreciate the illusion, you'll need to pay attention to your surroundings. If life's about the journey and not the destination, then so is the Walt Disney World Railroad. Those who just want a lift to Splash Mountain might miss out on the "magic" of the train that gets them there. The best way to ride these rails is to ride them full circle, from Main Street to Main Street. If you do, you'll find yourself on a train of thought, bound for an enlightening exploration of the interwoven story worlds that make the Magic Kingdom so stimulating.

WATCH THIS – Chitty Chitty Bang Bang (1968)

Many people mistakenly assume *Chitty Chitty Bang Bang* is a Disney movie. Understandable. Released just four years after *Mary Poppins*, the movie reunites much of the *Poppins* team. The Sherman Brothers, who wrote all of the *Poppins* songs, and Irwin Kostal, who penned its score, come together again to create the top-notch *Bang Bang* soundtrack. Dick Van Dyke, Disney's Bert, takes the lead role here as offbeat inventor Caractacus Potts. (Julie Andrews was reportedly asked to co-star as Truly Scrumptious but declined, passing the role to Sally Ann Howes instead.) It's not surprising then that the movie has a distinctly Disney charm about it.

Caractacus and his two children grow fond of Truly, the daughter of a big-time candy manufacturer. They drive out to the beach for a picnic one day, and when the tide comes in, their motorcar suddenly becomes a floating vessel. Clearly, the car, which they've nicknamed

> Chitty Chitty Bang Bang, has magical properties that can — and do — take them on a magnificent adventure into a world of fantasy.
> When riding the Walt Disney World Railroad, thinking about the train as a kind of Chitty Chitty Bang Bang can help us appreciate its trajectory. Though now an MGM film, *Chitty Chitty Bang Bang* was originally distributed to theaters by United Artists. It is currently distributed digitally and to home video by Twentieth Century Fox Home Entertainment (which means the home video rights are Disney's for the time being, even if the movie itself is not).

Sorcerers of the Magic Kingdom

Type: Live-action role-playing game
Duration: Unlimited
Height Restriction: None
Popularity/Crowds: Low to Moderate
FastPass+: No
Fear Factor: None
Wet Factor: None
Preshow: Optional training session (recommended for first-timers)
Best Time to Visit: Anytime
Special Comments: Lines fluctuate from one portal to the next throughout the day; if you arrive at a portal and there's a long line, you may wish to visit another attraction and return a little later.

Magic Kingdom plays to a broad crowd, but in February 2012, it introduced a different type of attraction to target a different type of audience: nerds. Happily, your author belongs to just such a group and can tell you all about it. Maybe I can even convince you that it's actually pretty cool, at least in a changes-how-you-think-about-Magic Kingdom kind of way.

One does not ride or watch Sorcerers of the Magic Kingdom. Rather, one plays it. This makes it different from most other attractions, especially within this particular park (though Adventureland does now offer a less elaborate adventure quest themed to Pirates of the Caribbean). Open to all guests at no additional charge, Sorcerers of the Magic Kingdom is an interactive card-trading and role-playing game with a storyline that incorporates four of the park's six lands. Playing requires a fair amount of foot travel and a willingness to be judged by others for looking decidedly dorky. If that's okay with you (and it is with me), then let's head together into Merlin's secret lair on Main Street, U.S.A.

That's where Sorcerers begins. The Main Street Fire Station, previously home to an unremarkable gift shop, is now headquarters for enlisting new sorcerers. A banner at the entrance reads, "Help protect our community!" Inside, we meet an animated Merlin (the wizard from Disney's *The Sword in the Stone*, appearing here in a rare nod to the oft-overlooked 1963 classic), who talks to us from a round video screen, which he calls a magic portal. He gives us a rundown on the war that's breaking out across the Magic Kingdom at this very moment.

We learn that Merlin is charged with guarding the Crystal of the Magic Kingdom, an almighty orb that protects the kingdom from evil forces and grants considerable power to whoever possesses it. When Hades (the arch-villain from 1997's *Hercules*) finds out about the Crystal, he sends his minions (Pain and Panic, also of *Hercules*) to steal it from Merlin's cottage in the woods. They're nearly successful, but Merlin catches them in the act. A scuffle ensues and the Crystal is accidentally broken into several pieces, four of which get scattered around the kingdom.

Now there's a race between Merlin and Hades, and whoever mends the Crystal first will determine the fate of the Magic Kingdom. Unfortunately, Hades has recruited a whole host of bad guys to aid in his quest. Being the lord of the underworld and all, he's even able to resurrect villains presumed dead. Merlin's no match for them alone, and that's where we come in. Armed with a little magic, we can help Merlin fend off the villains and recover each missing Crystal piece before it's too late.

Apparently, our wizard-in-chief created a whole network of mystic portals, just like the one we find inside the Main Street Fire Station, and he spread them throughout Magic Kingdom. When opened at the right time, the portals will "show you the thing you seek." It's a safe bet that the villains and their henchmen will be hot on our heels, tracking down the portals for themselves.

So how can we, mere mortals, possibly hope to open mystic portals and fend off mighty evildoers? Turns out all we need is every poindexter's favorite weapon — trading cards.

After Merlin recites his spiel, we move to the rear of the Fire Station, where cast members link our MagicBands to the game and hand us a shrink-wrapped set of five spell cards and a map. Practice portals in the firehouse let us get into the groove before going off to war. Just use the map to find the proper portal (always a video screen, sometimes cleverly concealed within building façades), hold your MagicBand up to the keyhole you find once you get there, and wait for on-screen instructions to appear. At any given portal, there's a good chance you'll be confronted by an on-screen villain, and if you are, you can defend yourself by holding up a spell card, which embedded cameras will recognize as a specific spell. Once you've defeated them, you'll hear the next part of the story and then be directed to a different portal, where your adventure will progress.

If this is all sounding like it's a little too involved for your taste, I regret to inform you we've just scratched the surface. But if it seems right up your alley, then put down your comics, tape up your glasses, and brace yourself, because we're about to take the nerdiness to warp speed.

As mentioned earlier, the game begins with a shrink-wrapped pack of five cards. Those are five *random* cards, out of more than 70 that exist. Every card features a different Disney character and a different spell. Not only that, they each fall into different categories and are assigned unique numerical values that make particular cards stronger in certain battles than in others. Some cards are quite common while others are extremely rare. Collecting them is a challenge in itself, one that thousands of people have already accepted — and with surprising exuberance, I might add.

But wait, there's more. You can *combine* cards. And when you combine them, they produce *new* kinds of spells. Some combinations are more potent when used against particular enemies, and the spells increase in strength and pizzazz the more you use them. If you want to defeat the game — that is, conquer every portal and recapture the Crystal pieces for Merlin — you'll eventually need to think critically about how you're casting your spells or else they won't measure up to the villains.

Collecting all the spell cards is easiest when you trade your duplicates with other players who have spares. It's not unlike trading baseball cards. Impromptu trading happens in the park all the time, usually near a game portal, outside the Main Street headquarters, or at Sorcerers' alternate HQ in Liberty Square. You can also turn to various internet fan forums to trade after you return home from vacation, or you can seek out rare spell cards for sale on sites like eBay.

There are three levels of gameplay — easy, medium, and hard.

Everyone starts on easy and it's pretty difficult to lose at that level, but as you work your way up, the battles become more sophisticated. Strategy is essential for victory at the most advanced level. If you want to play from beginning to end, you'll need to devote a considerable chunk of your day to it, and if you want to claim victory on all three difficulty levels, plan on coming back to Magic Kingdom for at least another day.

Some of Sorcerers' earliest and most ardent players were the *Dungeons & Dragons* meets "Big Bang Theory" types. But before long, something remarkable happened — Sorcerers started working its magic on the park's population at large. Today, the game has a healthy-sized following that includes hardcore fans and first-time park guests alike. From my observation, its appeal seems to be universal. Parents love playing it with their kids, while teens, singles, and young couples get into the spirit, too. You'll see soccer moms and grandfathers swapping cards with teenagers, all of them having a great time. Capitalizing on the success, the company has even rolled out merchandise, including apparel that can interact with the portal screens, as well as "booster packs" that allow easier access to those rare spell cards — for a price.

Disney clearly invested a great deal of imagination and resources in creating the game. The portals feature all-new animation, which varies wildly in quality but is sometimes quite good. Many of the original voice actors return to reprise their famous characters, including big names like James Woods (Hades), Anika Noni Rose (Tiana), Jodi Benson (Ariel), and Patrick Warburton (Kronk), among others. When substitutions are used, they're usually pretty close (a notable exception is the marvelous Jenifer Lewis, who lends her voice to two Sorcerers characters and can generally do no wrong but sounds nothing like Whoopi Goldberg as *The Lion King*'s Shenzi).

The game has a healthy respect for narrative. That's not to say it all makes sense. For instance, how exactly did the Crystal pieces get spread around the park? And if the Crystal's been keeping evil out of the kingdom, how do you explain villains turning up in meet-and-greets, parades, and stage shows? Maybe the Crystal lets them inside, but only on good behavior? (They never kill anyone in the parks, after all.) Also, why is Londoner Cruella de Vil the only villain we find on the U.S.-set Main Street?

The occasional plot hole aside, the narrative structure is impressive.

No matter where an individual gamer's quest begins, the adventure progresses in a way that makes sense. The Fantasyland storylines, which feature Ursula (*The Little Mermaid*) and Maleficent (*Sleeping Beauty*), are especially good. Hades may have enlisted his cads to help him capture the Crystal, but they enter the mix with double-crossing motives of their own, and that makes the game rather fascinating... even for those who are just tagging along and watching as their friends play.

The very idea of a story unfolding as we explore a theme park is intriguing in itself. Sorcerers is an extension of the premise we established inside Cinderella Castle, that this is a real kingdom, and it needs protection from outside threats. It turns the entire park into a game board, a stage on which we play a part in a story as it's being told. That gives us a sense of ownership in Magic Kingdom, which is a pretty nice feeling.

The game's map also reinforces an important idea we considered back in Liberty Square. Sorcerers of the Magic Kingdom doesn't acknowledge a distinction between Liberty Square and Frontierland at all. Geographically, both are there, and portals are found within each, but the game simply consolidates the two as a single setting for the same storyline. Why? Well, it could be that the game was designed for future implementation in Disneyland, which does not have a Liberty Square, or that dealing with one less land simply made Imagineers' lives a little easier. Whatever the reason, it lends newfound credence to the notion that Liberty Square and Frontierland are really one in the same, with nothing more than an arbitrary border to divide them.

Tomorrowland is neglected entirely. It's not on the map, there are no portals inside it, and not a single element of gameplay even references its existence. An explanation is elusive. Tomorrowland sees pretty heavy crowds, so could Imagineers have feared excessive congestion? Perhaps, but it's not as if other lands don't get crowded. Were the keyholes a thematic misfit for the future? (More of a misfit than *Monsters, Inc.!*?) Or maybe Tomorrowland portals are in store for some sort of Sorcerers 2.0 in the future. Without an official explanation, I like to think that the villains aren't able to access a "future that never was and never will be." We know that Merlin can time-travel (he returns from the twentieth century wearing Bermuda shorts in *The Sword in the Stone*), but it may be that Tomorrowland is not on his or anyone else's timeline.

Merlin isn't just the game's main character; he also appears on one of its spell cards. Many other deep-cut Disney icons feature too, the game far-reaching enough to include Colonel Hathi (*The Jungle Book*), Lythos the Titan (*Hercules*), and Doris (*Meet the Robinsons*), alongside scores of more popular personalities.[4] Like Mickey's PhilharMagic, Sorcerers brings a whole host of unrelated characters under one banner, and their interplay adds to the game's charm.

But I think there's quite a bit more to this game's appeal than the way it interfaces with the Magic Kingdom's cartography or its cast of characters. If gameplay is first and foremost an experiential activity, then there must be something about the action of this game that's speaking to its players. I suspect we can find the answer inside the castle. Not Cinderella's, though. Harry Potter's.

"You're a wizard, Harry." Those words in *Harry Potter and the Sorcerer's Stone* sparked an international obsession with spell casting and wand wielding that is likely to persist for a long time to come. Harry Potter instilled in many millions of us a desire to run around enchanted castle grounds, casting spells and heroically facing off against diabolical wizards.

Sorcerers of the Magic Kingdom offers that same kind of thing, essentially allowing us to live out the *Harry Potter* fantasy inside Magic Kingdom.[5] While *Potter* is not a Disney property (it's Disney's rival, Universal Orlando, that offers the Wizarding World of Harry Potter attractions), I don't doubt that J. K. Rowling's fantasy is alive and well in the subconscious of many a Magic Kingdomgoer. You might be able to find me a few people who haven't been enchanted by the *Potter* saga, but I doubt that Sorcerers' many bespectacled, card-carrying gamers and enthusiastic youths are among them.

In Sorcerers of the Magic Kingdom, we learn about different spells and are then turned loose to cast them in the acreage surrounding an enchanted castle. We encounter bad guys and peril along the way, always advancing in a storyline and drawing nearer to an ultimate showdown against evil. The parallels between our quest in the park and Harry's seven-year adventures connect themselves in our imaginations, where we're Gryffindors at heart, even in an environment that doesn't expressly acknowledge Rowling's mythos. All we need is a wand.[6]

Enlisting as one of Merlin's recruits is not unlike joining Dumbledore's Army, *Potter*'s band of students who teach themselves self-defense spells in order to battle against "the Dark Arts" in the fifth novel. The Dumbledore character does bear considerable resemblance to Disney's Merlin. Together, they might be culture's two greatest examples of the tall-hatted, long-bearded wizard archetype. The *Potter* texts are replete with Merlinian allusions, as are (to a lesser extent) the films. Rowling's characters recognize Merlin as one of the greatest wizards to ever live, and she makes much of Dumbledore belonging to the Order of Merlin, a society of sorts founded by the Arthurian wizard.

It stands to reason then that Sorcerers players, nearly all of them likely versed to some extent in *Potter* lore, will draw a connection between the game and Rowling's pervasive and wonderfully absorbing fantasy. Granted, the *Potter* connection is one for nerds to make and nerds alone, but if you're playing the game and getting into it, I've got some news for you about you. Welcome to the club, Sorcerer.

WATCH THIS - "Once Upon a Time" (2011)

ABC's hit primetime TV series isn't the first to ponder whether all the old fairy tales really were true, but it's probably the most clever and elaborate creation to do so. Bail bondswoman Emma Swan answers her door one day to find a young boy named Henry, who claims to be the son she gave up after his birth. He persuades her to take him home to Storybrooke, Maine, where she quickly crosses paths with the town's malevolent mayor, Regina.

Soon thereafter, Henry confides in Emma his belief that all the inhabitants in Storybrooke are actually real-deal fairy tale characters, trapped under a curse that won't let them remember who they are. Emma is Snow White's long-lost daughter, he tells her, and Regina is the apple-poisoning Evil Queen. Emma doesn't believe Henry (nor does anyone else), but those of us watching from home know the truth — he's right.

Created by two of the writers from "LOST" and produced by Disney's ABC Studios, "Once Upon a Time" is a riveting, complex, and brilliantly constructed fantasy soap opera capable of delivering mind-blowing twists and revelations week after week. Fairy tales and legends from different times and locales come together in an epic narrative mashup that rarely fails to amaze, even if the show's mid-budget special effects and occasionally contrived dialogue leave something to be desired.

Like the gamers in Sorcerers of the Magic Kingdom, Emma Swan is an ordinary mortal who must learn a thing or two about magic in order to track down mythical legends, unlock hidden portals, and face off against conspiring tag teams of villainy who are intent on manipulating her world for their own selfish ends. Harry Potter she is not, but she comes to encounter considerable sorcery inside a magic kingdom of her own. The fourth season even posits a theory for Cruella's appearance in America.

"Once Upon a Time" wrapped up in 2018, but complete seasons are available on home video and on various digital platforms.

Disney Festival of Fantasy Parade

Type: Parade
Duration: 14 minutes
Popularity/Crowds: High
FastPass+: Yes (reserved viewing area in the Hub); low priority
Fear Factor: 1 out of 5 (Villains and fire effects may frighten some children.)
Wet Factor: None (unless it rains)
Preshow: A Grand Marshal carriage escorts a specially chosen family down the route before some showings. Promotional "pre-parade" floats will occasionally feature as well. You might also catch the Main Street Philharmonic and/or visiting high school marching bands while you wait.
Best Time to Visit without FastPass+: For good views, claim your spot 30 to 45 minutes before the scheduled showtime.
Special Comments: The parade is usually offered once daily at 3 p.m. and typically begins in Frontierland and ends at the fire station at the front of Main Street. (Subject to change.) In the event of rain, Magic Kingdom may present the Rainy Day Character Cavalcade in lieu of either Festival of Fantasy or the "Move It! Shake It! MousekeDance It!" Street Party. The latter is a separate mini-parade/street party that performs several times throughout the day and can sometimes serve as a pre-show for Festival of Fantasy.

We could probably call all of Magic Kingdom a "Festival of Fantasy," but the park's newest daytime parade is slightly more specific than that. It's the answer to many a fan's prayer after the previous parade, Share a Dream Come True, stayed around longer than any before it, cycling through several progressively punier incarnations over the course of its thirteen-year run.

Festival of Fantasy is extravagance on wheels. Not since Prince Ali took to the streets of Agrabah with fifty-three purple peacocks and seventy-five golden camels has a single procession created such a spectacle. You won't find Aladdin here, though. Adventureland's laid claim to him, and Festival of Fantasy's purview is fixed on Fantasyland.

Which Fantasyland, exactly? That's not so clear. *Sleeping Beauty* is front and center, even though it's Disneyland that makes a big fuss over that particular fairy tale. Meanwhile, It's a Small World, arguably the most iconic attraction in any of the Fantasylands, is entirely absent.

Nevertheless, the parade is aesthetically fantastical in the Disney-est sense of the term. The whole affair is so lavish and grand that observing all its ornaments and intricacies in just a viewing or two is a challenge. Some of the costumes look like cupcakes. The floats are tall as turrets. There are so many moving parts that it practically qualifies as a ride. And it's all more colorful than a bowl full of Fruity Pebbles. This is the kind of show people expect to see when they visit Walt Disney World — spirited, spectacular, and larger than life. Magic Kingdom may have staged some mighty fine parades in its past, but this is the first in its daytime oeuvre to rival Macy's or a Christmas Day parade in terms of feeling special. It plays on the psychology of sensory overload, something the Disney Parks have always done well. Sight and sound bound down Main Street in an emotional whirlwind that sweeps the audience up in it and easily surpasses the mundane experience of everyday life outside The Most Magical Place on Earth. It isn't necessarily a difficult effect to achieve, but it takes a big budget. An established familiarity with onlookers doesn't hurt.

While Festival of Fantasy has earned near-universal acclaim, its few detractors take it to task for lack of narrative. To those critics' credit, there is no discernible story here. The Festival is just a festival, a random assortment of Disney characters sauntering down the street for fifteen minutes. And I'm not sure there's anything in the long and celebrated tradition of parades that requires them to be more than that. But story and narrative aren't the same thing, and what those who dismiss the parade as just a jumble of Disney-owned intellectual properties fail to realize is that Disney is itself a narrative... of sorts.

We can think of "narrative" as a storyline with a beginning, middle, and end... but we could also take a more scholarly approach to the term, in which "narrative" is a device we construct to help us understand morals, dilemmas, or ourselves. In that latter sense of the term, some of the basic conventions of culture are narratives. "Good triumphs over evil," for example, is a "narrative." Some would even call that a "master narrative."[7] Stories like *Sleeping Beauty*, then, are smaller narratives that exemplify and reinforce this larger, master narrative.

Now, let's think outside the box for a moment and consider "Disney" as one of these larger "master narratives." We might even call it a master-master narrative because it rolls so many of our culture's most potent master narratives into one: the victory of good over evil, the validation of faith, the escape from reality, the actuality of supernaturalism, the quest for self or truth, etc.

Maybe that's why our culture is so drawn to the allure of Disney. As a brand, it validates our conviction in our most cherished master narratives, bolstered by the power of nostalgia and some truly beautiful art in the form of movies, music, shows, and rides.

Like all narratives, the Disney master-master narrative is a construct. It has been created. Could that be why Disney parades like Festival of Fantasy are apparently capable of forging emotional connections that similar endeavors by the likes of Universal seemingly cannot? The Superstar Parade at Universal Studios Florida is — like Festival of Fantasy — a pageant of disparate characters with little in the way of storyline.[8] But while there's still some fun in watching that comparatively underwhelming parade pass by, it doesn't cast the same spell on its audience. Then again, Universal hasn't spent a half-century-plus purposely cultivating stories of common kind and creed. Disney has. Universal doesn't make it a priority to brand its characters as part of the same family. Disney does. People don't usually think of Beetlejuice and Spongebob Squarepants as belonging to the same brand whereas they more readily associate Peter Pan with, say, Winnie the Pooh or Merida from Pixar's *Brave*.[8]

So as we stand on the sidelines, watching Festival of Fantasy's reveling rumpus pass by, it is with very little legwork on our part that we can understand "Disney on Parade" not as a random collection of properties but as many arteries connected to the same heart. And more to the point, for the last fifty years or so, Americans have come to intuitively understand "Disney" as a kind of proxy for faith (broadly defined) and morality (at least inasmuch as Disney's productions have historically privileged traditional notions of goodness and virtue). We approach the parade already armed with universal familiarity with these characters, their tales, and the morals they uphold. Festival of Fantasy thrills us with a celebration of those morals, which it safely assumes we all embrace.

Cynics may shudder at the parade's "exploitation" of a value system that Disney itself has helped to perpetuate, but I reckon it's reasonable for people to celebrate beliefs they hold near and dear, even if they're as presumptively simple as "virtue" or "faith, trust, and pixie dust."

Festival of Fantasy's exuberance almost feels like an old church revival. There aren't any tents and I doubt any souls will get saved. Sleeping Beauty will, though.[9] And when she does, it means something to us, just as "Disney" means so many things to us at once — enough to fill a festival, even.

WATCH THIS – Hello, Dolly! (1969)

Like Main Street itself, *Hello, Dolly!* unfolds at the turn of the twentieth century. Its signature song, "Put on Your Sunday Clothes," has even been a part of Main Street's music loop for many years (long before it came to play an important part in Pixar's *WALL•E*). The rousing, show-stopping number begins with two young men in a turn-of-the-century supply shop, but it quickly grows into a full-blown parade right down the middle of a period-set street. It might as well serve as an alternative soundtrack to any given daytime Kingdom parade. The song speaks of strutting down the road to take a picture and riding around in horse-drawn cars. By the time it builds to a finale, an old-timey steam-powered train has rolled into town and Barbra Streisand is belting, "All aboard!" Later, a second parade becomes a pivotal plot point, accompanied by another classic number, "Before the Parade Passes By" (which also plays in the music loop, along with this film's "Elegance"). It's about as Main Street as movies come.

In 2019, *Hello, Dolly!*'s longtime close proximity to the Disney brand came full-circle when the Walt Disney Company acquired Twentieth Century Fox, the studio that produced it back in 1969. Now that it's technically a Disney movie, rumors are already flying about a possible remake or further incorporation of the movie on Main Street, U.S.A. Might we see Ms. Dolly Levi as a Citizen of Main Street in the future? Never put anything past her! In the meantime, the movie is still available on home video and digital platforms from Twentieth Century Fox Home Entertainment.

Happily Ever After

Type: Fireworks show
Duration: 18 minutes
Height Restriction: None
Popularity/Crowds: High
FastPass+: Yes (reserved viewing area in the castle hub); low priority
Fear Factor: 1 out of 5 (Fireworks scare some children.)
Wet Factor: None (unless it rains)
Preshow: Once Upon a Time (light-and-effects show projected onto Cinderella Castle, presented either before or after Happily Ever After, sometimes both — check the evening schedule)
Best Time to Visit without FastPass+: Arrive 25 to 35 minutes prior to the scheduled showtime (usually offered between one and two times a night).
Special Comments: For a better view of the castle projections, stand in the castle hub. For a better view of the fireworks, stand farther back on Main Street. For a "best of both worlds" view, stand somewhere in the middle. The show designers were purposeful in emphasizing projections during some portions and bursts during the other, so you'll get a good show no matter where you stand.

Could we end a day at Magic Kingdom with anything other than fireworks? This being Disney, can those fireworks be anything less than the best we've ever seen? Is it reasonable to think that a bunch of fire in the sky might make us cry? That we might walk away from a commercial nightcap with a renewed sense of purpose or a blueprint for changing our lives?

There are sensible people I know who would say that this is far from reasonable indeed — that Disney's sentimental, character-laden, soundtrack-oriented nighttime spectacular is nothing more than a three-hanky salute to consumerism, void of meaning or substance and a distraction from the bursts themselves.

Maybe. But if I find in these fireworks a message that resonates and millions of guests are similarly moved... if there is an argument in this presentation that takes more than a modicum of thought to digest... if these fireworks make more lasting an impact than those of all our collective county fairs, backyard barbecues, and Fourths of July... then maybe it's the cynics who are distracted, by just a touch of their own acrimony, from what's actually happening here in the castle hub.

Fireworks displays have for centuries marked the birth of a nation, a royal celebration, or the dawn of a new year. The idea of staging a full-scale display *every night*, though? That's relatively new. The Disney theme parks are renowned for their nightly pyrotechnics, and Walt Disney World just happens to be the largest single consumer of fireworks in the world. I suppose that's curious. Surely any given evening in a theme park is less momentous than Independence Day or New Year's Eve. Then again, the Magic Kingdom's guests aren't here by happenstance. The chance to stand in front of Cinderella Castle and see it with one's own eyes often represents years of working, saving, and planning for a family's once-in-a-lifetime vacation to The Most Magical Place on Earth. Each night, there are guests in this massive crowd who have truly been waiting their entire lives to be here. Magic Kingdom sends them off with a glorious celebration that recognizes and rewards everything it took to make that dream come true, a celebration of a day that will often rank among the most memorable in those guests' lives. Isn't that an occasion worth making a little noise for?

For many years, Magic Kingdom ended each evening with a fireworks show about *wishing* for happiness — Wishes: A Magical Gathering of Disney Dreams. Now it ends with a new show about *making* happiness happen, which is decidedly *not* how we're used to thinking about the three words that form its title: Happily Ever After.

The old show opened with Jiminy Cricket's disembodied voice calling out to us from the skies: "The most fantastic, magical things can happen — and it all starts with a wish."

In Happily Ever After, that wish comes to us not from the world of *Pinocchio* but from Tiana, Type-A princess and titular heroine of 2009's *The Princess and the Frog*. In an impressively projection-mapped sequence near the top of the show, Tiana sits on the castle's balcony ledge and sings, "The evening star is shining bright, so make a wish and hold on tight. There's magic in the air tonight... and anything can happen."

Here, as in her movie, those lines are a callback to *Pinocchio*'s "When You Wish Upon a Star," an anthem that looks to *fate* for dreams come true. It's our first clue that Happily Ever After has a different idea.

We might say that the show is divided into seven acts, approximating the classic "hero's journey" of literature, in which a reluctant or unlikely hero learns that they are called to greatness and then endures various trials and challenges in the quest to achieve it.[10] Disney doesn't name the acts, so I've given them titles of my own, each corresponding to an important part of the hero's journey.

The first act — *The Dream* — is the fireworks equivalent of an "I Want" song on Broadway, where we learn our protagonist is dissatisfied and harbors a daunting dream or desire. Act I is where Tiana makes her wish on that evening star. It's where we find Ariel, with her well-known dream of becoming human and engaging with a world that has captured her passion, and *Ratatouille*'s Remy, the rat who wants to cook you dinner. Rapunzel is there, ready for her life to begin, and so is Quasimodo, the disabled captive who wants to live life "out there, like ordinary men." (That *Hunchback* spends so long in the spotlight here is a real thrill to anyone who loves a deep cut.)

The second act — *A Call to Adventure* — is built around *Brave*'s challenge to "take hold of your own dream." A montage ensues with various characters taking the first steps in their respective journeys. When Moana shows up, the bursts take the shape of her story's Heart of Te Fiti, which just goes to show Disney's canisters don't come from Orlando's nearest TNT bargain tent.

"Trust me," Aladdin calls out from the sky, "having a best friend by your side opens up a whole new world of possibilities." This is Act III — *Meeting Mentors, Allies, and Supernatural Aids*. How interesting it is to hear Aladdin talk about "A Whole New World" in terms of Genie and Abu for a change. And how amusing to see *Tarzan*'s Terk toss dishes off into the air and see them "explode" as fireworks. How clever of this show to feature *Monsters, Inc.*'s Mike and Sulley while the chorus sings a line from *The Jungle Book* about opening a door — they know a thing or two about doors.

Speaking of doors, Act IV — *Love of All Kinds* — begins with a gorgeously stripped-down version of *Frozen*'s "Love Is an Open Door." This is an extension of the third act, showcasing affections both familial and romantic. It builds up to the dazzling ascent of a hundred projected lanterns, which dance along with Rapunzel's romantic epiphany in "I See the Light," the lyrics doubling as a comment on the bursts themselves.

We're taken by surprise when the castle lights up in red and gold to greet the seldom-seen Emperor from *Mulan*, who reminds us that "the flower that blooms in adversity is the most rare and beautiful of all."[11] This is the fifth act and the next stage in the hero's journey — *Enemies,*

Tests, and Temptations. It is a series of battles between good and evil: Eric against Ursula, Simba against Scar, Aladdin versus Jafar, and so on. In one memorable moment, Ping (that's Mulan in drag) fires a rocket that shoots off the castle and turns seamlessly into a real flare. There's also a Jack Sparrow sequence, the lone contribution from Disney's live-action catalogue, which we might accept as a reminder that the hero's journey is for antiheroes too. By confining his visage to a silhouette, the show at least gives him the texture of animation, and his shadow quickly gives way to the hand-drawn outlines of others as the castle appears to be engulfed in flames.

When the fire is over and the ashes have cooled, Mufasa speaks to us from beyond the grave: "You are more than what you have become. Remember who you are." This is Act VI, *The Return.* The hero's journey is complete. The castle is slowly repaired, its broken bricks replaced with gold trimming and stained glass, each window honoring one of the characters we encountered along the way. The tip-top window belongs to Tiana, who appears just as the narrator addresses us directly. "Grab hold of your dreams," he says, "and *make* them come true, for *you* are the key to unlocking your own magic."

I was watching Happily Ever After from Main Street one night and was struck by how quickly this noisy crowd had fallen to a relative hush. But when we reached the stained-glass climax, a man beside me leaned over to his wife and said, "Tiana's on top, right where she belongs." I laughed and figured she must be his favorite, but then it occurred to me: he's right. It is no coincidence that the hero's journey opens and closes with Tiana.

The Princess and the Frog is not quite like the Disney princess stories that came before. Tiana's big "I Want" song is about opening a restaurant and baking beignets, and it's not even so much an "I Want" song as a "Here's How I'm Gonna Get It" song.

"Fairy tales can come true," she sings, almost in answer to Jiminy Cricket, "but you've got to *make* them happen. It all depends on *you*. So I work real hard each and every day... and I'm almost there."

This is the message of Happily Ever After, and as it happens, it's also the truth about life. It is a truth which, for all their other virtues, Disney's stories haven't always hammered home.

In literature, the hero's journey is charted as a circle, and when the hero returns at the end, it is specifically a return with new knowledge. This, I think, is the new knowledge that Happily Ever After wants to leave us with: "Each of us has a dream, a heart's desire. It calls to us. And when we're brave enough to listen, *and bold enough to pursue*, that dream will lead us on a journey to discover who we're meant to be."

It reminds me of the message that Oprah Winfrey (coincidentally, the voice behind Tiana's mom) imparted when ending her 25-year TV run: "We all are called. Everybody has a calling. And your *real* job in life is to figure out what that is and get about the business of doing it."

Walt Disney said something similar: "The way to get started is to quit talking and begin doing." It echoes a line from the flying song in *Peter Pan*: "There's no better time to start." And that's the very song we hear as the show swells into Act VII — *Flight* — our finale. It begins with a shooting star that crests over Tiana in that stained glass window, a reminder of what she told us about fairy tales coming true. Then the music swells. The castle goes all gold and red. The bursts start to shoot upward directly from the forecourt, each successive stream moving closer to the castle and higher into the air. "Look up and reach to the sky," we hear. "We all have the courage to fly." The key modulates. "You can fly." It moves up another step. "You can fly." Higher still. "You. Can. Fly!" It's the moment we forgot we were waiting for. From the highest spire, Tinker Bell takes flight at last, the sky behind her erupting in a spreading landscape of color and fire.

And there, in that overwhelming moment, amidst the cheering and applause, and the sniffling of a crowd moved to tears, with the whole horizon lit up in front of us, we see just how right Walt was about getting started. Wishes-come-true aren't merely the things of make-believe. As Tiana concedes, they can come true. But they are the manifestation of hard work, human ingenuity, and divine inspiration, the very things that Walt Disney acted on when he boldly pursued the dreams that led up to this single moment in the Magic Kingdom nearly a century later. He was born into poverty but made the most of the meager opportunities available to him, eventually overcoming his circumstances to build an entertainment empire that has been a source of joy and inspiration to the whole world.

All of the multi-billion-dollar spectacle and unforgettable euphoria of the theme park around us is there because of his vision, perseverance, and faith. Main Street, U.S.A. wasn't just a dream. The Happiest Place on Earth was no wish upon a star. Mickey Mouse was much more than a happy accident. Walt Disney — with the help of friends and family and maybe even a gift from God — *made* these things happen. He figured out his calling, and he got about the business of doing it. So must we. Happily Ever After tells us how. It is both a benediction and a call to action. "We're changed by the way we live every day," it tells us. As we end our walk around this park together, let us take that to heart. The next time we meet here for a Happily Ever After, let's all have taken a step closer to our own.

WATCH THIS – Magic Kingdom (Date Unknown)

Happily Ever After is all about being bold and moving forward. It's in that spirit that I close this book with a recommendation for a movie that hasn't been made yet. For many years, Walt Disney Pictures has had a major live-action movie in the works, tentatively titled *Magic Kingdom*. It's about a family that finds itself still in the park after closing... and things start to come to life. Director Jon Favreau (*Iron Man*, *Elf*) is set to co-write and direct.

On the heels of his *Jungle Book* remake in 2016, Favreau said part of the reason that movie was made was to develop new CGI technology for use in *Magic Kingdom*. But then *Jungle Book*'s success meant Favreau got snatched up for 2019's *The Lion King* almost right away (and Disney's Marvel Cinematic Universe has kept him plenty busy too). Nothing else has been announced about *Magic Kingdom* since then, not even a year for release (the studio says it wants to give the project all the time it needs), nor has there been any official clarification as to whether it will be set in California or Florida.

In the past, Favreau has promised that his *Magic Kingdom* will stay away from *Night at the Museum* territory and will avoid crossing too far into other Disney franchises, like *Pirates of the Caribbean*. That was before Disney acquired *Night at the Museum* and announced a remake for Disney+, and before 2020's *Jungle Cruise* movie earned an official spot on the release calendar. So where does the project stand now? In the spirit of Tiana, let's hope somebody makes it happen.

In an interview with *Geek Time* on SiriusXM, Favreau said, "I want to make it a little bit spookier, like the old Disney movies were," he said, "I really want to focus on the classic stuff like *Dumbo*, *Steamboat Willie*... all the Fantasyland stuff. I think there was something timeless about what Walt Disney did... There is such a weird, shared experience that any of us who's ever gone to Disneyland feels, that I don't think has really been mined yet. It's this collective subconscious that we have."

That collective subconscious is what allows something like Happily Ever After to work so powerfully. If Mr. Favreau continues to pursue the project with that kind of insight and passion, then this project may find its happily ever after yet.

Notes

Chapter 1: Adventureland

1. Marc Davis (1913 - 2000) began his Disney career as an animator on films like *Snow White and the Seven Dwarfs* and *Bambi*. He went on to become one of Walt's "Nine Old Men," the studio's core group of animators. In later years, he worked on attractions like Jungle Cruise, the Haunted Mansion, Walt Disney's Enchanted Tiki Room, Pirates of the Caribbean, It's a Small World, the Carousel of Progress, Ford's Magic Skyway, and the Country Bear Jamboree, among others. He was named a Disney Legend in 1989.
2. One of my favorites came from Mikey of the *Magic City Mayhem* video podcast. He drew a sketch of the likely perpetrator: the Dreamfinder, a long-lost and iconic Epcot character who, like the original Tiki birds, had been silenced when Disney updated his attraction. So why the Dreamfinder? Well, not only does he have the revenge motive, but there's his signature theme song, too: "One Little Spark."
3. Prior to February 6, 1986, The Walt Disney Company was known as Walt Disney Productions. Originally founded in 1923 as the Disney Brothers Cartoon Studio, the partnership became The Walt Disney Studio in 1926, and then Walt Disney Productions, Ltd. in 1929, before later merging with several other Walt-owned enterprises to form Walt Disney Productions in 1938.
4. The Tiki Room's Sunshine Pavilion is not to be confused with the Sunshine Tree Terrace dining location (also in Magic Kingdom's Adventureland) or The Land Pavilion's Sunshine Seasons in Epcot (formerly the Sunshine Season Food Fair).
5. The show's opening line, "Ohhh, buenos días, señorita, my siestas are getting shorter and shorter," is one of the more famous Disney attraction quotes.
6. The term "tree house" is properly written as two words. Disney, however, uses the

unconventional "Treehouse" spelling in the official title. Accordingly, I will use "Treehouse" when referring to the attraction name and "tree house" when speaking more generally.

7. Wyss' *The Swiss Family Robinson* (published in 1812) is a reworking of the original English novel, *Robinson Crusoe*, by Daniel Defoe, which was in turn inspired (in part) by the real-life adventures of Alexander Selkirk, who in 1704 was a castaway for four years on an uninhabited island off Chile. Today, that island is known as Robinson Crusoe Island.

8. *Variety* announced in late 2004 that a major live-action remake of 1960's *Swiss Family Robinson* was in production at the Disney Studios, and in June 2005 confirmed that Jonathan Mostow *(U-571, Terminator 3: Rise of the Machines)* had signed on as director. Production was repeatedly delayed as story and casting plans changed and other projects interrupted progress. At one point, Lindsay Lohan was reportedly in talks to star. In 2009, news broke that Will Smith, Jada Pinkett Smith, and their three children, Trey, Jaden, and Willow, would star in *The Robinsons*, presumably a new title for this same project. I asked Mostow for an update on *The Robinsons*' status during a virtual press junket in January 2010, but he would neither confirm nor deny any forward momentum. News was slow to follow. Then, in 2014, Disney announced a new movie with a comical twist on the same concept: *Brooklyn Family Robinson* starring Steve Carell, lingering in "development hell" ever since. It's unclear whether *Brooklyn* is the end result of the Mostow project (he's not involved) or a different project altogether.

9. Between The Magic Carpets of Aladdin and the Tiki Room's "Under New Management" phase, *Aladdin* has not fared well in Adventureland, despite the film's popularity. A dining experience-turned-storytelling show called Aladdin's Oasis struggled in Disneyland's Adventureland too and ultimately closed. It's had better luck elsewhere, though. Disney's Aladdin: A Musical Spectacular first caught on at Disney California Adventure and is currently showing on Disney Cruise Line.

10. *One Thousand and One Nights* is one of several accepted titles for a collection of short stories and folk and fairy tales that were probably first gathered and anthologized during what is known as the Islamic Golden Age, as far back as the ninth century or even earlier. The work's history is uncertain and complex, and numerous versions exist. Many scholars believe that its three best-known stories, "Aladdin and the Enchanted Lamp," "Ali Baba and the Forty Thieves," and "The Seven Voyages of Sinbad the Sailor," did not exist in the original Arabic texts but were added by French translator Antoine Galland (and possibly some of his contemporaries), though there is little doubt as to the stories' origins in authentic Arabic or Persian folklore. The other stories are believed to have originated in the ancient or medieval Middle East or South Asia. Galland's 1704 translation is considered extremely influential as a part of the collection's legacy, and it was followed two years later by the first English translation,

entitled *The Arabian Nights' Entertainment*. The English-speaking world has commonly referred to the work as *The Arabian Nights* ever since. Disney's *Aladdin* and especially its progeny in the studio's *Aladdin* franchise draw inspiration from the "Enchanted Lamp" and "Ali Baba" tales, among others, though the film diverges from the original tale in a number of ways. In *The Arabian Nights*, for example, "Aladdin" unfolds in China.

11. Alan Menken (born 1949) is an eight-time Oscar-winning composer of songs and scores for film and the stage. His first big break came with Off-Broadway productions *God Bless You, Mr. Rosewater* in 1979 and *Little Shop of Horrors* in 1982, the latter of which was adapted for a major motion picture. He is best known, though, for his work in Disney animation, where he was instrumental in the renaissance of animated filmmaking during the late 1980s and 1990s, beginning with *The Little Mermaid* in 1989. He worked with lyricist Howard Ashman until the latter's death, and their partnership produced the acclaimed soundtracks for *Beauty and the Beast* and *Aladdin*. Menken's later films include *Pocahontas*, *Hercules*, *Enchanted*, and *Tangled*, among others, and his recent stage work includes the Broadway adaptations of the 1992 Disney-studio films, *Aladdin*, *Sister Act*, and *Newsies*. In addition to his Oscars, Menken has seven Golden Globes and a Tony Award to his credit. He was named a Disney Legend in 2001.

12. Sabu Dastagir (1924 - 1963) was an Indian actor who enjoyed a vogue in British and American films of the 1930s and 1940s. He was typically billed by just his first name. Notably, Sabu's next two film credits were as Mowgli in a live-action version of *The Jungle Book* (1942) and as Ali Ben Ali in *Arabian Nights* (1942), also inspired by *One Thousand and One Nights*.

13. Conrad Veidt (1893 - 1943) was a German actor who specialized in playing villains. Although vehemently anti-Nazi, he is perhaps best remembered by American audiences as the Nazi Major Strasser in *Casablanca*.

14. I first started thinking about Pirates of the Caribbean's use of time travel to take us *in medias res* after reading Steven Johnson's essay on the use of a similar device — flashback (albeit not time travel) — to take us *in media res* in Broadway's *Hamilton*, particularly in the song "Satisfied." See: Johnson, Steven. "Work, Work: Repetition and Circular Songwriting in 'Hamilton.'" *Pop Culture Pundit*. 27 June 2016. Web. 10 Aug. 2019. <bit.ly/2MPfwip>.

15. The building's name and design were inspired by the Castillo San Felipe del Morro, also known as Morro Castle, in San Juan, Puerto Rico. In Spanish, "Castillo del Morro" means "Castle of the Point" or "Castle of the Promontory." The name is not related to the so-called "Moors," a questionable and sometimes controversial term used to identify certain Northern African populations, despite that term's occasional correlation with piracy.

16. There is much to be said about the changes made to the ride's "Bride Auction" scene and whether those changes were warranted. I recorded a podcast on the topic when the

changes were first announced (but before they had been implemented). In light of the importance of this topic, I feel it is one that can only be discussed at length if it is to be discussed at all. The podcast format has allowed for a more extensive discussion on this particular topic than the constraints of this book will allow. I invite anyone interested to listen. See: "Redheads Tell New Tales" (Season 13 of *On Main Street with Aaron Wallace*, originally released as Episode #80 of *Zip-A-Dee-Doo-Pod* on July 13, 2017; available for free on most major podcast services and at www.AaronWallaceOnline.com). For those curious, I must confess I am largely won over by the changes as implemented. I hope the framework presented in this episode will be helpful for others who wish to work through the issue on their own, or as a framework that might be applied to similar issues in the future.

17. I will concede that there is a distinction to be made here. The Jungle Cruise is different from Pirates of the Caribbean in that the former features a live performer (the skipper). Still, is it not true that the scenes we encounter on Pirates of the Caribbean are staged in front of us — in other words, "live on stage" — even if the performers themselves are not alive? That distinction might mean a ride like Pirates is different from theatre in the traditional sense, but it also means these rides are not quite a like movie or any other artform either. Only the concert, the lecture, the exhibition, and the play put us face-to-face with performers, and all of those things speak to us on the day they are performed. It stands to reason that theme park rides (at least ride-along narratives like the traditional dark ride) must also speak to us as of the day we ride them.

18. Disney has adapted its own live-action version on film: *Rodgers & Hammerstein's Cinderella* (1997), starring Whitney Houston, Brandy, Jason Alexander, Whoopi Goldberg, Bernadette Peters, Natalie Desselle, Victor Garber, and Paolo Montalban. Disney's version cost $12 million to make — an unheard-of sum for television productions at the time — and brought in over 60 million viewers when it premiered on ABC, making it one of the most-watched broadcasts of all time. The musical *first* premiered in 1957 as a made-for-TV production starring Julie Andrews, later adapted for the stage. A 1965 television remake put veteran Disney star Lesley Ann Warren in the title role. However, Disney did not get involved until 1997 and has not attempted another adaptation since. Stage versions date back to London in 1958, with a number of big-name stars appearing in off-Broadway adaptations over the years too, but it did not enjoy its first full-fledged Broadway run until 2013.

19. "In Walt's Own Words: Plussing Disneyland." *The Walt Disney Family Museum*. 17 July 2014. Web. 10 Aug. 2019. <bit.ly/33n0Mx7>.

20. A brief note on the history of Pirates of the Caribbean: originally intended as a walk-through wax museum, the concept eventually evolved into the large-scale dark ride we know today. Disneyland's opened first, in 1967. Travelers who have visited both U.S. Disney resorts are quick to call Florida's version of the ride "Pirates Light." With

Disneyland boasting several additional scenes and nearly double the duration, it's easy to see why. Still, the Magic Kingdom edition has a treasure trove all its own in the queue — not only are there two routes to the loading platform but they are also more elaborately themed than the single queue at Disneyland. Magic Kingdom was never supposed to get a pirates ride at all. Assuming the Sunshine State was too close to the Caribbean for Floridians to care, Imagineers were planning an altogether different ride called Western River Expedition for Magic Kingdom in Pirates' place. But when Magic Kingdom opened and crowds were bigger than anyone anticipated, Disney decided to shelve the Western River Expedition and build Pirates, with its ready-made blueprints, instead. (Western River Expedition is probably the most famous and influential Disney attraction never to be constructed. Original story and show elements from the ride are today found not just in Big Thunder Mountain Railroad, which is covered in *Chapter Two*, but in numerous other attractions in Walt Disney World and around the globe, including Splash Mountain, Tom Sawyer Island, The Great Movie Ride, Living with the Land, Phantom Manor, and Expedition Everest. It continues to inspire new ideas for future attraction development.) The ride remained unchanged on both coasts for many years. In the 1990s, the company started to make some light-handed changes to address concerns about the violence, villainy, and gender roles in the ride. X Atencio, who had scripted the original ride, famously complained that it was becoming "Boy Scouts of the Caribbean" instead. Later, a different kind of change would prove even more controversial: following the immense success of the *Pirates of the Caribbean* film series, Walt Disney World answered fan demand by welcoming the movie's Captains Jack Sparrow and Hector Barbossa to the ride's Caribbean shores. For a few years, the movies' Davy Jones and Captain Blackbeard turned up too as projections on mist, but the powers that be finally realized that meeting movie characters in the caverns (i.e. the present day) disrupted the time travel narrative.

21. Marc Davis was one of the principal creatives in Pirates of the Caribbean's development at Disneyland. For more on Davis, see: *Chapter One*, Note 1.
22. For a historical deconstruction of the jokes included in the original Pirates of the Caribbean "Bride Auction" scene (e.g. "Shift yer cargo dearie, show 'em your larboard side;" "Belay there, ya fo'c'sle swab;" "Strike your colors, ya brazen witch, no need to expose your superstructure;" etc.), refer to the podcast episode cited in Note 16 above.
23. See: Smith, Paige. "This Is Your Brain on True-Crime Stories." *The Huffington Post*. 5 April 2018. Web. 10 Aug. 2019. <bit.ly/2KBlhxk>. See also: McCarthy, Erin. "12 Reasons We Love True-Crime, According to the Experts." 10 Oct. 2018. Web. 10 Aug. 2019. <bit.ly/31xEeIe>.
24. Prince, Kira. "Why Is Pirates So Good?" *Theme Park Concepts*. 17 Oct. 2017. Web. 1 July 2019. <bit.ly/2Md9TLu>. Note: Prince argues, convincingly, that the ride's "expertiential immersion" is more effective at Disneyland than at Magic Kingdom.

Chapter 2: Frontierland

1. Then again, there *are* those out there who hate It's A Small World (for shame!). I suppose the title of "Most Divisive" might be up for grabs.
2. Disneyland's expectations for the Country Bear Jamboree were so high, based on its success in Florida, that they built *two* theaters for it right away. Inexplicably, whether due to its location or some other variable, the show was never as popular in Disneyland as it was in Walt Disney World and that extra capacity went largely unneeded. When Splash Mountain opened there, Bear Country became Critter Country instead, and the Bears' popularity declined even further. Disneyland shuttered the attraction in 2001 to make way for The Many Adventures of Winnie the Pooh. Ironically, many Disneyland fans now pine for the Jamboree, while Walt Disney World's guests generally express less passion for it. Perhaps absence makes the heart grow fonder.
3. Big Al is voiced by actor and country music star Tex Ritter (1905 - 1974), and it is he who performs "Blood on the Saddle" in the show. Ritter had performed the song earlier in his career, including in the 1937 Western film, *Hittin' the Trail*, and as the lead track on his 1960 album, *Blood on the Saddle*. While there is some dispute as to the song's origins, it was most likely written in the 1920s by Everett Cheetham and first recorded by Ritter. For more, see Herndon, Jerry A. "'Blood on the Saddle': An Anonymous Folk Ballad?" *The Journal of American Folklore* 88.349 (1975) : 300-04. Print.
4. In June 2019, Walt Disney World took the rare step of publicly denouncing a well-known Walt Disney World fan site that had claimed to have inside information about Walt Disney World's plans to close the Enchanted Tiki Room and the Country Bear Jamboree. Condemning the fan site's reporting "unscrupulous," Disney confirmed that the Jamboree will remain open at least through the resort's fiftieth anniversary on October 1, 2021 and that, at least as of June 2019, the company had no plans to close the Tiki Room either. See: Smith, Thomas. "'About Our Country Bears…'" *Disney Parks Blog*. 28 June 2019. Web. 28 June 2019 <bit.ly/33pU7SH>. See also: Smith. "A Little Birdie Told Us." *Disney Parks Blog*. 26 June 2019. Web. 28 June 2019 <bit.ly/2yNcpPM>.
5. The Golden Horseshoe is a lunch-and-dinner theater that has operated in Disneyland's Frontierland since 1955. Magic Kingdom initially opened with its own version, the Diamond Horseshoe Saloon, which sits on the border between Frontierland and Liberty Square and has been officially designated as belonging to one or the other at various times in its history. The stage show there ran under several names until it was replaced in 2003 by "Goofy's Country Dancin' Jamboree," a line-dancing character show that went unaccompanied by any dining menu and ended in 2004. The Diamond Horseshoe no longer appears on the attractions roster and has remained mostly closed since 2004, opening only for special events or for occasional counter or table service dining (without live entertainment) during the busiest days of the year.

6. "The Country Bears (2002)." *RottenTomatoes.com*. Flixster, n.d. Web. 23 Apr. 2015. <bit.ly/1GbiCiz>.
7. Fess Parker (1924 - 2010) was an actor best known for playing the title hero in Walt Disney's "Davy Crockett" television series. He also starred in several Disney feature films, including *Old Yeller*, *The Great Locomotive Chase*, and *Westward Ho, the Wagons!* He was inducted as a Disney Legend in 1991.
8. The mine train is a common type of steel roller coaster in which the vehicles are shaped like mine cars and appear to be pulled by a steam locomotive at the front. They typically feature steep banks and sharp turns but few drops. Mine train coasters outside of the Disney parks include The Runaway Mine Train at Six Flags Over Texas (built in 1966 and often credited as the very first mine train coaster); the Carolina Goldrusher at Carowinds Park in Charlotte, North Carolina; Thunder Run at Canada's Wonderland in Vaughan, Ontario; and Thunderation at Silver Dollar City in Branson, Missouri (note the thunder motif in this particular genre of coasters). While these other mine coasters may be charming in their own right, they feature a standard, exposed-steel design with only modest detail in comparison to Big Thunder Mountain Railroad.
9. Tony Baxter (born 1947) is the former Senior Vice President of Creative Development at Walt Disney Imagineering and is one of the most famous and celebrated living Imagineers. He began his career at Disney in 1965, working as an ice cream scooper on Main Street in Disneyland while also studying for a degree in theater design at California State University, Long Beach. He worked his way up the company ladder, where his ingenuity caught the attention of WED Enterprises, the precursor to Walt Disney Imagineering. Big Thunder Mountain Railroad was his big break in terms of creative control, and he has since been heavily involved in the design of Splash Mountain, Indiana Jones Adventure: Temple of the Forbidden Eye, the original Journey Into Imagination, and many other attractions, in addition to Disneyland's overhauls of Fantasyland in 1983 and Tomorrowland in 1998, not to mention the overall design of Disneyland Paris.
10. Joel Chandler Harris (1845 - 1908) was an American writer born in Eatonton, Georgia. A white man, Harris spent his teenage years working as a printer's devil (a printing press apprentice) for Turnwold Plantation just outside of Eatonton, where he spent much of his time with slaves, befriending them and learning their speaking and storytelling styles. Later, he moved to Atlanta, where he developed two careers under two names. As Joe Harris, he was a journalist and an associate editor of the *Atlanta Constitution* newspaper, in which he became known as an outspoken voice in favor of racial reconciliation and certain minority rights during the Reconstruction era and the years following. As Joel Chandler Harris, meanwhile, he was the best-selling author of *Uncle Remus: His Songs and His Sayings* (1880). It is the latter for which he is most commonly remembered today. Despite what he professed to be his earnest disdain

for racism, Harris's work as both a folklorist and a political advocate is the source of ongoing academic criticism and controversy. Some scholars defend his writings as important milestones in the history of black literature, while others accuse him of paternalism toward black citizens and theft of black storytelling. Still others have called into question the authenticity of his folklore.

11. *Song of the South* takes place after slavery was abolished, and so there is no indication that Uncle Remus is enslaved at any point during the film (though it's reasonable to infer that his character would have lived in slavery just a few years earlier, perhaps on the very same plantation). While most of the movie's informed critics readily concede that point, they still take issue with Uncle Remus's apparent satisfaction with his lot in life. Unquestionably, his were not happy circumstances in which to live. Other objections have been lodged against the film too, including what some have called the racial stereotyping of Aunt Tempy (McDaniel) and several of the animated characters.

12. Given the constraints and purpose of this book, I am content to raise these questions without endeavoring to fully answer them here. It is often the purpose even of scholarship merely to interrogate and inquire. I believe this is the first book to ask these specific questions, and I pose them in the hopes that others will see fit to pursue them, as I may some day as well. There is surely a world of academic intrigue to be found in their answers.

13. Michael Eisner and Frank Wells became the new CEO and President/COO, respectively, of The Walt Disney Company in 1984. Interestingly, it was Walt's nephew, Roy E. Disney, (along with fellow shareholder Stanley Gold) who recruited the two men for the jobs, which meant that Walt's son-in-law (and Roy E.'s cousin-in-law), Ron W. Miller, lost his position as company head.
Under the leadership of Eisner and Wells, The Walt Disney Company radically changed, transforming from a movie-and-rides studio to a mighty multimedia conglomerate and introducing an unprecedented decade of success in numerous new ventures. Wells died in a helicopter crash in 1994 (he was posthumously inducted as a Disney Legend the same year), and Eisner's later years as the corporate head honcho were less successful, ultimately resulting in Roy E. and Gold's "Save Disney" campaign to oust their own handpicked CEO from his job. The campaign was effective, and Eisner bowed out from the Mouse House in 2005, handing the CEO reigns to his successor and the current head, Bob Iger. For more on this, one of the most fascinating sagas in media history, see Stewart, James B. *DisneyWar*. New York: Simon & Schuster, 2005. Print.

14. Walt Disney Pictures launched its Touchstone Pictures subsidiary in 1984, intended for material too edgy for Disney's family-friendly brand. Its first film was the PG-rated *Splash* (1984), a box office titan that paved the way for future Touchstone titles like *Pretty Woman*, *Sister Act*, *Who Framed Roger Rabbit*, *Armageddon*, and many more. As

Touchstone is merely a distribution and marketing label, there is no real difference between a Touchstone film and a Disney film at the studio level. Often, movies are well into production before a final decision is made as to which brand will be applied. Touchstone is also designee for much of Disney's broadcast television programming. The number of Touchstone releases has slowed in recent years, Disney having cut back on its annual output while also welcoming some PG-13 fare in its native brand.

Chapter 3: Liberty Square

1. Frontierland is the only land in Magic Kingdom not directly accessible from the Castle hub, and that is significant. To get there, guests must start at the beginning of the story by entering through Liberty Square (or cheat and take a backdoor shortcut through Adventureland). The park map draws a seemingly arbitrary boundary between the two worlds; in the park, the transition is marked on the ground by a strip representing the Mississippi River and an out-of-the-way Frontierland entrance sign, both easy to miss.
2. When referring to them as a brand, Disney capitalizes both words in "The Muppets." That's also the title of a TV show and a feature film from Disney. When referencing any of the above, I will capitalize both words. But when talking about the characters generally, I will refer to them simply as the Muppets.
3. Jim Henson (1936 – 1990) was the filmmaker, screenwriter, voice actor, and puppeteer who created the Muppets and shows like "Fraggle Rock" and "Sesame Street." He was the creator and original voice actor and puppeteer for Kermit the Frog and various other Muppet characters. Beyond those properties, his feature films include *The Dark Crystal* (1982), *Labyrinth* (1986), and *Emmet Otter's Jug-Band Christmas* (1977). Despite having been generally in good health, he died suddenly at the age of 53 as a result of toxic shock syndrome from a rare but rapidly developing bacterial infection. His death shook the world, and he remains a fondly remembered giant of the entertainment world of the 1950s, '60s, '70s, and '80s. His business interests, including The Jim Henson Company, continued on after his death and many are still in operation to this day. In 2004, The Walt Disney Company acquired The Muppets from The Jim Henson Company, the culmination of a long partnership between the two companies that traced back to Henson himself.
4. See, for example: Fenzel, Peter. "A Muppet of a Marxist, or a Very Marxist Muppet?" *Overthinking* It. 6 Dec. 2011. Web. 3 Aug. 2019. <bit.ly/2KdvuRr>.
5. The Muppets aren't merely guests in Magic Kingdom. Sam the Eagle actually has a job in Liberty Square! He is this land's counterpart to the Royal Historians of Arendelle at Disney's Hollywood Studios. And in this show, the Muppets make use of the two lamps that have long been a part of Liberty Square lore, hanging in a window there as a tribute to Paul Revere for many years. Who knew that Liberty Square would be an even better fit for the Muppets than Hollywood Studios? Seeing them integrate so naturally

in Magic Kingdom must go a long way toward "Disney-fying" them for anyone who never fully embraced Disney's acquisition of the brand.

6. In fairness, the material covering Henson's Muppets is closer to fleece than felt, made with a flocked foam that gives them their signature look. Stevens, Elizabeth Hyde. "Millennials Just Don't Get IT! How the Muppets Created Generation X." *Salon.* 6 April 2014. Web. 3 Aug. 2019. <bit.ly/2ZvNJ9Z>.

7. "A Salute to All Nations, But Mostly America" is a fictitious show that Sam the Eagle plans (but never stages) as part of the plot of Muppet*Vision 3D, a short film that plays at Disney's Hollywood Studios.

8. Paul Revere shares at least one thing in common with Walt Disney: their most famous quotes aren't quite what they're believed to be. Walt Disney isn't the one who said, "If you can dream it, you can do it." (That was Tom Fitzgerald, writing the script for Epcot's Horizons ride.) Likewise, Paul Revere's "The British are coming!" isn't quite right, and "one if by land, two if by sea" isn't quite how it happened. All of that comes from a colorful interpretation of the events by poet Henry Wadsworth Longfellow in "The Midnight Ride of Paul Revere." For a fun, brief read on the real story, see: "Midnight Ride of Paul Revere." *Boston Discovery Guide.* n.d. Web. 3 Aug. 2019. <bit.ly/2Ylh3Uh>. See also: Leehey, Patrick M. "The Real Story of Paul Revere's Ride." 16 April 2015. Web. 3 Aug. 2019. <bit.ly/2Kf7I7J>.

9. Robert Newman (1752 – 1804) was a sexton and an American Patriot during the Revolutionary War. He was the one responsible for hanging the lanterns in the famous Paul Revere story, and that's essentially who Fozzie plays in Liberty Square. Newman famously lived with his mother for much of his life. I can't help but think of the relationship between Fozzie and his mom in *A Muppet Family Christmas* (1987).

10. One nice thing about the Muppets: they're so silly that they can make anything seem ridiculous without coming across as combative or nasty — even American politics!

11. Following the advent of the printing press, town criers were also responsible for posting written proclamations in town centers. It's one of the reasons some of our newspapers today call themselves *The Post*.

12. Disney has a long list of town crier-type characters. Find them in Spaceship Earth, *Newsies*, *Cinderella* (both 1950's and 2015's), *The Princess Diaries 2: Royal Engagement*, *Johnny Tremain*, Mickey's Royal Friendship Faire, etc. Earlier, I mentioned that Liberty Square never had an official town crier until the Muppets came along, and that's true, but you sometimes find cast members effectively playing that part at two of Liberty Square's restaurants: Liberty Tree Tavern and Columbia Harbour House.

13. To quote Fenzel (Note 4 above), "The Muppet Show is not a variety show, it is a backstage show about putting on a variety show — you do not get the finished product of the labor of the Muppets as your entertainment to consume — you get a chance to connect with them and move past your own alienation by connecting with them."

14. The puppets (if you'll forgive my use of so pedestrian a term) look *sensational* in person. The ones used here are just slightly larger than those used in most Muppet TV shows and movies. But believe it or not, they are performed by live puppeteers right here in the park each and every time. These are not Audio-Animatronics! The show's vocals are pre-recorded, but you're otherwise seeing something very close to real-deal Muppeteering right where you stand.
15. President Trump is the 45th President, but there are only 44 in the Hall of Presidents because Grover Cleveland served two non-consecutive terms.
16. *Johnny Tremain* (1957) featured Walt's daughter, Sharon Disney, in a small supporting role.
17. Vagnini, Steven. "The Hall of Presidents Story." *D23*. n.d. Web. 3 Aug. 2019. <bit.ly/1mx5ZeN>.
18. See Vagnini, Note 17, above.
19. Abraham Lincoln was Disney's first human Audio-Animatronic, but he wasn't the first U.S. President sculpted for Disneyland. That honor belongs to Andrew Jackson. Frontierland briefly featured a mannequin in the seventh president's likeness (though it was presented as Major General Jackson, not yet President Jackson).
20. Maya Angelou (1928 – 2014) was a renowned poet, memoirist, and activist. Throughout the 1990s and afterward, she was closely associated with the Clinton family, having recited a poem at Bill Clinton's first inauguration and later campaigning on behalf of Hillary Clinton. She would go on to endorse and campaign for Barack Obama. During Obama's Presidency, in 2011, Angelou was awarded the Presidential Medal of Freedom. Both Bill Clinton and Michelle Obama spoke at Angelou's memorial after her passing in 2014.
21. Around the time of Trump's debut in the attraction, I wrote a light-hearted, tongue-in-cheek reflection on his Audio-Animatronic's countenance. See: Wallace, Aaron. "13 People Who Look More Like Disney's Donald Trump Animatronic Than Donald Trump Does." *Aaron Wallace Online*. 21 Dec. 2017. Web. 3 Aug. 2019. < bit.ly/2ODIQuR>.
22. Ambramovitch, Seth. "Vice Retracts Report of Trump Turmoil at Disney's Hall of Presidents Attraction." *The Hollywood Reporter*. 27 June 2017. Web. 3 Aug. 2019. <bit.ly/2OEK4WG>.
23. Tillett, Emily. "Trump to Have Speaking Role in Disney World's 'Hall of Presidents.'" *CBS News*. 26 June 2017. Web. 3 Aug. 2019. <cbsn.ws/2YFBvi2>.
24. Smith, Thomas. "Latest on Enhancements to The Hall of Presidents at Magic Kingdom Park." 27 June 2017. Web. 3 Aug. 2019. <bit.ly/2OE0uhN>.
25. Mazza, Ed. "Trump Wanted His Disney Animatronic To Brag About His Skyscrapers, New Book Says." *The Huffington Post*. 25 Jan. 2019. Web. 3 Aug. 2019. <bit.ly/2LWk6eU>.

26. J.D. Hall (born 1947) is a voice actor whose credits include "Spider-Man: The Animated Series" and "Star Trek: Enterprise." He narrated The Hall of Presidents at Magic Kingdom during George W. Bush's time as president, from 2001 to 2009. Given his last name, you might say he's *the* Hall of Presidents.
27. Fjellman, Stephen M. *Vinyl Leaves: Walt Disney World and America.* Boulder, Westview Press, 1992, pp. 68-71.
28. In fairness to the 1993-2009 versions of The Hall of Presidents, the issue of federal executive power is central to any study of Abraham Lincoln and his policies concerning the Civil War, so to some extent, the prevalence of that theme reflects the attraction's origins as a show about Lincoln and Lincoln alone. Notably, many presidents, and especially the George W. Bush Administration, have cited Lincoln's actions in the Civil War in defense of their own uses of executive power. But that is precisely why the issue is so controversial, and the twenty-three-minute Hall of Presidents probably doesn't have the capacity to address it adequately.
29. Morgan Freeman (born 1937) is an Oscar-winning actor best known for his roles in *Driving Miss Daisy* (1989), *The Shawshank Redemption* (1994), *Bruce Almighty* (2003), *Million Dollar Baby* (2004), and *The Dark Knight* (2008). In 2018, he starred in Walt Disney Pictures' live-action fantasy film, *The Nutcracker and the Four Realms.*
30. For an example of President Obama warning about populism, see: Kilpatrick, Ryan. "Barack Obama Warns Against the Rise of Populism During a Speech in Montreal." *Time.* 7 June 2017. Web. 3 Aug. 2019. < bit.ly/2YGyVIu>. For an example of political analysts observing populism in Obama's campaigning, see: Thrush, Glenn. "Obama the Reluctant Optimist." *Politico.* 21 Jan. 2012. Web. 3 Aug. 2019. <politi.co/2yzvSDm>. See also: Cohen, Michael A. "Obama's New Populism." *The Wall Street Journal.* 23 Feb. 2008. Web. 3 Aug. 2019. < on.wsj.com/2GMWc1j>.
31. Joy Vandervort-Cobb is an actress and voiceover artist who is perhaps best known for her recurring appearances on TV's "Army Wives" and for voicing the current iteration of The Hall of Presidents during the presidency of Donald Trump. She is also the voice of the official U.S. Capitol Building orientation film. She describes her voice as having "warm, dulcet tones." See: "Joy Vandervort-Cobb." *Voice123.com.* n.d. Web. 3 Aug. 2019. < bit.ly/2KpNrLA>.
32. Alternatively, could it be that Morgan Freeman refused to come back in and record an introduction for Donald Trump? Or that he and Disney had reached some other disagreement? When asked about the reason for the change, Freeman's publicist told the *Tampa Bay Times,* "Ask Disney." The *Times* did ask Disney; they didn't respond. Spata, Christopher. "I Sat Through Disney's Hall of Presidents Five Times. It Says More About Us Than Trump." 15 Feb. 2018. Web. 3 Aug. 2019. <bit.ly/2PC74FW>.
33. In the current version of the show, the narrator talks about Lincoln as a "master of words," as opposed to a "plainspoken" candidate as described in previous iterations,

almost in direct answer to Fjellman's criticism in *Vinyl Leaves*, where he had noted that Lincoln's speech in this attraction was anything but plainspoken. (See Fjellman, Note 13, above.) We might read this change in light of Trump too, as he is also sometimes described as plainspoken, for better or for worse. Might it be that Disney no longer wanted to highlight plainspokenness as a virtue?

34. Walt wanted you to smell burning cordite in the theater too… an idea that never made it to The Hall of Presidents. (See Vagnini, Note 17, above.)
35. In late 2017, a viral video showed a man heckling the Trump animatronic inside The Hall of Presidents. See: Wolf, Colin. "Disney World Guest Chants 'Lock Him Up' During Donald Trump's Robot Speech at Hall of Presidents." *Orlando Weekly*. 28 Dec. 2017. Web. 3 Aug. 2019. For more anecdotes about interactions and incidents at The Hall of Presidents, see: Spata, Note 32 above.
36. Paul Frees (1920 - 1986) was an actor best known for his versatile voice work. His many credits with Disney include the Ghost Host in Haunted Mansion, the Auctioneer in Pirates of the Caribbean, the narrator for Adventure Thru Inner Space, and the voice of cartoon character Professor Ludwig Von Drake. Frees is also a staple of the Christmas season, having voiced memorable holiday characters that include Burgermeister Meisterburger in *Santa Claus Is Comin' to Town* and a number of characters in *Frosty the Snowman, Mister Magoo's Christmas Carol, The Little Drummer Boy*, and many more. He was named a Disney Legend in 2006.
37. Claude Coats (1913 - 1992) worked as a background artist on many Disney films, including *Snow White and the Seven Dwarfs, Pinocchio, Fantasia*, and *Cinderella* before joining WED Enterprises in 1955 to aid in the design of Disneyland. His tenure there lasted until his retirement in 1989, during which time he worked on attractions such as Mr. Toad's Wild Ride, Snow White's Scary Adventures, Haunted Mansion, It's a Small World, and many more. He was named a Disney Legend in 1991.
38. See *Chapter One*, Note 1.
39. Xavier Atencio (born 1919), more commonly known as simply X Atencio, came to Disney as an animator, most notably working on *Fantasia* and the Oscar-winning *Toot, Whistle, Plunk, and Boom*. But he made his biggest impact as part of WED Enterprises, where he wrote "Yo Ho, Yo Ho A Pirate's Life for Me" and co-wrote "Grim Grinning Ghosts." He also penned the scripts for Pirates of the Caribbean and Adventure Thru Inner Space, among other notable contributions to the parks. He retired in 1984 and was named a Disney Legend in 1996.
40. Haunted Mansion is found in New Orleans Square in Disneyland, Liberty Square in Magic Kingdom, and Fantasyland in Tokyo Disneyland, while the Parisian counterpart, Phantom Manor, is located in Frontierland in Disneyland Paris. Hong Kong Disneyland's is called Mystic Manor, located in Mystic Point (a new, supernatural rainforest-themed land).

41. The company has proffered variations on its own Mansion backstory over the years, with different accounts turning up in backstage tours, assorted publications, and Eddie Murphy's *Haunted Mansion* movie. Cast members working the attraction have espoused plenty of their own theories, too. The details of these narratives vary and they can all probably be best regarded as supplementary and non-canonical. As an audience, we are empowered to make our own meaning out of what is — and perhaps more importantly, what isn't — made apparent as part of the actual attraction experience.

42. One possible reading for this scene is that when the Doom Buggies fly out of the window, they actually fall to the ground, suggesting that the guests have just died (either because they committed suicide or were pushed out of the window by the evil bride). There's nothing in the ride to establish that narrative as definitive, and I'm not sure I subscribe to it, but it *would* explain why the ghosts suddenly seem so happy to see us (perhaps they're welcoming us to the afterlife) and why a mortal groundskeeper is shaking in his boots when he sets eyes on us (though he could just be frightened by the ghosts behind us).

43. Shakespeare's full verse reads:
"*Look, how the world's poor people are amaz'd*
At apparitions, signs, and prodigies,
Whereon with fearful eyes they long have gaz'd,
Infusing them with dreadful prophecies;
So she at these sad sighs draws up her breath,
And, sighing it again, exclaims on Death.
'Hard-favour'd tyrant, ugly, meagre, lean,
Hateful divorce of love,'— thus chides she Death, —
'Grim-grinning ghost, earth's worm, what dost thou mean
To stifle beauty and to steal his breath,
Who when he liv'd, his breath and beauty set
Gloss on the rose, smell to the violet?" (925-936).

44. Thurl Ravenscroft (1914 - 2005) was a successful singer and voice artist who first became associated with Disney as part of The Mellomen, a singing quartet he co-founded in 1948. In addition to singing backup for the likes of Elvis Presley, Rosemary Clooney, Bing Crosby, and Peggy Lee, The Mellomen also contributed songs to a slew of Disney productions, including "Zorro," *The Jungle Book*, and *Peter Pan*. For Disneyland, they recorded the now-classic "Meet Me Down on Main Street." Meanwhile, in his individual capacity, Ravenscroft lent his voice to dozens of Disney films and attractions, with Splash Mountain, Pirates of the Caribbean, and Walt Disney's Enchanted Tiki Room among them. Notably, his face is projected onto one of the singing busts inside Haunted Mansion. It was, however, his work outside the Disney studio that brought him his greatest fame. In 1966, he recorded the sneering anthem for Chuck Jones's classic *How*

the Grinch Stole Christmas!, and for more than 50 years, he provided the voice of Frosted Flakes mascot Tony the Tiger. His signature phrase, "They're Grrrrreeeat!" left an indelible mark on popular culture. He was inducted as a Disney Legend in 1995.

45. For more on Disney's fan-favorite Halloween comedy *Hocus Pocus* (1993) and the bond it formed with audiences by scaring them, surprising them, or setting them on edge, see: Wallace, Aaron. *Hocus Pocus in Focus: The Thinking Fan's Guide to Disney's Halloween Classic*. Orlando, Pensive Pen Publishing, 2016.

46. For many years, there was something very ring-like in the pavement just outside Haunted Mansion's exit, often said to have been the remnant of an old pole. Still, rumors persisted that this was the bride's wedding ring, either intentionally placed there by mischievous cast members/Imagineers or somehow supernaturally reappearing. It came and went at least a couple of times over the years but has now seemingly disappeared for good. A similar ring, however, appears in the attraction's new queue (unveiled in 2011), this one apparently permanent and unquestionably purposeful.

47. For one such photograph, see "Truly Haunted Haunted Mansion Photo." *WDWMagic – Unofficial Walt Disney World discussion forums*, 4 Dec. 2004. Web. 17 Dec. 2012. <bit.ly/V3HyQJ>.

    I'm not signing on as a believer in the ghost quite yet myself, but the attraction *does* feel just real enough to make one wonder...

Chapter 4: Fantasyland

1. In 2015, Magic Kingdom officially unveiled a new interactive queue outside of Peter Pan's Flight, intended to make the very long wait a little more bearable. The queue takes us through the Darling nursery, which comes to life with impressive effects. It is curious, though, that we should explore the Darling nursery and exit it only to reenter during the ride itself. It is even more curious that this nursery looks very different — and smaller — in the ride than in the queue. We might explain that as an illustration of the way children see spaces (big and magical) vs. adults (smaller and linear). Or the way women process stories vs. men. Or maybe there's some sort of time lapse that happens between the queue and the ride. Perhaps the Darlings remodel the nursery before we get onboard? Straining plausibility as we might, it's probably best to see this particular queue as its own entity — a kind of trailer, tribute, or promotional exhibit — and not a part of the essential ride narrative, though I acknowledge that many park fans insist that divorcing a queue from the overall storyline is disingenuous or even impermissible.

2. The dark ride concept predates Walt Disney's birth, tracing all the way back to the late nineteenth century. A popular precursor was the "Old Mill," typically an indoor, waterborne boat ride through a dark and spooky environment. Just such a ride was among the earliest offerings at Coney Island's Sea Lion Park, which opened in 1895 to become the world's first permanent, enclosed amusement park. Likewise, the "Tunnel of Love,"

originally a boat ride, has long been a staple of carnivals and fairs. (One of Disney's first encounters with the dark ride came when a jealous Donald Duck followed Daisy into a Tunnel of Love in 1946's *Donald's Double Trouble*, nine years before Disneyland opened.) What we might call the modern dark ride premiered in 1928 at the Tumbling Dam Park in New Jersey. The park's developers, Leon Cassidy and Marvin Rempfer, wanted to replicate the Old Mill experience in their park, but without the expense of water canals. As a result, Cassidy patented the first-ever electric dark ride, an Old Mill concept using a single floor-mounted rail as opposed to water boats. Though initially untitled, the ride became known as the Pretzel after one guest said he felt like the twisting track had bent him into one. Soon thereafter, the Pretzel Amusement Ride Company went into business and Cassidy's single-rail dark ride — complete with large, cast-iron pretzels on the vehicle's sides — took the world's fairgrounds and amusement parks by storm. For more on the history of the dark ride, see Luca, Bill. "Send 'Em Out Laffing!: William Cassidy and the Pretzel Amusement Ride Co." *Laff in the Dark*, n.d. Web. 7 June 2015. <http://bit.ly/VOdBF3>. See also "Laughter in the Dark: A History of Dark Rides." *Entertainment Designer – Theme Park and Museum Design News*, 18 July 2011. Web. 7 June 2015. <bit.ly/SOaKRC>.

3. Disney's *Peter Pan* most directly descends from Scottish playwright J.M. Barrie's 1904 stage play, *Peter Pan, or The Boy Who Wouldn't Grow Up*, but the character's lineage is somewhat more complicated. He first appeared two years earlier than that as a small part of Barrie's 1902 adult novel, *The Little White Bird*. In 1906, the play having already been a smash on both London's West End and Broadway, the Pan portions of *White Bird* were excerpted, slightly reworked, and republished as *Peter Pan in Kensington Gardens*. Then, in 1911, the original play was novelized and released as *Peter and Wendy*, which is often retitled *Peter Pan* today. The script for the play itself was finally published in 1928, the same year Mickey Mouse made his debut. Each of those versions remains in print, having seen various abridgements, expansions, illustrations, and annotations over the years. Disney has itself continued the tradition with a new line of young adult novels that began in 2004 with *Peter and the Starcatchers*, written by Dave Barry and Ridley Pearson. Coming full circle, *Starcatchers* inspired a 2009 musical play that opened Off-Broadway in 2011 and transferred to Broadway in 2012, winning five Tony Awards. It closed January 20, 2013.

4. I define the First Golden Age of Disney Feature Animation as beginning in 1937 with *Snow White and the Seven Dwarfs* and concluding with *Bambi* in 1942; the Second beginning with *Cinderella* in 1950 and ending with *The Jungle Book* in 1967; and the Third beginning in 1989 with *The Little Mermaid* and ending with either *Tarzan* or *Fantasia 2000* in 1999. Accordingly, we might refer to the intervening eras as the First, Second, and Third Dark Ages of Disney Animation, respectively. A Fourth Golden Age may very well have begun in the late 2000s, inclusive of films like *Meet the Robinsons*,

The Princess and the Frog, Wreck-It Ralph, Tangled, Frozen, and *Big Hero 6.* (I note that Pixar films are not a part of Disney's Feature Animation canon.)

5. The theme of masculinity probably rivals mortality/immortality and the transition from childhood to adulthood as the most-tackled issue in scholarship on *Peter Pan* (these discussions often segue into interrogations of femininity vis-à-vis Wendy and Tiger Lily and racial/ethnic bias with respect to the other tribal characters). One early work, "J. M. Barrie: a study in fairies and mortals" by Patrick Braybrooke, was published in 1924 and opened with an Author's Note in which Braybrooke asked only two things of Barrie: one, to finish another of his works, and the second, to never let Peter Pan be played by a woman again. "There is no character of Barrie's so essentially masculine as 'PETER PAN'," Braybrooke wrote, "yet the part is played by actresses who are in every sense horribly and inevitably grown up." Naturally, not all the scholarship shares Mr. Braybrooke's perspective. For a survey of *Pan* in its various academic contexts, including multiple considerations of the masculinity theme, see Barrie, J.M. *Peter Pan.* Ed. Anne Hiebert Alton. Toronto: Broadview Press, 2011. Print.

6. The Disney studio's decision to cast a boy as Peter Pan might seem natural now, but that wasn't necessarily true in the early 1950s. For nearly a half-century, Pan had been played on the stage by adult women. The first movie adaptation, Paramount's 1924 silent film, kept with tradition and chose actress Betty Bronson for the lead role (Bronson was in her late teens at the time). When Walt cast Bobby Driscoll, previously known for his lace collar and boyish charm in 1946's *Song of the South*, he broke from convention, presenting the public with a fully male Peter Pan for the first time. Walt's decision set the course for Hollywood in each of the major film adaptations that would follow. The silver screen's Peters include Robin Williams (*Hook*, 1991); Blayne Weaver (*Return to Neverland*, 2002); and Jeremy Sumpter (*Peter Pan*, 2003). On the stage, however, tradition has held firm. Arguably the most prominent theatrical take on the play is Broadway's *Peter Pan*, a musical first staged in 1954 (just one year after the Disney film). Mary Martin headlined the original production, which enjoyed several television broadcasts and an eventual home video release. Later, Sandy Duncan and then Cathy Rigby took over the role in a series of successful revivals. In 2014, NBC stuck with stage convention and cast Allison Williams in the lead for the enormously successful *Peter Pan LIVE!* To date, Broadway has yet to welcome a man in Peter's role for any major staging of the play. But then on the other hand, the Disney parks use male cast members for Peter in all of their meet-and-greets, stage shows, and parades. It isn't quite clear why the cinema prefers men for Peter while the live theater has favored women. Perhaps the answer lies in the difficulty of keeping child actors on the stage for hours (a challenge other shows have managed to overcome), or in the power of tradition. Whatever the reason, the conundrum certainly adds to scholars' fascination with *Peter Pan*.

7. Disney often styles the attraction name as "it's a small world," using all lower-case

letters. The company is hardly consistent with that — various Disney publications use capital letters — but the park maps, resort websites, and the signs on the attraction itself use the lower-case styling. Arguably, then, that's the official name. While that works from a marketing perspective (emphasizing the "small" in the name), it doesn't make as much sense in a commentary on the attraction, so I will use capital letters for It's a Small World in this book.

8. In 2010, Magic Kingdom slightly rerouted the Small World queue so that the entryway now wraps behind the clock tower. As a result, guests' view of the smiling face is somewhat obstructed as they board the boats. Happily, the impressive display is still visible when guests walk in, and on a busy day, the line extends far enough to afford a great view to those waiting.

9. Magic Kingdom now serves alcohol at select table service dining experiences, but the menu is limited to wines and beers. The drinks cannot be taken outside of the restaurant. Spirits (i.e. hard liquor) are not served anywhere in the park except for inside the Magic Kingdom's Club 33, an exclusive (and pricey) private club. Alcohol (including hard liquor) has always been served in all of the other Walt Disney World theme parks and most other Walt Disney World Resort locations.

10. Coca-Cola reigns supreme in Disney theme parks today, but it hasn't always been that way. When Walt Disney World opened, guests there (and at Disneyland) had their choice of Pepsi or Coke. Pepsi had sponsored a handful of Disney attractions in the past, the Country Bear Jamboree and The Golden Horseshoe among them. It wasn't until 1985 that the Disney Parks signed a global exclusivity deal with Coca-Cola, making the soda giant the resorts' sole provider of carbonated soft drinks. Legend has it that Disney was running low on syrup one weekend and called Pepsi for an emergency supply, but a company representative told the Mouse they'd have to wait until after the weekend. In a bind, Disney called Coke instead, which arranged for their delivery men to make an urgent shipment. Disney cut their ties with Pepsi on the spot, or so the story goes. That rumor, despite its persistence among Disney fans, almost certainly isn't true, but Coke nevertheless maintains its tight grip on Disney's soda fountains today. In the late '90s, Disney Regional Entertainment (DRE) inked a new deal with PepsiCo that gave the latter a hold on DRE's properties, which included Club Disney, DisneyQuest, and the ESPN Zone. DRE dwindled over the years, turning DisneyQuest over to the Parks and Resorts division and seeing most of its ESPN Zones either rebranded or handed off to third parties, dashing Pepsi's hopes of getting its foot back in Disney's door. As it happens, while writing this very note, I'm sitting in Walt Disney World's ESPN Club restaurant, sipping an ice-cold Coca-Cola Classic.

Even as Disney has distanced itself from the Coke-vending McDonald's fast food company, which once had a sizeable presence in Walt Disney World, Coke products remain as visible and ubiquitous in the parks and dining districts as ever. The All-Star

Sports hotel features giant, multi-story Coke cups (it would take 20 million soda cans to fill one of them). Epcot is home to Club Cool, an attraction featuring free samples of Coca-Cola products from around the world (currently closed and undergoing changes). Disney Springs is home to the multi-story Coca-Cola Store and rooftop bar. While Coke's Mickey monopoly will surely dismay Pepsi fans (and thrill Coke loyalists like myself), it is unquestionably a union of two iconic American brands.

11. There are two ways to spell "carousel" and the Magic Kingdom uses them both. In Tomorrowland, Walt Disney's Carousel of Progress uses the standard single-r spelling, while Fantasyland opts for the less conventional double-r with Prince Charming Regal Carrousel. The antiquated "rr" just feels so much more majestic, doesn't it? It fits Fantasyland's vibe.

12. Incidentally, Griffith Park is now home to Walt Disney's Carolwood Barn, often called "the birthplace of Imagineering." Walt used the barn as a machine shop for the Carolwood Pacific Railroad, a fully functioning, one-eighth scale locomotive track that ran in the backyard of his home in California. The train there eventually inspired the Disneyland Railroad and many of the train-based attractions in the Disney parks around the world. After Walt's death, his family had the barn relocated to Los Angeles's Griffith Park, where it's occasionally open to the public as a free-of-charge museum, the result of a collaboration between The Walt Disney Family Foundation, the Carolwood Foundation, the Carolwood Pacific Historical Society, the Los Angeles Live Steamers, and the City of Los Angeles. For more on Griffith Park and other items of interest to Disney fans while visiting Southern California, allow me to suggest my trip report podcast, "The Walt Disney Pilgrimage" (Season 11 of *On Main Street with Aaron Wallace*, originally released as Episode #72 of *Zip-A-Dee-Doo-Pod* on August 4, 2015; available for free on most major podcast services and at www.AaronWallaceOnline.com).

13. Prince Charming Regal Carrousel's backstory may not be apparent to riders, but Disney did share it with the public on May 25, 2010, in a post on its online Disney Parks Blog.

14. Some of these movies, like *Beauty and the Beast*, did in fact employ some early computer animation, though they were all primarily hand-drawn.

15. *Working for Peanuts* was the opening act for a movie called *Magic Journeys*, which originally opened in Epcot as Disney's first 3-D film made especially for a theme park. *Journeys* played in Epcot until 1986, when *Captain EO* took over. But it wasn't until *Journeys* reopened in Magic Kingdom's Fantasyland Theater in 1987 that *Working for Peanuts* joined it. Both closed in 1993 so that Legend of the Lion King could move into Fantasyland Theater, which today is home to Mickey's PhilharMagic. Before playing in Fantasyland, *Peanuts* had premiered in actual theaters back in 1953, one of Hollywood's first 3-D short films to earn wide distribution. It returned to the big screen in front of *Meet the Robinsons* in 2007, this time projected in Disney Digital 3-D. As one of the rare Disney cartoons to screen both in and outside of the theme parks, it's a fitting precursor

to PhilharMagic's Imagineering/Feature Animation collaboration.
16. Beast's castle is itself a nod to da Vinci. Beauty and the Beast's animators modeled it after Château de Chambord, which many historians believe da Vinci helped design.
17. The Imagineers have never revealed the mechanics behind the effect, but for a plausible theory about how it might have been achieved, see: Hernandez, Gary. "Thorough Explanation of Magic Mirror Effect in the New FantasyLand at Disney World." *YouTube*. 25 Oct. 2012. Web. 30 Aug. 2014. <bit.ly/1qQlDx2>. (Warning: spoilers.)
18. Take, for example, Alice in *Through the Looking Glass*. Other notable magical mirrors in fantasy include The Mirror of Erised (*Harry Potter*), the Magic Mirror (*Snow White and the Seven Dwarfs*), the imprisoned Ozma (*Return to Oz*), and the handheld mirror in Disney's original *Beauty and the Beast*.
19. There is a small error in the retelling. Lumière says, "One night, when her father was away on a journey, Belle heard the sound of galloping... it was her father's horse, Philippe, returning to town." That scene did not take place at nighttime in the film.
20. We did have to walk through a mirror, the narcissist's favorite friend, to find Belle.
21. Enchanted Tales replaced a similar, albeit much simpler, production entitled Storytime with Belle. It took place in a small nook near Cinderella Castle, where Belle would appear a few times a day to quickly recount her story with the help of a few young volunteers. That show took place after the events of the film, so it didn't have the narrative weirdness of Enchanted Tales, but also none of the flair. Storytime closed on September 12, 2010 to make way for Enchanted Tales, which began previews in November 2012 and officially opened on December 6, 2012.
22. There's a lot to be said about the contractual issues in The Little Mermaid. In fact, the film is often used to teach first-year law students about contract enforcement. For more, see: Kprofs2013. "Contracts and 'The Little Mermaid.'" *ContractsProfBlog*. Ed. Telman, D. A. Jeremy. 7 Oct. 2013. Web. 23 Apr. 2015. <http://bit.ly/12M29F8>.
23. In the ride, as in the film, "Part of Your World" and "Under the Sea" are in conversation with one another. The former says "go up there" while the latter counters with "stay down here." Simply by locating those songs in consecutive scenes, the ride succinctly helps uninitiated guests understand Ariel's burden of choice. Then again, whereas Ariel looks rather reluctant at times in the film's sequence, her exuberance in the ride's "Under the Sea" might leave some guests confused as to her final decision on the matter.
24. The Ursula character was modeled after drag queen performer Divine (1945 – 1988), best known for appearances in a number of John Waters films, including the role of Edna in *Hairspray* (1988), released one year prior to *The Little Mermaid*. (For more, refer to the audio commentary on the film's 2006 Platinum Edition DVD or 2013 Diamond Edition Blu-ray/DVD.)
25. In Hans Christian Andersen's original fairy tale, The Little Mermaid longs for a human

soul because they are eternal (unlike mermaids') and bound for Heaven.

26. Another matter of critical interest in The Little Mermaid is a female blackfish, which appears in the film's "Under the Sea" sequence as Sebastian says, "the blackfish, she sings." Many argue that the character's design reinforces certain racial stereotypes and that her name works as a racially charged pun. The blackfish is absent from the ride, though two other characters sometimes cited as racist — the Fluke (referred to in the song as "The Duke of Soul") and Sebastian himself (because he extols the virtues of work-free living in a Caribbean accent) — do turn up, perhaps because the blackfish has taken the bulk of the criticism over the years.

27. Earlier proposals for the ride called for a more story-centric approach. Plans for a *Mermaid* dark ride go back to at least the early 1990s, but it took decades for Under the Sea to materialize. (It first opened as The Little Mermaid ~ Ariel's Undersea Adventure at Disney California Adventure in 2011, later replicated in almost identical form at Magic Kingdom in 2012.) When Disney Home Entertainment released the movie's Platinum Edition DVD in 2006, it included a bonus feature ride-through of the proposed Mermaid dark ride, recreated through animation, complete with optional audio commentary by Imagineering and a featurette on those plans. The ride we know today differs in a number of key respects, but many fans believe that the strong response to the bonus feature ultimately paved the path for Ariel's Undersea Adventure. The ride-through can also be found on the film's Diamond Edition Blu-ray, along with a newer featurette in which Jodi Benson (original voice of Ariel) goes for a ride on Under the Sea.

28. Snow White's poisoned apple bite parallels the Genesis account of Eve's eating the forbidden fruit in the Garden of Eden.

29. In November 2018, at the themed entertainment industry's annual IAAPA conference, Chairman of Disney Parks, Experiences, and Products Bob Chapek announced that the upcoming *Guardians of the Galaxy*-themed roller coaster at Epcot will have the world's first "storytelling vehicles." "We call it a 'storytelling coaster,'" Chapek said. "On most coasters, the vehicles point straight ahead throughout the ride, but on this attraction each individual cab will be programmed to direct your eye to the story happening around you." (Nolfi, Joey. "Disney Unveils Spinning *Guardians of the Galaxy* roller coaster cars, new ride details." *Entertainment Weekly.* 15 Nov. 2018. Web. 10 Aug. 2019. <bit.ly/2yQzOQd>.) It remains to be seen whether the distinction from Seven Dwarfs Mine Train as the first "story coaster" is meaningful or mere puffery.

30. Over in Disneyland, Snow White's Scary Adventures has traveled a similar trajectory over the years. The ride still runs there today, with a presentation that more closely resembles Magic Kingdom's original 1971 version. Paris and Tokyo have each also retained the ride in their parks.

31. For an incredibly rich and thorough chronicle of Snow White's Scary Adventures

and its history in Disney parks around the world, see Sundberg, Kenneth. "KenNetti Proudly Presents: Snow White's Scary Adventures: The Tribute." Rev. ed. 10 Sep. 2012. Web. 23 Apr. 2015. <http://bit.ly/1IN2fvr>.

32. Carrillo, Jenny Cooney. "The Steven & Stanley Story." *Urban Cinefile*. 6 Sep. 2001. Web. 23 Apr. 2015. <http://bit.ly/1DEJW7f>.

33. Mine Train pays homage to Snow White's Scary Adventures with several Animatronics recycled from the ride, including the vultures on the first lift hill and the dancing dwarfs and Snow in the final cottage scene

34. When Walt Disney acquired the rights to Milne's *Pooh* characters, his intention was to develop a feature-length film right away. During a staff meeting, however, the studio decided it might be best to administer *Pooh*'s simple, easy temperament to American audiences in smaller doses. Accordingly, they scrapped plans for an immediate feature-length project and embarked on a longer-term production schedule in which they would release a series of *Pooh* cartoon shorts over the course of several years. Ultimately, three cartoons premiered in theaters between 1966 and 1974 before the full-length *The Many Adventures of Winnie the Pooh* debuted in 1977. For an excellent history on Pooh's early development at Disney, as well as a guide to many other fantastic *Pooh*-related resources, see Gray, Richard "Loomis." "The Ultimate Guide to Pooh: Winnie the Pooh, From A.A. Milne to Disney – History, Commentary, and Filmography." *DVDizzy.com*, n.d. Web. 22 Apr. 2015. <bit.ly/UAwLPD>.

35. In the years after *Pooh's Grand Adventure*, Disney increasingly marketed Pooh & Co. to an exclusively preschool audience. That changed to some extent with 2011's *Winnie the Pooh*. Like *Grand Adventure*, the new *Pooh* is a sequel to the original *Many Adventures* film. It marks the first time that the Walt Disney Animation Studios (formerly called the Feature Animation division) created an all-new *Pooh* movie for theaters from beginning to end. Alas, it underperformed at the box office (thanks primarily to head-on competition from *Harry Potter and the Deathly Hallows – Part 2*), but as a hilarious and charming adventure with lovable characters, it succeeds beyond any other Hundred Acre Wood outing since the original. Its "Top Critics" rating on RottenTomatoes.com stands at a most impressive "97% fresh"!

36. While critics split over Burton's *Alice in Wonderland*, the movie fared well at the box office and on the awards stage. It was nominated for three Golden Globes and three Oscars, winning two of the latter (Art Direction and Costume Design). As of early 2015, with a global gross of more than one billion dollars, it is the 17th highest-grossing film of all time worldwide (and the 31st, domestically).

37. The Skyway was an opening day attraction at Magic Kingdom, basically a clone of the same ride that opened in Disneyland in 1956. Gondolas traveled through the sky along a cable lift with guests riding inside them, offering a rare view of the park below. There were two stations: one beside It's a Small World (where it was called Skyway

to Tomorrowland) and the other next to Space Mountain (Skyway to Fantasyland). Disneyland's closed in 1994 and Walt Disney World's in 1999. Both Magic Kingdom stations remained intact until Tomorrowland's was completely demolished in 2009. Fantasyland's followed suit in 2011 as part of the New Fantasyland project.

38. Mickey's Toontown Fair initially opened as Mickey's Birthdayland on June 18, 1988. It was renamed Mickey's Starland on May 26, 1990. Three years later, Disneyland opened its own Toontown on January 24, 1993. Then, on October 1, 1996, Florida's Starland became Mickey's Toontown Fair, where characters from Disneyland's much more lavish Toontown would supposedly come for vacation. Magic Kingdom's Toontown was always intended as a temporary land, but somehow it stuck around for 13 years. Now it exists as Storybook Circus, no longer an independent land but rather an incorporated district within Fantasyland. Fairs and circuses are not dissimilar, so one can naturally still find remnants of the old Toontown Fair, but Storybook Circus has the look and feel of permanency that this part of Magic Kingdom never enjoyed before.

39. "Forced perspective" is one of Disney Imagineering's favorite and cleverest tricks. In a nutshell, they make an object appear bigger or smaller (or closer or farther away) than it really is by gradually changing the scale or angle of construction, or by surrounding it with things that are deceptively different in size. For example, the shops on Main Street look taller than they really are because the second story is actually shorter than the first and the third story smaller still. Likewise, the bricks and décor of Cinderella Castle shrink in size as they get higher, and the few trees near it are proportionally much shorter than the castle itself.

40. It may seem strange to find Dumbo back in a circus, now that he's a free elephant. Circus life was never very kind to him, after all. But then we see Mrs. Jumbo, his mother, watching over him. Golden busts of Mrs. Jumbo's loving face adorn the newly outfitted Dumbo hubs in Storybook Circus. She is the mother who protected him. He is her "Baby Mine." Seeing her there reminds us of Dumbo's freedom and reassures us that the circus is a better home for him now than it was in the film.

41. The official entrance sign presents the attraction as The Barnstormer Featuring Goofy as the Great Goofini. Meanwhile, as this book goes to press, the Magic Kingdom park map and official website present it simply as The Barnstormer. For brevity's sake, I'll generally use the shorter title throughout this book, making reference to the lengthier locution as needed.

42. The attraction was almost always referred to as The Barnstormer at Goofy's Wiseacre Farm, including on Disney's park maps and websites and in several of its official books. The name painted in multiple places on the barn itself, however, used a slightly different locution — Goofy's Wise Acres Farms. Perhaps the idea was that Goofy couldn't get the name of his own barn right. Either way, most guests simply called it "Goofy's Barnstormer" (and many still do).

43. Mickey's PhilharMagic is another Fantasyland attraction starring characters from "the fab five," but as previously noted, PhilharMagic's storyline is steeped in magic and fantasy.
44. The cartoon short has enjoyed a modest resurgence in recent years, thanks in large part to John Lasseter's commitment to the short film format in his role as Chief Creative Officer at Pixar and Walt Disney Animation Studios. Lasseter also serves as Principle Creative Advisor for Walt Disney Imagineering.
45. The "Cinderella" story was first published in the late seventeenth century and Disney's film can probably be assumed to be set during that time as well. However, Imagineers actually looked to many different castles from various eras when designing Cinderella Castle, some dating as far back as the thirteenth century. For more on the architectural inspirations for Cinderella Castle, see Mongello, Louis A. *The Walt Disney World Trivia Book: Secrets, History & Fun Facts Behind the Magic.* Branford: The Intrepid Traveler, 2004 : pp. 77-78. Print.
46. Charles Perrault (1628 - 1703) was a French author and one of the founding fathers of the fairy tale genre. The child of wealthy parents, he studied law and served as the secretary to Jean Baptiste Colbert, an advisor to King Louis XIV, before turning to writing later in life. In 1697, he published *Histoires ou contes du temps passé*, better known in English as *Mother Goose Tales* (some English printings use variations on that title). In addition to "Cinderella," *Mother Goose* included "Sleeping Beauty," "Little Red Riding Hood," and "Puss in Boots," among other well-known fairy tales. Though Perrault is frequently cited as the original author of "Cinderella," the story's origins undoubtedly predate him. The idea of a missing shoe that sparks a royal search for its wearer can be traced all the way back to ancient China and Greece, with variations on the tale emerging and evolving from different cultures over the centuries. "Cenerentola," written by Italian poet Giambattista Basile and published posthumously in 1634, appears to have inspired Perrault's version, but it was Perrault who gave us the glass shoes, the fairy godmother, the bewitched pumpkins, and the enchanted animals as coachmen, all essential elements of the "Cinderella" story today.
47. The castle is now known as Cinderella Castle, but in accordance with the fairy tale and the Disney film, it belongs to Prince Charming and his royal family. (Renaming a palace after a princess is a historical anomaly, but then how many people would travel to visit the Charming Castle?) Presumably then, the King's Gallery was a reference to Prince Charming's portly father, who isn't given a name but nonetheless plays a memorable part in Disney's *Cinderella*. He does actually handle a sword in one of his funniest scenes, a disagreement with the Grand Duke, but his silliness results in a few too many close calls with the blade. Actor Luis van Rooten voiced both the Grand Duke and the King.
48. Securing reservations at Cinderella's Royal Table requires greater diligence than any

other dining experience at Walt Disney World. For more on exactly how to get yourself a seat, see Barrett, Steven M. *The Hassle-Free Walt Disney World Vacation*. Branford: The Intrepid Traveler, 2011 : p. 55. Print.

49. The Cinderella Castle Dream Suite is reportedly still used on occasion for VIPs and the like, and I've even heard (unconfirmed) reports of Disney randomly surprising guests with an overnight stay in the years since the "Year of a Million Dreams" ended, but the suite is no longer part of any ongoing promotion and remains inaccessible to the general public.

50. Trying to situate Fantasyland within a single era or artistic/historical moment is probably as futile as it is silly. Cinderella Castle is the centerpiece and Perrault's "Cinderella" was published in France at the tail end of the Renaissance. However, Fantasyland's other story worlds come from many different periods, some having emerged as recently as the twentieth century (*Peter Pan*, *Dumbo*, and *Winnie the Pooh*, for example). Architecturally, the village festivals and fairs of the Medieval and Renaissance eras inspire much of the land, resembling at times a sanitized version of the modern-day Renaissance fair (which is typically set in either England or France). Jousting, a sport associated with both the Middle Ages and the Renaissance, appears as something of a motif throughout the area. But as previously noted, Cinderella Castle emulates a wide array of castles from various eras (see Mongello, above, pp. 77-78). And as for geography, while England and France are clearly important progenitors of Fantasyland's central storylines, other parts of Europe and even the United States show up, too. The Pinocchio Village Haus bears a distinctly German influence, and It's a Small World travels all around the globe. The land is probably best thought of as a primarily European pastiche of the Middle Ages, the Renaissance, and the Early Modern Era with an infusion of innumerable other geographies, eras, and styles, including Modern and Contemporary periods. Of course, it should be noted that there is no clear consensus among historians on a single chronology of the world's historical periods and that diverging movements and periods often overlap, making any definitive timeline for Fantasyland elusive.

51. With the New Fantasyland expansion, Magic Kingdom added additional castle courtyard walls, which open up to the Enchanted Forest behind them. I suppose that makes them a little more vulnerable to attack, but then surely Charming's guards could barricade the gates should any villains get too close for comfort.

52. Taylor, Blake (disney_blake). "On this day — June 17, 2016...." *Instagram*, photographed by Blake Taylor. 17 June 2019. <bit.ly/2YTe70t>.

53. One of the tragedies of that week involved the terrible loss of a young boy's life in an alligator attack on Walt Disney World property on June 15, 2016. Responding quickly and out of sensitivity to the family, Magic Kingdom producers quietly made changes to the already-rehearsed-and-ready-to-premiere Mickey's Royal Friendship

Faire. Among the characters scripted as part of that show was Louis, the oversized alligator from *The Princess and the Frog* (2009). The show premiered without Louis or his character's pre-recorded dialogue, the cast modifying their performances at the last minute accordingly. Louis was later added to the show after a period of mourning and discretion. The other high-profile tragedies of that week in Orlando included the mass shooting at Orlando's Pulse nightclub on June 12 and the murder of young recording artist Christina Grimmie at Orlando's The Plaza Live concert venue on June 10.

Chapter 5: Tomorrowland

1. A version of this quote is on a plaque at the entrance to Disneyland's Tomorrowland, but it substitutes the word "ideas" for "ideals." It's a one-letter discrepancy, but it arguably changes Walt's meaning. A Tomorrowland focused on ideals (like "progress"), rather than on ideas (like "high-definition TV"), might be less prone to growing stale with the passage of time.
2. Some of those dioramas can now be seen along the path of the Disneyland Railroad.
3. The PeopleMover is still casually referred to by some as the "Skyway" in both Disneyland and Walt Disney World, but it should not be confused with the ski lift-style Skyway attraction that ran at both U.S. Resorts as well as Tokyo Disneyland until the 1990s. See also: *Chapter Four*, Note 37.
4. In keeping with Disneyland's PeopleMover Thru the World of *Tron*, I propose that Walt Disney World's ride be officially renamed the Tomorrowland Transit Authority PeopleMover Thru the Worlds of Space Mountain and Buzz Lightyear's Space Ranger Spin... WEDWay.
5. While passing Walt Disney's Carousel of Progress, guests riding the TTA from 1994 to 2009 heard, "Paging Mr. Morrow, Mr. Tom Morrow, your party from Saturn has arrived. Please give them a ring." When the page returned on June 16, 2010, it was moved inside the Space Mountain building, where you'll now hear, "Paging Mr. Morrow, Mr. Tom Morrow. Please contact Mr. Johnson in the Control Tower to confirm your flight to the moon." Mr. Tom Morrow was a character in Flight to the Moon, the original attraction standing where Stitch's Great Escape is now. Mr. Johnson was a similar character (with the same voice actor, George Walsh) in Mission to Mars, an updated version of Flight to the Moon that ran from 1975 to 1993. Fans are divided on whether the new page is an acceptable substitute for the older one.
6. It would appear that Walt may have used the phrase at least twice in his public comments, once as part of a 1965 presentation entitled "Total Image," in which he said, "There's really no secret about our approach. We keep moving forward — opening up new doors and doing new things — because we're curious. And curiosity keeps leading us down new paths." This line was quoted by former Disney CEO Michael Eisner in his introduction to *Walt Disney Imagineering: A Behind the Dreams Look at Making the Magic*

Real (Disney Editions, 1998) as well as in *The Quotable Walt Disney*, compiled by Disney archivist Dave Smith (Disney Editions, 2001). The other instance is quoted using on-screen text in Disney's *Meet the Robinsons*— "Around here, however, we don't look backwards for very long. We keep moving forward, opening up new doors and doing new things… and curiosity keeps leading us down new paths," though the film offers no independent citation for this similar-but-different presentation.

7. "Animated Classic" is an objective categorization of animated (or at least predominately animated, as opposed to live-action) films from the studio's Feature Animation division (now known as Walt Disney Animation Studios). The company officially canonizes movies as part of its "Animated Classic" lineup, so when I refer to a movie with that label, I don't always mean that it's a film classic in the sense that *Citizen Kane* is one. Rather, a Disney film is an "Animated Classic" simply because Disney says so.

8. For more information about the 2003 "Save Disney" campaign that ultimately led to Eisner's eviction from the Mouse House in 2005, see *Chapter Two*, Note 13.

9. When entering the attraction, guests pass through what appear to be high-security clearance doors and walk through a long, narrow hallway. When they emerge, they sense that their proportions have changed. All around them are toys like the View-Master, Etch A Sketch, and the one and only Buzz Lightyear, each as tall or even taller than the guests themselves. The suggestion is that entering Star Command has shrunk the humans down to the size of a toy. Other visual cues, like a sprawling instruction sheet on the wall and a screwdriver head, reinforce that idea. Disney has used similar tricks in other *Toy Story* attractions around the world, including those in Toy Story Land (Florida, Shanghai, and Hong Kong) and Toy Story Playland (Paris).

10. Slightly different versions of Buzz Lightyear's Space Ranger Spin exist in Disneyland and Hong Kong Disneyland (as Buzz Lightyear Astro Blasters), Tokyo Disneyland (as Buzz Lightyear's Astro Blasters), and Disneyland Paris (as Buzz Lightyear Laser Blast). A different attraction, Buzz Lightyear's AstroBlaster, ran at Walt Disney World's DisneyQuest (a five-story, interactive, indoor "theme park" located in Downtown Disney) until it closed on July 2, 2017.

11. Ten years after Buzz Lightyear's Space Ranger Spin, Walt Disney World unveiled the next generation of the video game ride in its Hollywood Studios theme park. Inspired by the same series of films, Toy Story Mania! is a substantial technological advancement from Space Ranger Spin and has arguably rendered the Tomorrowland ride obsolete. Nevertheless, the Buzz Lightyear ride's unique story and charm help explain why it's still running, even if it might become a prime candidate the next time Magic Kingdom looks to replace an attraction.

12. It isn't necessarily clear in the *Toy Story* films whether, within their story world, Buzz Lightyear was first a video game (or cartoon) star that inspired a popular action figure, or vice-versa. Certainly, we see him in all those environments throughout the *Toy Story*

saga. Even if, for the sake of argument, the character did not originate in a video game, his game identity nevertheless clearly contributes to his popularity with Andy and the other children in that fictional universe.

13. The term "laser tag dark ride" or "shooting dark ride" is sometimes applied to this hybrid, though one wouldn't be incorrect to simply refer to it as a "dark ride." Interestingly, an attraction like Toy Story Mania, which involves backstory and gameplay similar to Space Ranger Spin's but puts less emphasis on a "front story" and doesn't use lasers, would probably still qualify as a "dark ride" and a "shooting dark ride" but not a "laser tag dark ride," suggesting that this lattermost term is too specific to be helpful in classifying attractions by ride type.

14. Many of the roadways that today comprise the U.S. Interstates already existed but were not formally part of the Dwight D. Eisenhower National System of Interstate and Defense Highways until at least 1956.

15. In Disneyland, the Tomorrowland Autopia opened in 1955. It was followed by a similar ride in Fantasyland, Junior Autopia, in 1956. Junior Autopia closed in 1958 and reopened as the expanded Fantasyland Autopia in 1959. The latter was known as the Rescue Rangers Raceway from 1991 to 1992 (essentially the same ride, but with a "Rescue Rangers" overlay). It was then redubbed the Fantasyland Autopia until 1999, when both the Fantasyland and Tomorrowland versions were permanently closed. In 2000, the two tracks were reworked and combined to create today's singular Autopia (officially a Tomorrowland-only attraction). In addition to those, a no-grown-ups-allowed version of the ride, called Midget Autopia, ran in California's Fantasyland from 1957 to 1966 (it was later donated to Walt's hometown of Marceline, Missouri, where it briefly ran until maintenance grew too costly). Around the world, one can also find Autopia-type rides in Disneyland Paris and Hong Kong Disneyland.

16. See *Chapter Four*, Note 38.

17. The spinning planet effect has been known to start working again for brief periods of time in recent years, but it never seems to last for long.

18. Many fans have noted that, as abridged, the attraction name creates some unfortunate and unintentional acronymic innuendo… probably not something the average guest notices, but enough to keep fans on Twitter plenty amused.

19. A number of official Disney publications provide varying and conflicting dates for Space Mountain's official opening in Walt Disney World, ranging from early 1974 to early 1975. The January 15, 1975 date appears to be the most widely cited and is consistent with major newspaper reports.

20. The attraction never gives us a last name (we just know his first name is John), and some have speculated that might mean this isn't the same family we're seeing from one scene to the next, but the weight of the evidence suggests otherwise. John Progress, then, isn't an official name, but it's one that many fans have embraced.

21. Disney had Audio-Animatronics on display in several World's Fair attractions, including It's a Small World, Great Moments with Mr. Lincoln, and Ford's Magic Skyway. For more on the technology's reception, see: Brady, Hillary. "Walt Disney's Progressland." *Smithsonian Institute Archives*. 21 July 2016. Web. 3 Aug. 2019. <s.si.edu/29R61II>.
22. For more on the history of the attraction: Smith, Martin. "Carousel of Progress WDW – Martins Ultimate Tribute." *YouTube*, uploaded by MartinsVidsDotNot. 17 Oct. 2015. Web. 3 Aug. 2019. <bit.ly/2T3Wplw>. See also: "Yesterworld: The History of The Carousel of Progress (Disney Attraction Evolution)." *YouTube*, uploaded by Yesterworld Entertainment. 27 Nov. 2018. Web. 3 Aug. 2019. <bit.ly/2Kiev0J>.
23. Moore, Thomas Gale. "The Meaning of Progress" in "On Progress: Its Reality, Desirability, and Destiny." n.d. Web. 3 Aug. 2019. <stanford.io/2T39vja>. Note also the discussion, beginning on page 12 in Moore's chapter cited here, about how the annual wage growth rates in America might have contributed to an evolving view of "progress" in the United States during the 1960s and '70s.
24. Incidentally, this is precisely why Barbara Walters becoming the first female anchor was such a big deal, and part of why she's an official Disney Legend.
25. The fact that the dog's name used to vary between some of the scenes only adds to our confusion about this family's curious progression through time. Was the dog dying and being replaced by an identical dog every 20 years or so? If that's the case, why didn't the rest of the family age along with them? But even more interesting is that the dog's *gender* used to change too, from Sport (presumably male) to Queenie (presumably female). This changes how we read the 1975 version of Act II, in which Queenie grumbles in support of Jane.
26. Fjellman, Stephen M. *Vinyl Leaves: Walt Disney World and America*. Boulder, Westview Press, 1992, p. 216.
27. See Moore, Note 23 above.
28. When honoring actress Emma Thompson at the National Board of Review awards in 2014, actress Meryl Streep called Walt Disney a "gender bigot." Thompson was starring in Disney's newly released *Saving Mr. Banks* at the time, a film in which her character is sometimes at odds with Walt Disney during the 1950s and '60s. The explosive comment attracted tremendous media attention and led to intensive debate about Walt Disney's life and legacy, with many rushing to his defense and many others joining in Streep's sentiments. In fairness to Streep as it relates to our discussion about the Carousel of Progress, her comments were more squarely aimed at this company's employment practices at the time, but they also included broader-view disparagements of Walt Disney's character and beliefs. The Walt Disney Family Museum responded with a stinging public review, laying bare many of the inaccuracies that Streep had asserted in her speech. Floyd Norman, a legendary Disney animator who worked with Walt Disney,

published his own op/ed joining in the Museum's defense.
29. For more on these and other ideas for improving the fourth act in Carousel of Progress, see: Heaton, Dan. "5 Ways to Fix the Carousel of Progress' Final Scene." *The Tomorrow Society*. 10 July 2016. Web. 3 Aug. 2019. <bit.ly/2OU563N>
30. As Douglas Adams wrote in *The Salmon of Doubt*: "I've come up with a set of rules that describe our reactions to technology:
    (1). Anything that is in the world when you're born is normal and ordinary and is just a natural part of the way the world works.
    (2). Anything that's invented between when you're 15 and 35 is new and exciting and revolutionary and you can probably get a career in it.
    (3). Anything invented after you're 35 is against the natural order of things."
31. Rubin, Gretchen. *Happier at Home: Kiss More, Jump More, Abandon Self-Control, and My Other Experiments in Everyday Life*. New York, Three Rivers Press, 2012, p. 263.
32. Until the fall of 2011, Walt Disney's Carousel of Progress was the *only* attraction in Walt Disney World to bear Walt Disney's name in its official title. When The Enchanted Tiki Room reopened in August 2011, it added the name as a reminder that the original attraction was Walt's personal property (for more, see *Chapter One*). Technically, the Walt Disney World Railroad bears his name too, but the effect there is to designate the railroad as belonging to the Florida Resort, whereas Walt Disney's name in the Carousel of Progress is intended as a personal tribute to the man who created it.
33. The attraction has been altered and redressed many times since Progressland and its days in Disneyland, with whole scenes rebuilt since Walt passed away. But surprisingly, many of the props and set pieces on display in Magic Kingdom's ride are reportedly still the original ones used in New York in 1964. It's almost chilling to sit there and think about that.
34. Fantasound was a stereophonic sound system developed by the Disney Studios in conjunction with RCA for use in *Fantasia* (1940)'s original theatrical distribution. Fantasound made *Fantasia* the first major movie released in stereo sound and is considered a precursor to surround sound and many of the home theater technologies we know today. (Director Jon Favreau and composer John Debney sought to recreate the Fantasound experience when mixing the soundtrack for their 2016 film, *The Jungle Book*). Technicolor was one of the first widely adopted systems for producing color movies in Hollywood, best known for its vibrant, ultra-saturated color. Though the Disney studio didn't invent it, Walt was an early adapter, using it for many of his short films in the mid-1930s and again in 1937 for *Snow White and the Seven Dwarfs*. Walt's full-fledged embrace of the format is credited with helping to popularize Technicolor as the industry's most widely used color process during the 1930s, '40s, and early '50s. The storyboard is a planning process that filmmakers use during pre-production and production in order to visualize a scene before filming it. Walt Disney and his team

developed it for their animated films, but the process soon spread to live-action pictures and to other studios. It is widely used today. The monorail is a single-rail train system used for public and private transit. Though its origins trace back to the 1800s, it was Walt Disney who opened America's first daily operating monorail at Disneyland in 1959. Disney's monorail systems are arguably the best-known in the world, and they have been credited for popularizing this form of transportation around the world. The multiplane camera was developed at the Walt Disney Studios by Ub Iwerks and has since been used in countless film productions. The camera allowed animators create a sense of depth ("parallax") when shooting two-dimensional animation. The Experimental Prototype Community of Tomorrow was the name for Walt Disney's original concept for a futuristic city. He passed away during its development, but the idea later evolved into the theme park we now know as Epcot. For more, see: Wallace, Aaron. *The Thinking Fan's Guide to Walt Disney World: Epcot*. Orlando, Pensive Pen Publishing, 2017.

35. According to podcaster and author Lou Mongello, Walt Disney personally requested that the Carousel of Progress never cease operation. "Walt Disney's Carousel of Progress." *WDW Radio*. 16 Sep. 2007. Web. 3 Aug. 2019. <bit.ly/2YF53fL>.

Chapter 6: Main Street, USA

1. Out of deference to Disneyland's most faithful fans, I note that "The Happiest Place on Earth" is a term first applied to the Disneyland park and is the official tagline of the Disneyland Resort in Anaheim, CA. Magic Kingdom's tagline, meanwhile, is "The Most Magical Place on Earth." Despite that technical distinction, the former slogan is part of the national vernacular and is often applied informally to Magic Kingdom too. While I acknowledge Disneyland's more credible claim to that title, I think it's fair to use the two interchangeably, at least in the course of everyday conversation. Both parks seem plenty happy *and* magical to me. (But if you're a proud Disneylander reading this and shuddering at the thought, believe me, I understand!)

2. The entire area surrounding the train station is themed as Carolwood Park, a fictional public park that has supposedly been taken over by the Storybook Circus. The bathrooms next door are located behind a Carolwood Fire Dept façade. The Carolwood name comes from Walt Disney's own *Carolwood Pacific* railway, which also inspired the real-life Carolwood Barn in California (a fact that makes The Barnstormer's location in Storybook Circus especially appropriate). For more on these connections and the history of the Carolwood Pacific, see *Chapter Four*.

3. In an effort to mitigate the uncomfortable "othering" that used to happen in this scene (complete with an out-of-context ballad from Pocahontas), the narration now reminds us that the Native Americans were here long before the rest of us. Still, we might

call the whole scene into question, along with some of the other Native American stereotyping at work in Frontierland and at Disney's Fort Wilderness Resort). See *Chapter Two* for more.

4. Perhaps surprisingly, the game leaves out two of Disney's most popular sorcerer characters, Sorcerer Mickey and Yensid, both of *Fantasia* (1940). Each appears on a separate spell card in the game, but they are not otherwise part of the storyline and they never appear on any portal screens. Maybe the Imagineers decided that with all the attention paid to *Fantasia* and its "The Sorcerer's Apprentice" segment elsewhere in the Disney theme parks, it was appropriate to focus on less ubiquitous properties here.

5. I don't mean to imply that Disney intentionally created or designed Sorcerers of the Magic Kingdom in order to replicate or even borrow from the *Harry Potter* experience. Nor am I certain that the Imagineers developed Sorcerers as a means of competing with Universal Orlando's Wizarding World of Harry Potter. Intentional or not, Sorcerers does manage to tap into a shared, underlying pop-cultural desire to live out the *Potter* fantasy. It may be that the game's development and popularity are simply symptomatic of the profound impact *Potter* has had on the world.

6. Kyle Burbank of *The Disneyland Gazette* and LaughingPlace.com presented me with a brilliant idea while touring Magic Kingdom — affixing Sorcerers playing cards to the tip of the Potter wands sold inside Universal's Wizarding World for ultimate spell-casting legitimacy. Or "metanarrative," as some scholars use that term — a grand story informed by numerous, smaller stories.

7. Or "metanarrative," as some scholars use that term — a grand story informed by numerous, smaller stories.

8. I offer Universal only as a convenient example. We can say the same of the other major creators of mass-entertainment. Hanna-Barbera, Rankin/Bass, etc. might be exceptions, but they also aren't the big-house major players that Disney is, nor have they had nearly the same level of cultural penetration/saturation. In making the observation, I don't mean to suggest that Universal necessarily should do these things. Their brand, business model, purview, and cultural positioning differ from Disney's. I merely note that these differences account for the different relationship they have with their respective audiences.

9. While the parade may not tell a story, so to speak, it does have one notable "plot point" in the middle, a briefly dark sequence in which Prince Phillip saves Sleeping Beauty by battling an enormous, fire-expelling, dragonish Maleficent through bramble with blade. It is the highlight of the whole parade, artfully achieved with amazing costume craft. Strikingly, the dragon's heart (visible through her steampunk-flavored design) is the tale's infamous spinning wheel, continuously turning to keep her on her wicked way.

10. Also known as the "monomyth," the hero's journey is a narrative template or pattern occurring across a wide range of media in which a reluctant hero goes on adventure,

encounters conflict or crisis along the way, and returns transformed. For an analysis of Walt Disney World attractions through the lens of the hero's journey, see: Berger, Adam M. *Every Guest Is a Hero: Disney's Theme Parks and the Magic of Mythic Storytelling.* Orlando, BCA Press, 2013.

11. In his essay on Happily Ever After, Disney fan columnist Blake Taylor suggests that the show's appeal to millennials (by way of these "deep cut" properties that resonate most immediately with our generation) is more than just fan service, arguing that the script taps into one of millennials' "greatest joys… identifying the skillsets within ourselves and learning how to use them best." Taylor, Blake. "Review — 'Happily Ever After' Fireworks Is Provocative, Millennial-Charged Knock-Out." *WDW Radio.* 3 July 2017. Web. 4 Aug. 2019. <bit.ly/2ODMIM4>.

Index

A

ABC 36, 80, 82, 222
Admiral Joe Fowler 75
Adventureland 14, 21-46, 50, 107, 112, 216, 223
Adventures of Bullwhip Griffin, The 60
Adventures of Huckleberry Finn 63, 68, 137
Adventures of Tom Sawyer, The 68
African Lion, The 26
African Queen, The 26
Aladdin 9, 21, 28, 37-39, 118, 120, 223, 229, 230, 236, 237
Alice in Wonderland 126-127, 146-148, 256
Alice in Wonderland (2010) 126, 148
Allen, Rex 194
American Dream, The 206
Andrews, Julie 81, 83, 215
Angelou, Maya 90, 245
Apple Dumpling Gang, The 57
arcades 48, 58-60, 173
Archie Bunker 195, 201
Ariel's Grotto 19
Armstrong 31, 63, 94, 181
art (qualifying rides as) 42-44
Ashman, Howard 130-131
Astro Jets. *See* Astro Orbiter
Astro Orbiter 10, 37, 165, 169, 179-181

Atencio, X 98-99
Audio-Animatronics 16, 23, 27-29, 31, 51-52, 64, 66, 75, 81, 86-90, 93, 119, 125, 133-134, 144, 190, 193
Aunt Polly's Dockside Inn 68
Autopia 177-179

B

Babes in Toyland 34
backstory 16, 17, 31, 55, 56, 97, 115, 116, 133, 155, 168, 174
Bambi 106, 137,
Band Concert, The 119, 122
Barnstormer, The 104-105, 154-158
Barrie, J.M. 106-107, 110
Baskett, James 61-62
Baxter, Tony 54-56
Bear Country 49
Beauty and the Beast 104, 118, 123, 126
Bedknobs and Broomsticks 122
Be Our Guest Restaurant 104, 124
Bibbidi Bobbidi Boutique 159, 160-161
Big Bird 84
Big Thunder Mountain Railroad 48, 54-59, 70, 75, 133, 185-186, 214
Big Wash, The 158
Blackbeard's Ghost 46
Black Hole, The 189
"Blood on the Saddle" 50

Boys: The Sherman Brothers' Story, The 113-14
Bradbury, Ray 139
Brother Bear 121
Burton, Tim 126, 148
Bush, George W. 88-90, 92
Buzz Lightyear's Space Ranger Spin 165, 170-175, 183

C

Candleshoe 100
Carolwood Pacific 213
Carousel of Progress, Walt Disney's 165, 169, 190-207
Casey Jr. Splash 'N' Soak Station 150
Castillo del Morro 40
Castle Courtyard 104, 115
Chaplin, Charlie 69
children's entertainment 107, 135, 137
children's literature 63-64, 97, 137, 138, 141
Chip (*Beauty and the Beast* character) 123, 126
"Chip 'n Dale Rescue Rangers" 64
Chitty Chitty Bang Bang 215-216
Christianity 137
Christopher Robin 140-145, 173
Cinderella (1950 film) 106
Cinderella Castle 17, 74, 103, 121, 149, 159, 161-163, 180, 220, 227-228
Cinderella Castle Suite 161
Cinderella III: A Twist in Time 126
Cinderella's Golden Carrousel 115
Cinderella's Royal Table 159, 161, 258
Citizens of Main Street 211
Civil Rights Act of 1964 112
Clinton, Bill 88-89, 92
Clinton, Hillary 88
Coats, Claude 96
Compton Wynyates manor 101
Connecticut Yankee in King Arthur's Court, A 78, 117

Conway, Tim 57
Country Bear Jamboree 48-53, 58, 142
country music 50-51
Cruella de Vil (character) 136, 219
Crystal Arcade 58

D

Dapper Dans 210
dark ride 16, 127, 129, 131-132, 134-135, 142, 172, 174
da Vinci, Leonardo 124
Davis, Marc 23-24, 46, 96
Davy Crockett 15, 53, 58-59
Davy Crockett's Pioneer Mercantile 58
Dead Poets Society 64
Defoe, Daniel 33
denying disbelief 151
Depp, Johnny 26, 44, 46, 110
Diamond Horseshoe Saloon 58
Dinosaur (attraction) 24
Disney+ 14, 53, 63, 179, 185, 233
Disney bubble, the (concept) 133, 210
Disney California Adventure 16, 185
Disney difference, the (concept) 118
Disneyland 15-16, 21, 23, 26, 28-29, 33-35, 38, 40, 46, 47, 49, 52-55, 58-59, 64, 68, 73, 75, 86-87, 93, 96, 97, 103, 112, 114-15, 117, 121, 127-28, 134-36, 139, 142, 147, 151-53, 160, 165-68, 177-78, 180, 185-86, 192-93, 203, 206, 209, 211, 213, 220, 224, 233
Disneyland Paris 16, 54, 68, 96-97, 112
Disneyland, U.S.A. (1956) 153
Disney-MGM Studios. *See* Disney's Hollywood Studios
Disney mountains (concept) 185
Disneynature 23
Disney Parks Blog 89, 90
Disney, Roy E. 171
Disney, Roy O. 213

INDEX

Disney's Animal Kingdom 16, 23, 37, 151, 185
Disney's Fort Wilderness Resort 266
Disney's Hollywood Studios 16, 130, 151
Disney Springs 16
Disney, Walter Elias 15, 16-18, 21, 22, 23, 29, 32-34, 43-44, 46-47, 49, 53, 57-58, 61, 63-64, 66, 69, 73, 82, 86-87, 91-93, 96, 99, 103, 105-106, 109, 112-116, 121, 135-138, 141, 146, 151-53, 157, 160-61, 165, 167, 169-71, 177, 179, 181, 185-86, 188, 192, 194-95, 199, 202, 204-07, 209, 211-14, 231-33
Dobkin, Lawrence 90
Donald Duck (character) 118
DoomBuggies.com 100
Downtown Disney (Disneyland Resort) 16
Dream Along with Mickey 162
Driscoll, Bobby 61
Dumbo the Flying Elephant 104, 134, 149-53, 156, 157, 179

E

Ebert, Roger 62
Edison Square 192
Eisner, Michael 64, 171, 189
Elliott, Ted 46
Emperor's New Groove, The 184
Emporium 58
Enchanted (2007) 163
Enchanted Forest 104, 116, 124, 127
Enchanted Tales with Belle 10, 104, 123-26
Enchanted Tiki Room 21, 27, 29, 30, 33
Estefan, Gloria 29
E-ticket 17, 38, 54, 55, 61, 105, 150, 176, 185, 187
Even Stevens Movie, The 32

Experimental Prototype Community of Tomorrow 206

F

fables 42
Fantasia 106, 118, 119, 137, 146, 147, 247, 250, 264, 266
Fantasound 206, 264
Fantasyland 14, 19, 37, 64, 65, 97, 103-164, 186, 214, 220, 223-24, 233
Fast & Furious — Supercharged 176
FASTPASS 19
Favreau, Jon 233, 264
Festival of Fantasy Parade, Disney's 11, 122, 223, 224, 225, 226
Fey, Tina 83
Finding Neverland 109, 110
fireworks 22, 120-122, 134, 159, 210, 211, 213, 227-233
Fjellman, Stephen M. 90, 202
flat ride (ride type) 37, 152
Forbidden Journey, Harry Potter and the 130
Ford Magic Skyway 166
Foster, Jodie 70, 100
Fox, Twentieth Century 65, 131, 216, 226
Fozzie Bear (character) 50, 80, 81, 84
Freeman, Morgan 246
Frees, Paul 95
Freewayphobia 179
"Friends" (TV show) 84
Frontierland 14, 46-71, 73, 74, 75, 77, 97, 151, 153, 185, 214, 220, 223, 240, 243, 245, 247, 266
Frontierland Shootin' Arcade 48, 58-59
Frontierland Shootin' Exposition 59
Frontierland Shootin' Gallery. *See* Frontierland Shootin' Arcade

G

Garland, Judy 212
Gaston's Tavern 104
gender 31, 107-08, 192, 195, 199, 201, 202, 205, 239, 263
General Electric 193
"Glee" (TV show) 131
Goldberg, Whoopi 117, 219
Golden Ages of Disney 107
"Golden Girls, The" (TV show) 84
Golden Horseshoe Saloon 52
Gonzo (character) 80-81, 84
Goofy (character) 104, 118-119, 122, 154, 155-58, 179
Grandma Duck's Barn 154
Grand Prix Raceway. *See* Tomorrowland Speedway
Great Goofini. *See* Barnstormer, The
Great Moments with Mr. Lincoln 87
Griffith Park 253
"Grim Grinning Ghosts" 99
Grimm, Brothers 138
Grizzly Peak 185-86

H

Hall of Presidents, The 74, 77, 79-80, 85, 86-89, 91-94, 144
Hamilton 81
Happiest Millionaire, The 94
Happiest Place on Earth, The (slogan) 211-212, 232
Harris, Joel Chandler 61, 63
Harry Potter 104, 120, 130, 137, 221, 223
Hawn, Goldie 94
Hayes, Helen 100
"Heigh-Ho" 32, 133
Hello, Dolly! 226
Henson, Jim 79
Hercules 217, 221
hero's journey, the (concept) 229

Hibler, Winston 153
Hocus Pocus 99
Hogwarts Express, The 215
Honey, I Shrunk the Kids 64
Hong Kong Disneyland 16, 35, 68, 96, 112
hub-and-spoke 38, 151, 179

I

Iger, Bob (Robert) 88-89, 170-71
I Love Liberty 84
Imagineering 16-17, 46, 54-55, 88-89, 96, 109, 119, 124, 129, 130, 158, 213
immersion (theme park design concept) 21, 41, 45, 151, 152, 173
in medias res 40-41, 44
Interstates 177
"It's a Good Time" 212
It's a Small World 104-105, 110-14, 224

J

Jackson 5 63,
Jackson, Andrew 90, 91
Jiminy Cricket 122, 228, 230
Johnny Tremain 86
jukebox musical 129
Jungle Book, The (2016) 233
Jungle Cruise 21-27, 30, 43, 58, 59, 152, 233
Jungle Cruise (2020) movie 233

K

"Keep Moving Forward" (phrase) 121, 170
Kermit the Frog (character) 50, 80-84
Kid in King Arthur's Court, A 78, 117
King Arthur Carrousel 115
King's Gallery, The 160, 258
Knight in Camelot, A 78, 117

Knotts, Don 57, 181
Kostal, Irwin 215

L

Lady and the Tramp (1955) 146
Lansbury, Angela 44
Lear, Norman 84
LeFou's Brew 104
Legend of the Lion King 120
"Let It Go" 131
Lewis, Jenifer 219
Liberty Belle. See Liberty Square Riverboat
Liberty Square 14, 71-101, 214, 218, 220
Liberty Square Riverboat 9, 74-78, 214
Lily Belle 213
Lincoln, Abraham 69, 85-87, 92,
Lion King, The 28, 120, 219
Lion King, The (2019) 233
Little Mermaid, The 64, 104, 127-30, 138, 220
Lonesome Ghosts 97
Longfellow, Henry Wadsworth 80
Looney Tunes (characters) 120
"Lost" (TV show) 36
Love Bug, The 121

M

Mad Tea Party 10, 104, 146-48
MagicBands 217-18
Magic Carpets of Aladdin, The 9, 21, 37-39, 236
Magic Kingdom (movie) 233
Main Street Cinema 210
Main Street Fire Station 217
Main Street Penny Arcade 58
Main Street Philharmonic 210, 223
Main Street Shooting Gallery 58
Main Street Trolley Show 210
Main Street, U.S.A. 14, 19, 58, 86, 150, 160, 209-233

Maleficent (2014) 126
Maltin, Leonard 62
Mama Rose (character) 44
Many Adventures of Winnie the Pooh, The 104, 129, 139-45
Marceline, Missouri 15, 209, 211-12
Mark Twain Steamboat 75
Mary Poppins 34, 60, 66, 114, 121, 215
masculinity 107, 251
master narratives 225
Matterhorn Bobsleds 112, 151, 185-87
McDaniel, Hattie 61, 242
meet-and-greets 17, 19, 108, 127, 135, 150, 156
Meet Me in St. Louis 204, 212
Meet the Robinsons 170, 171, 221
Melody Time 58, 60
Merida (character) 108, 225
Miami Sound Machine 29
Mickey Mouse (character) 15, 19, 53, 64, 106, 119, 122, 140, 150, 154, 213, 232
"Mickey Mouse Club, The" (TV show) 15, 53, 64, 122
Mickey's Christmas Carol 122
Mickey's Philharmagic 104, 118-22
Mickey's Revue 119
"Mickey's Royal Friendship Faire" 159, 162-63
Mickey's Toontown Fair 104, 150, 154-56
millennial 195
Milne, A.A. 140-45
Minnie Moo 154
Miss Piggy (character) 50, 80, 84
monorail 57, 80, 206
Monsters, Inc. 165, 182-85, 220, 229
Monsters, Inc. Laugh Floor 165, 182-85
Moon Pilot 181
Moore, Thomas Gale 194-95, 202
Moses, Robert 87
Most Magical Place on Earth, The (slogan) 13, 211, 224, 228, 265

Move It! Shake It! MousekeDance It! 159, 212, 223
Mrs. Potts (character) 123-24
Mr. Toad's Wild Ride 127, 142
Mr. Tom Morrow (character) 169
"Muppet Babies" (TV show) 82
Muppets from Space 82
"Muppet Show, The" (TV show) 81, 83, 84
Muppets Present... Great Moments in American History, The 9, 18, 74, 79-85
"Muppets Reenact the Continental Congress" (TV segment) 84
"Muppets, The" (2015 TV show) 82
Muppets, The (2011 film) 82
Muppets, The (characters) 18, 50, 74, 77, 79-85
Muppets' Wizard of Oz 82
Muppet*Vision 3D 24
My Disney Experience (MDX) 19
MyMagic+ 19

N

narrative 16, 17, 38, 40-41, 56, 65, 76, 93, 110, 116, 121, 126, 128-31, 152, 159, 162, 167, 172-74, 187, 205, 215, 219, 222, 224-25
narrative revision (cinematic trend) 126
Native American stereotyping 43, 266
New Fantasyland 104, 116, 126, 128, 131-32, 135, 157
New Orleans Square 54, 87, 97
New Tomorrowland 168, 173, 178
New York World's Fair (1964-65) 86, 112, 166, 192
Night at the Museum 233
Nixon, Richard 87, 92
"No One Is Alone," 131

O

Obama, Barack 88, 90, 92, 93
"Once Upon a Time" (TV series) 132, 222
One and Only, Genuine, Original Family Band, The 94
One Thousand and One Nights 38, 39, 236, 237
On the Record, Disney's 129
othering 265

P

Pandora — The World of Avatar 151
Parade of Dreams 121
Parker, Fess 53
"Parks and Recreation" (TV show) 84
Paul Revere 74, 79-81
Pecos Bill 52, 60
Pecos Bill Tall Tale Inn and Café 52
People and Places 153
People for the American Way 84
PeopleMover. *See* Tomorrowland Transit Authority PeopleMover
Perrault, Charles 160, 258-59
Peter Pan (character and film) 43, 61, 104-110, 118, 120-121, 129, 131, 150, 225, 231
Peter Pan's Flight 104-110, 129, 131
Peter Pan (stage musical) 43
Peters, Bernadette 44
Pinocchio 106, 111, 136, 228
Pinocchio Village Haus 111
Pirates of the Caribbean 21, 26, 40-46, 54, 68, 81, 98, 121, 130, 144, 216, 233, 235, 237, 238, 239, 247, 248
Pirates of the Caribbean and the Curse of the Black Pearl 44
Pluto (character) 156, 212
Pocahontas (character) 237, 265
Pollyanna 207

Pooh for President (campaign) 140
postmodern 76-77, 126, 128, 151, 215
Prince Charming Regal Carrousel 10, 104, 114-17, 160, 253
Prince, Kira 45
Princess and the Frog, The 228, 230, 251, 260
Princess Fairytale Hall 19, 135
progress (concept) 194-95, 202, 205, 207
progressivism 31, 91, 192, 195, 198
Progressland 193, 196-97, 201
Progress City 204, 206
Psycho 137

R

"Rainbow Connection" 131
Rainbow Ridge 153
Rainy Day Character Cavalcade 223
Ravenscroft, Thurl 99
Reddy, Helen 84
Richard F. Irvine 75
Richards, Keith 46
Rivers of America 56, 68, 75
Robinson Crusoe 33
Rocket Rods 167
Rodgers and Hammerstein 43, 113
Rodgers & Hammerstein's *Cinderella* 43
Roosevelt, Theodore ("Teddy") 91
Rossio, Terry 46
Rubin, Gretchen 205, 264
Russell, Kurt 94

S

Sam the Eagle (character) 50, 79-80, 84
Seven Dwarfs Mine Train 104, 132, 138
Seven Seas Lagoon 159
Shanghai Disneyland 16, 176, 213
Share a Dream Come True (parade) 223
Sherman Brothers, The 70, 94, 111-13, 193, 206, 215

"Silly Song, The" 138
Sinatra, Frank 84
Skeleton Dance, The 97
Sleeping Beauty 34, 108, 115-16, 123, 137, 160-61, 220, 224, 226
Sleepy Hollow Refreshments 74
Snow White and the Seven Dwarfs 15, 23, 43, 105, 127, 129, 131-32, 134-35, 137-39, 151, 222
Snow White's Scary Adventures 127, 129, 131, 135, 138, 151
Something Wicked This Way Comes 139
Song of the South 61-64, 66
South Pacific 21, 113
Space Mountain 10, 55, 165, 168, 170, 176, 179, 180, 185-89, 193, 257, 260, 262
Spielberg, Steven 109, 137
spinners (ride type) 37
Splash Mountain 48, 61-66, 149, 214, 215
Star Jets. *See* Astro Orbiter
Star Tours — The Adventures Continue 130
"Star Trek" (TV show) 189
Star Wars: Galaxy's Edge 151
Steamboat Willie 15, 233
Sting (singer) 185
Storybook Circus 104, 139, 149, 150, 152, 154-58, 214
"story coaster" (marketing term) 132-33
Streisand, Barbra 84, 226
SuperSpeed Tunnel 166
Superstar Parade (Universal Orlando) 225
suspending disbelief 143, 151, 152
sustaining disbelief 151
Sweatbox, The 185
Swiss Family Robinson 33-36
Swiss Family Treehouse 21, 33-34, 36, 205
Sword in the Stone, The 117, 217, 220
synergy 118-20

T

Tangled 104, 162, 229
Tarzan (1999) 35, 229
Tarzan's Treehouse 35
Taylor, Blake 162
Technicolor 43, 53, 153, 206, 264
Thief of Bagdad, The 39
"30 Rock" (TV Show) 83
Tiana (character) 162, 219, 228-31, 233
Tiki Room. *See* Enchanted Tiki Room
Tinker Bell 19, 23, 107, 121, 231
Tokyo Disneyland 16, 54, 64, 68, 96-97, 112
Tom and Huck 68, 69, 70
Tomorrowland 10, 14, 37, 59, 112, 149, 165, 166, 167, 168, 169, 170, 171, 172, 173, 175, 176, 177, 178, 180, 181, 182, 183, 184, 186, 188, 189, 193, 202, 203, 204, 206, 207, 213, 220, 241, 253, 257, 260, 261, 262
Tomorrowland (film) 189
Tomorrowland Jets. *See* Astro Orbiter
Tomorrowland Speedway 165, 176-79
Tomorrowland Transit Authority PeopleMover 59, 165, 166-71, 180, 184
Tom Sawyer (1973 film) 70
Tom Sawyer Island 48, 67-71, 75, 77, 214
Touchstone 64
town criers 81-82
Toy Story (franchise) 172-74
TriceraTop Spin 37
Tron 166, 175-76, 178, 189
Tron: Legacy 175-76, 189
Tropical Serenade 28
True-Life Adventures 23
Trump, Donald 81, 88-92
Tumbleweed 55-57, 59
Twain, Mark 45, 63, 68-71, 75, 76, 78, 117

20,000 Leagues Under the Sea 34
Typhoon Lagoon 64

U

Uncle Remus 61-63, 66
Under the Sea ~ Journey of the Little Mermaid 104, 127-31
Unidentified Flying Oddball 78, 117
Universal Orlando Resort 104, 173, 176, 221
Universal Studios Florida 225

V

Vandervort-Cobb, Joy 91
Van Dyke, Dick 215
video gaming 59, 171-75

W

Walt Disney's Carousel of Progress. *See* Carousel of Progress
Walt Disney's Enchanted Tiki Room. *See* Enchanted Tiki Room
Warner Brothers 120
Warren, Lesley Ann 94, 238
WDI. *See* Imagineering
weenie (theme park design) 17, 180
Wells, Frank 64
Western River Expedition 54-55
Westward Ho Refreshments 53
Westward Ho, the Wagons! 53
"When You Wish Upon a Star" 103, 228
Williams, Robin 84
Winfrey, Oprah 231
Winnie the Pooh (character) 104, 129, 139, 140-45, 225
Wishes: A Magical Gathering of Disney Dreams 228
witches 29, 99, 128-29, 133-34, 136, 138

Wizarding World of Harry Potter,
    The 104, 130, 221
Working for Peanuts 158, 253
Wyss, Johann David 33

Y

Year of a Million Dreams, The 161
"Yo Ho (A Pirate's Life for Me)" 41, 45

Z

"Zip-A-Dee-Doo-Dah" 66

Acknowledgements

This book would not have been possible without the support and encouragement of so many people in my life. I would first like to thank Kelly Monaghan and Sally Scanlon at The Intrepid Traveler for believing in this project, helping to bring it into reality, and making a dream come true. I would also like to thank my in-park research assistants – Joshua Aguilar; Rev. Courtney Lambert; Reuben Gutierrez; and Rebekah Mlinarcik – as well as the other great friends who have traveled to the Disney Parks with me over the years and helped inspire my ponderings there: Aaron and Krista Berlin; Devon Derrow; Christopher Disher; Josh and Drea Harper; Casey Jennings; Laura A. Jones; Dr. Selena Lane; Adam Lutterloh; Claire Nader; Jenna Pennell; Lindsay Purnell; Emily Thornton; and Lily Wagner.

I must also acknowledge my writing teachers, especially Erin Mackie and Daniel Wallace, for helping me find and understand my writing voice, as well as Dr. Laurie Langbauer at the University of North Carolina at Chapel Hill, for encouraging me to investigate the academic dimensions of Disney's productions when so many scholars scoffed at the idea and for first sparking my critical interest in the parks' written-word roots with her scholarship in children's literature.

I would not have been in the position to write this book if not for the opportunities afforded me by Luke Bonanno and the staff at DVDizzy.com; Jesse Obstbaum, who gave me my first podcasting gig and helped paved the way for my own unofficial Disney discussion show; Jeff Falvo and Michael Fenyes, who've made me a part of the wonderful community of producers at The Disney Podcast Network; and the panelists on *The Hub Podcast*: Matt Osborne, Keegan Cooke, Greg McNaughten, Will Jensen, Michael Fenyes (Mike from *MiceCast*), and "Earl," as well as all of our recurring and special guests.

Writing is a fulfilling but lengthy and demanding process. Thank you to all of those who provided me emotional support, words of encouragement, feedback, or just a friendly ear during this undertaking: My family, especially my parents, sister, grandmother Dolores Finger, and aunt Debra Finger; everyone at The Law Offices of Amos & Kapral, LLP;

the entire student and professional staff of Wake Forest University, and especially Nicole A. Rodriguez-Pastor for her friendship and ongoing support in so many arenas of my academic, professional, and personal life; the many baristas who took such a friendly and genuine interest in my work as I toiled for endless hours with a latté in hand; and all of my amazing friends, especially the Aguilar family, Kyle Burbank, the entire Disney Podcast Network family; Matthew Fletcher, Amy Gates, Blake Gates, Adam Jass, the Lambert family, Anthony Lane, Emily Mabry, Luke Manning and the entire staff at *The Disneyland Gazette*, Alexandra McVetty, Renata Olson, Caitlin Overend, Nikki Pollard, Tommy Sanford, Katrina Schaffhouser, Patrick Westmoreland, and so many others.

Finally, I want to thank: you, the reader, for taking this adventure with me; every listener and fan of my other work in print and online; the entire Disney fan community for being so warm, accessible, embracing, and friendly; the Cast Members of the Disney Parks around the world for excellence in magic making; and Roy O. Disney and his younger brother, Walt, for a legacy that has meant the world to me and so many others in it.

2020 Edition Acknowledgements

My endless thanks to Jonathan Harvill, Albert Gutierrez, and Reuben Gutierrez for your help with this latest edition. Thanks also to Rob Yeo for designing a cover I love so much. Finally, thanks to everyone who has shown me more patience than I deserve during this process. And to the reader, thank you for continuing to be a part of this journey.

www.ingramcontent.com/pod-product-compliance
Lightning Source LLC
Chambersburg PA
CBHW020418010526
44118CB00010B/308